The Health of Nations

The Health of Nations

A North–South Investigation
by MIKE MULLER

faber and faber

First published in 1982
by Faber and Faber Limited
3 Queen Square London WC1N 3AU
Printed in Great Britain by
Redwood Burn Ltd, Trowbridge, Wiltshire

British Library Cataloguing in Publication Data

Muller, Mike
The health of nations: a North-South investigation.
1. Underdeveloped areas—Medical care
2. Drug trade   3. International business enterprises
I. Title
362. 1'09172'4   RA394

ISBN 0-571-11888-7
ISBN 0-571-11956-5 Pbk

For Carol

Contents

Foreword and Acknowledgements

When it was first proposed that I should write this book, I approached the idea with some hesitation. It is, by common consent, easier to write books about the developing world from outside it, and I was to be based in Mozambique for the duration. Worse, the book was to be not just about the developing world but also about the institutions of the rich world. In the event, instead of making a quick safari to a few of the more accessible developing countries and returning to write, close to the resources of London's libraries, I have had to stand the process on its head. The perspective is thus a different one, but perhaps more appropriate.

The extensive documentation that is now available on pharmaceuticals and the Third World has helped greatly. When I first took an interest in the subject in the early 1970s there were perhaps five key documents to read. Today the debate about pharmaceutical policy threatens to get bogged down under the sheer weight of the new literature. Fortunately, it has not been submerged. Indeed, one of the problems I have faced, writing to the leisurely tempo of book publication, is that, as Michael Peretz of IFPMA, the international drug companies trade association, told me would happen, I have been on a moving staircase. (He was talking authoritatively, since in his desk drawer at the time were drafts of IFPMA's next two position papers.)

Given the pace at which the debate is developing, this book cannot be a comprehensive, up-to-date review of its subject. What I have attempted instead is to chart the course which it is taking, illustrating some of the life-and-death issues which literally underlie its often dry language, and indicating which issues will grow in importance in the 1980s. So as well as acknowledging my sources as completely as possible—which will, I hope, make this book useful for reference —I have also used their words extensively where this will better convey their tone.

This kind of writing is always a parasitic, if not downright exploitative, business. I have been more than usually dependent on the friends and acquaintances around the world who helped by finding much of the material I needed, as well as those who looked after me so well during my European safari. So my thanks (and apologies in some cases) to them and to the many other people who responded to specific requests for information. I am also grateful to those people in the pharmaceutical industry who took the time and trouble to present their points of view. It may appear that I treat them harshly in the text, but to judge from what they themselves told me about their public relations strategies, I suspect they would be disappointed were it otherwise.

M. M.
January 1982

Note on Terminology

The terminology available to describe pharmaceuticals as a class of products is as imprecise as their use. *Pharmaceuticals, medicines,* and *drugs* have been used interchangeably—the case for restricting the last to alcohol, nicotine, caffeine and 'narcotics' is weak since these are used, often more rationally, for purposes as 'medical' as many pharmaceuticals.

Drugs have been referred to by preference by their *generic,* non-commercial names although the strict INN usage has not been followed in all cases. Commercial names have been used as well, with the generic equivalent indicated and differentiated in most cases, for example, Valium (diazepam). To avoid confusing readers who are also not medically trained, I have avoided a profusion of products in the text, with the same drugs used as examples in a number of different contexts.

Similarly, to avoid entanglement in unproductive debates implicit in the use of *developing, underdeveloped* and *less developed countries* (DCs, UDCs and LDCs) as well as *Third* or *poor world,* the terms have been used interchangeably. (The *Fourth World* that creeps in with the quotations is to be found to a greater or lesser extent in all developing countries and is not a particularly useful concept to express the division between the haves and have-nots in them.) *Rich world* and *developed countries* follow from these usages. The countries themselves have, almost without exception, decided which side of the *North–South dialogue* they are on.

Multinational has been used in preference to *transnational* to describe the pharmaceutical *companies* or *corporations.* (The latter two terms are used interchangeably.) The case for *ultranational* is made in the final chapter.

Last, where Portuguese words are used without translation, it is because they mean exactly what they appear to mean in English, with the exception of *bairro* (a district or suburb).

Abbreviations

ABPI	Association of British Pharmaceutical Industries
AID	Agency for International Development (USA)
ALIFAR	Association Latinoamerica de Industrias Farmaceuticas
CEME	Central de Medicamentos (Brazil)
CPR	Centre for Public Resources (USA)
FDA	Food and Drugs Administration (USA)
IFPMA	International Federation of Pharmaceutical Manufacturers' Associations
INN	International Non-proprietary Name
IOCU	International Organization of Consumer Unions
LDC	Less Developed Country
MIMS	*Monthly Index of Medical Specialities*
OECD	Organization for Economic Cooperation and Development
PHC	Primary Health Care
PL 480	Public Law 480 ('Food for Peace' scheme under which American farm surplus is sold abroad at concessional prices)
PMA	Pharmaceutical Manufacturers' Association (USA)
SMON	Subacute Myelo-Optico-Neuropathy
UNCTAD	United Nations Conference on Trade and Development
UNICEF	United Nations International Children's Emergency Fund
UNIDO	United Nations Industrial Development Organization
WHO	World Health Organization
World Bank	International Bank for Reconstruction and Development. This is one of the financial institutions established at the 1944 Bretton Woods Conference and, as a rich world controlled agency, is not to be confused with the agencies of the United Nations which are increasingly controlled by the developing countries.

Part I: The 1970s

One: The Issues

The pharmaceutical company of Hoffmann-La Roche has its headquarters in Basle, Switzerland. At the centre of its office complex is a steel and glass tower, the kind that in the early 1960s symbolized science and progress. I visited it in 1976 to talk to the Roche management about their role in meeting the health needs of the Third World. It was a surreal experience. We talked in the offices of senior management, then passed through their impressive anterooms, discreetly planted with tropical plants, to the laboratory block where white-coated scientists and technicians were performing strange rituals in search of new drugs. In one lab, they had nurtured aquaria full of snails to harbour the water-borne parasites of schistosomiasis. Successive cohorts of identical white rats were baptized, in order to be exposed to these parasites; then they were killed and dissected. It was hoped that one of their varied chemical diets would yield a substance effective against the parasite which afflicts more than 200 million people in the Third World. Higher up in the research tower, an earnest economist was arguing passionately that the governments of Third World countries should pay for their medicines and let Hoffmann-La Roche get on with the self-imposed task of developing the drugs which the people of these countries need.

This was all so distant from Segbwema, a small town in Sierra Leone, where, a few months before, I had discussed the benefits bestowed by Hoffmann-La Roche on a poor Third World community. The doctor at the small mission hospital there had been telling me about the strange cocktail of largely trivial drugs that he received from European wellwishers, the dregs from household medicine chests, the unwanted free samples collected from doctors' surgeries, all the latest remedies for the diseases of degeneration and depression with which the affluent world is ridden. Well represented in his collection were Roche's famous money-spinners, Valium and Librium, the rich world's favourite tranquillizers. These were surely not much use in rural Africa, I ventured. But the answer was to the contrary.

In the children's ward of the hospital, the doctor showed me what he meant. Among the thirty or so patients were five infants, only a few weeks old, lying motionless in their cots. Their weak breathing was obstructed by the tubes which passed through their noses to their stomachs. They lay still, but not relaxed. Their tiny bodies were contorted by the spine-twisting spasm of tetanus.

Neonatal tetanus occurs commonly in communities where children are born at home, often straight on to a mud floor, with only the help of an old woman as midwife who, after cutting the umbilical cord with an old knife or piece of glass, will staunch the bleeding with mud or cow dung. The disease contracted as the result of the infection is usually fatal. But in Segbwema's hospital, those discarded Roche tranquillizers were being administered to the babies in massive doses to ease the spasm. And perhaps half were surviving.

So Valium, the drug which more than any other symbolizes the affluent world's pill-for-every-ill culture was, here, saving lives. Perhaps what they said in Basle was true. The Third World should leave the drug industry to get on with its job of developing even better new drugs. It is a tempting conclusion but a misleading one. The drug helped in the management of neonatal tetanus, but half the babies still died. The health workers at that little hospital had a more ambitious target. They were trying, by reaching out to the old women who traditionally act as midwives, to deal with the problem at its origin, at that critical moment in life when the umbilical cord is cut and the baby, suddenly alone, faces a dangerous world for the first time. They were attempting to offer a simple technical solution which could mean the difference between life and an extremely brutal death. What they gave the old women were little plastic packets containing sterile razor blades, string and cotton wool. The midwives were being encouraged to use these instead of old knives and cow dung, and to deliver the babies on to something other than a bare mud floor—a clean piece of newspaper, perhaps. Preliminary signs were that the campaign was being successful, if success could be measured by a halving of the number of new cases of neonatal tetanus admitted.

The management of the disease in a hospital—the manipulation of naso-gastric tubes, the calculation and administration of the right drugs and diet—is skilled work with only a modest success rate. The prevention of the disease is more difficult. It requires social and political talents as well as technical skills; the ability to enter the world of the old women and talk to them for hours about the problems of delivering babies in a village environment which, for them, is plagued by hostile spirits. The difference between these approaches is one focus of this book, for it is not possible to discuss the relationship between a multinational pharmaceutical company like Hoffmann-La Roche and a poor Third World country like Sierra Leone without distinguishing between the practice of technical, curative medicine and the attack on the social and economic origins of a community's disease.

To these cases of neonatal tetanus in Sierra Leone, Roche made a real, if limited, contribution. It was not a unique contribution—other drugs with similar sedative effects are available—nor could Roche claim that Valium would ever have been developed if its only market were in this type of application. The benefit to Sierra Leone was a chance by-product of Roche's profitable preoccupation with the rich world's anxieties. And Sierra Leone's best approach to the problem of tetanus is clearly preventive rather than curative.

What this book seeks to examine, however, is not just the proposition that the contributions of the multinational pharmaceutical corporations to Third World health are coincidental by-products of their activities in the developed world, although this is one part of it. The more fundamental question is whether their positive contributions are not in fact outweighed by, and are incidental to, the damage they do and the bad health care they promote; in economic terms, whether the resources they have captured would not generate more benefit to their consumers if applied in other ways.

The idea that the activities of the drug companies and better health for the Third World are not necessarily related has been widely formulated and argued. Professor Julie Sulianti Saroso of Indonesia's Ministry of Health put it succinctly when, speaking to assembled leaders of the industry in Tokyo in 1978, he said: 'Undoubtedly there are mutual interests between the pharmaceutical industry and the Third World but until now only the differences have been obvious.'[1]

Three years earlier, Dr Halfdan Mahler, Director General of the World Health Organization (WHO), had summarized some of these differences in his report to the World Health Assembly:

> Drugs not authorized for sale in the country of origin—or withdrawn from the market for reasons of safety or lack of efficacy —are sometimes exported and marketed in developing countries; other drugs are promoted and advertised in these countries for indications that are not approved by the regulatory agencies of the countries of origin. Products not meeting the quality requirements

of the exporting country, including products beyond their expiry date, may be exported to developing countries that are not in a position to carry out quality control measures. While these practices may conform to legal requirements, they are unethical and detrimental to health.[2]

Resources for health care were very limited, Dr Mahler pointed out:

The need to optimize expenditure on drugs . . . is therefore vital for developing countries. Resources are often wasted in the purchase of expensive drugs that are only marginally useful or even totally irrelevant to the solution of the countries' main health problems, whereas large segments of the population are in urgent need of essential drugs for disease control and primary health care. In many instances, the lack of these essential drugs is an important constraint on the solution of the health problems of the populations in need.

Around the same time Dr Sanjaya Lall in a report published by the United Nations Conference on Trade and Development (UNCTAD) wrote that the transnational pharmaceutical companies were making excessive profits from their trade with the developing countries and that the health needs of the world's poor were being ignored by corporate research programmes.[3]

The indictment was pretty damning. It provoked, as was intended, a fierce debate within and between the United Nations organizations, pharmaceutical companies, governments and other interest groups in both developed and developing countries. In the pages that follow, these accusations will be examined in detail. It will be necessary, too, to examine the nature of pharmaceutical company operations in the rich, developed world since many of the abuses noted in the developing countries are the direct consequence of the transfer of inappropriate technical and commercial ideologies developed in environments of relative affluence.

To understand, for instance, why the contribution of the pharmaceutical companies to better health in the developing world must be limited, it is helpful to look at the historical contribution of these same companies to the undoubted improvements in health that have been achieved in the industrialized world. This is a point about which I feel keenly. While writing this book, I have been sharing the responsibility for the water supplies of about 300,000 people in Mozambique's Sofala province, the population of the city of Beira and the lucky minority of rural dwellers with access to piped water. In this position, I have been linked to the daily lives of some of those people in whose interests the pharmaceutical companies say they operate.

There is an air of absurdity about this. Watching the women and children, straight-backed and straining under their burden of 30 litres of water as they carry it carefully through the makeshift settlements on the swampy outskirts of the city, seeing the intimate interplay of water and dirt, food and excrement during the rainy season when the *bairros precários* are awash with sticky, smelly mud, I am struck by the grand paradox of the existence of an assertive drug industry with its powerful armoury of products alongside this sanitary chaos with its almost total absence of the physical and economic structures essential for 'health'. Just how relevant to health could the products of the research-based pharmaceutical industry be in a community in which the supply of enough food to meet even minimum energy needs cannot yet be assured?

In the rich world, 'health' as measured by stark statistics like the birth rate, the death rate and the expected length of life, was not the product of any dramatic therapeutic advances either by the pharmaceutical industry or by medical science in general. The advent of truly active drugs with which it was possible to combat effectively a wide range of diseases can be dated as late as the 1930s, by which time the drama was almost at its end. This barely defined 'health' was almost entirely the product of the century-long development of a sanitary infrastructure, based on national economic growth which had, at the same time, made it possible for the majority of the population of the rich world to reap its benefits. The claims of the pharmaceutical companies are those of the upstart actor who had just two lines in the last act and is now trying to steal the scene at curtain call.

Medical historian Professor Thomas McKeown gives a clear analysis of the course of the infectious diseases that, up until the beginning of this century, determined the health of the now 'developed' world: 'The first and most important reason for the decline of infectious diseases was improvement in nutrition,' he writes. 'Second only to nutritional influences in time and probably in importance, were the improvements in hygiene introduced progressively from the second half of the nineteenth century.' Drugs—indeed, most of what is traditionally seen as medicine—were of little importance. 'The influence of immunization and therapy on the death-rate was delayed until the twentieth century and had little effect on national mortality trends before the introduction of sulphonamides in 1935.'[4]

The poor world, as the United Nations has emphasized by its declaration of this (the 1980s) as the water and sanitation decade, has yet to benefit from the hygienic improvements which McKeown highlights, and many hundreds of millions of its people are still inadequately fed. So there is no historical reason to expect the availability of modern drugs to transform the health prospects for those women waiting patiently, since before sunrise, in the queue at the public tap. For that listless child squatting beside the road, its life draining slowly away with its diarrhoea, the idea that some new drug, synthesized in a laboratory halfway round the world, will somehow help it over the multiple hurdles of malnutrition and infection to its fifth birthday is preposterous.

Health care, which may include some drugs, will play a part. But it will not be the type of health care with which the western reader is familiar—a relatively accessible doctor who perhaps still makes home visits, backed up by hospitals whose specialists have all the technical means for diagnosis and treatment. That is out of the question. For a start, few developing countries will ever be able to afford this type of care for all their people, although in many, a large proportion of health budgets is spent on providing it for a privileged minority.

Some countries have already developed systems of primary health care which reach right down to the country village where most people in the Third World live, rather than stopping at the district hospital. With the backing of the WHO, others are following their lead. To extend care so far, few of the health workers will be doctors, and the tools at their disposal will clearly be limited. Their medicines, for instance, will have to be fewer and cheaper, and their safety and efficacy will have to be appropriate to their conditions of use. By their temerity in pointing this out, the WHO and its allies provoked an outcry from the pharmaceutical industry; the suggestion that poor countries should restrict the drugs they use to a short list of essential products was regarded as a frontal assault on the companies.

It is important at this point to recognize that the so-called Third World is a diverse collection of countries which to a greater or lesser extent have yet to achieve (the term could be disputed) the industrialization, social development and accumulation of wealth of the rich countries of Europe and North America. Countries such as Mexico and Brazil, nominally part of the Third World, have in many ways more in common with the USA than with Mozambique, Kenya, Bangladesh, Sri Lanka or El Salvador. Within the countries, too, the divides are often more evident than the unity—divides between rich and poor, town and country, men and women.

In many countries, medicine helps to define the divides. As Doyal and Pennell put it for those with a taste for class analysis, medicine is just one more luxury for the bourgeoisie to indulge in:

> There is an important sense in which western scientific medicine, with its associated apparatus [and this clearly includes its drugs] represents yet another item of luxury consumption for the few who can afford it . . . Such a pattern of medical care does of course have advantages for a class which has the personal resources to pay for it and which is protected from the life-threatening environmental conditions to which the bulk of the population is exposed. Thus the exclusive residential areas formerly occupied by the colonialists have now been taken over by the national bourgeoisie and with them, the mentality of the *cordon sanitaire*.[5]

Again, the point is one on which I have personal feelings. My house in Beira, in Mozambique, is in a part of the city where the better-off Portuguese lived during colonial times. Like the others in the street, it is served by piped water, sewers and electricity. The rubbish is collected every night. Beyond the backyard wall, among the cashew and mango trees, another community begins, the *bairros precários* built by black Mozambicans during Portuguese rule, illegally (and thus impermanently), without planning and without any thought for the provision of 'essential services'. Still further back begin the swamps which play a vital part in the economy of this other community, since, during the rainy season, they are almost permanently flooded and make excellent rice paddies. They also provide an ideal breeding ground for mosquitoes. Not surprisingly, malaria is rife. Mosquitoes are democratic insects—they bite rich and poor alike. It takes a strong sea breeze to keep them from my house and although the netting on the windows is in reasonable repair, some always penetrate the defences and many more wait for me outside. So I should acknowledge the contribution of the pharmaceutical industry whose anti-malarials, part of my own *cordon sanitaire*, make it possible for me to obtain my historical perspectives at close quarters without risking the fevers which always blunted the colonial advance on this coast.

For those of us living in the *cimento*, the cement city, who contract one of the diseases fostered by the lack of sanitation in the *bairros precários* on the periphery—through contaminated food perhaps, or by swimming in a sea polluted by their sewage—a visit to a health centre, maybe some laboratory tests as well, may indicate the cause and an appropriate pill. Sometimes this medicine will also help those who live on the other side of the divide. In post-colonial Mozambique, the aim is to give peasants in the countryside and dwellers in the *bairros precários* the same access to available medical facilities as *cimento* residents, filtered first through front-line health posts and health centres. There are few illusions at policy-making levels about the value of this curative medicine in the absence of measures to eradicate the conditions which permit constant exposure to reinfection by infectious and parasitic diseases. Prevention is thus seen as more important than purely curative activities.

In most Third World countries, even those where health care is not just a commodity to be commandeered by the richest and most powerful groups, this is not the case. There remains a powerful and understandable belief that the simple extension of the hospital and drug-based medicine which the policy-makers rely on for their personal health can equally meet the needs of their less fortunate compatriots. The pharmaceutical companies, by no means without vested interests in the matter, have not lost opportunities to promote this point of view. But if the companies have helped to reinforce the divides within nations, they themselves straddle the global divide between the poor world and the rich. World pharmaceutical trade is dominated, as we shall see, by a few dozen multinational enterprises, typical of the giant companies which control so much of world business. Just as it is impossible to discuss the anatomy of modern medicine without an understanding of its industrial base, so too any dissection of the pharmaceutical multinationals must verge into the anatomical study of the species as a whole.

The pharmaceutical industry has become a laboratory in which new mechanisms for the control of multinational company operations in the developing world are being tested. United Nations agencies have joined with various Third World governments in an action programme whose positive objective is to give them the means to get the essential drugs needed to bring primary health care to the majority of their people. This is a direct challenge to the companies in whose immediate economic interest it has been to sell smaller quantities of their more expensive new products.

The challenge has been accepted. What is now occurring provides a fascinating study of the ability of large international corporations to adapt their unwieldy structures to survive in a changed environment. It is an open question whether they have the flexibility to make the changes; if they do, will it be viewed as the democratic response of good corporate citizens to political demands made by their society, or the selfish adaptation of a parasite the better to exploit its host? With other industries, the relationship between corporate activities in a developing country and the net benefits to its citizens is usually complex and open to endless dispute. The pharmaceutical industry deals directly in measurable benefits, the health and physical well-being of its consumers. We can see who they are, we can see whether they benefit. We can measure the contribution of the industry to life's quality in the Third World more easily than in most other areas of endeavour.

The challenge to the industry is part of a broader challenge by the poor world to the rich. Can you show that the thesis of the Brandt Commission—in essence, that the economic well-being of the rich world will best be assured by promoting that of the poor world —holds in practice?[6] Will the multinationals find a strategy which will enable their drugs to be delivered to the people who need them? Or will the poor countries have to develop an industry of their own, more appropriate to their needs? To begin to answer these questions, we have to lurch back again from the global to the individual and see what happened when Carol, to whom this book is dedicated, took a pill for her headache.

Two: Safety

When, one lunchtime in August 1979, Carol knocked at the door of my office at the water company to ask for a lift home, she was not looking at all well. She had been plagued by a headache for a week or so, had since developed a sore throat, and was running a high temperature. I drove her home, she went to bed and, over the next few days, got steadily worse. When her headaches had started, she'd gone round to a local pharmacy where she had been advised to try a popular painkiller called Cibalgin, just the thing for her. A *consulta* with a doctor at the local health centre would have meant some hours off work, and she was conscientious about her teaching. So the tablets seemed a sensible response.

Before she came to see me, she had tried a course of chloroquine, everybody's reflex response to fever in malaria-ridden Beira. It hadn't helped. Now she started to develop cold sores around her mouth. The next time she came to my door it was late one night, and by now she was panicking; she wanted a lift to the home of a local dentist to see if he was still awake; her gums, she said, were coming off on her toothbrush.

He wasn't awake, so we returned home. Events moved swiftly. The course of antibiotics prescribed for her had no effect. Far from getting better, the infections in her mouth were worsening. Her face swelled beyond recognition and new, painful infections developed along the veins of her arms. After a blood test showed her white blood cell count to be precariously low, she was admitted to hospital, too weak to stand.

Beira, as Mozambique's second city, provides a far better standard of health care than most of the country, since its hospital serves three provinces. Still, it could boast only twenty-five doctors for the local population of 200,000. And there were no facilities at the hospital to diagnose anything other than simple parasitic and bacterial diseases. There was, for instance, no way of discovering whether Carol's agranulocytosis—the pathological depression of the white blood cell count—resulted from one of the several rare viral diseases that were possible causes.

As she showed no sign of improvement, it became clear that her life was in danger. So she was flown to Johannesburg, in isolation, and admitted to the Fever Hospital. There she came under the care of a team from the National Institute of Virology which included international authorities on the exotic arboviruses such as Lassa Fever and Marburg Disease which could not be ruled out as the cause of her illness. By now, Carol's condition was critical. The infection which had started in her mouth had erupted all over her body and x-rays revealed abscesses on her lungs too. Her lips fell off, the flesh completely decayed, as were her gums. The jaw bone, now exposed to view, also proved to be diseased—the teeth were so loose that a doctor examining her mouth pulled one out by mistake. The Johannesburg team ran a series of tests that ruled out a viral cause, but their laboratories were able only to diagnose the unusual bacteria responsible for the infections which had resulted from the catastrophic drop in the protective white blood cell numbers. With carefully selected antibiotics, administered and monitored hourly to maintain the correct, precise blood concentrations, they halted the infections.

Once their patient was on the mend, the doctors continued their attempts to establish the cause of her illness. The next step was to ask what drugs she had taken. She mentioned Cibalgin and there was no need to look any further. Ciba-Geigy's local office apparently had no knowledge of the product. Its sale is not allowed by the South African drug authorities. Amidopyrine, the active ingredient of Cibalgin, had first been shown to cause agranulocytosis fifty-eight years before.

An avoidable cause of death

Amidopyrine is a textbook example of an iatrogenic (disease-producing) drug. One authority says: 'amidopyrine carries too big a risk of agranulocytosis to be useful as a mild analgesic.'[1] Or, to turn to Dr Hugh-Jones's *Lecture Notes on Hematology*: 'The first drug to be incriminated [as a cause of agranulocytosis] was amidopyrine and although the compound is no longer prescribed, it is still available in some proprietary preparations in certain parts of the world.' The package of Cibalgin that Carol bought was in fact labelled for sale in Central American countries such as Nicaragua, El Salvador and the Netherlands Antilles.

In many countries of the developed world, national authorities had long ago taken action to limit the damage done by the drug. It was placed under prescription control in the United States as early as 1938 and banned completely in Australia in 1964. It was little consolation for Carol to know that the *British Medical Journal* of 14 June 1952 included a paper entitled 'Agranulocytosis caused by amidopyrine—an avoidable cause of death' in which the author pointed out that amidopyrine-containing drugs were still causing problems 'when prescribed under a proprietary name by a practitioner who does not know that it contains amidopyrine'. To avoid this kind of confusion the drug was shortly afterwards withdrawn from the market. It continued to be widely available in the developing countries and, it should be added, in West Germany, Switzerland and Japan.

The manufacturers of products containing amidopyrine—they included companies in the world top ten such as Hoechst and Sandoz—steadfastly refused to accept that the risks were as great as stated by their critics, some of whom estimated that as many as one in every 120 patients who had taken regular courses of amidopyrine had suffered adverse reactions.[2] In 1977, however, Ciba, Hoechst and Sandoz announced the withdrawal of all their products containing amidopyrine after it was shown that they might form carcinogenic by-products in the body.[3] The withdrawal and reformulation of the products (with other active ingredients whose relative safety is still held to be questionable) proved to be less than a top priority. The 1979 *Dictionary of Medical Specialities* for the Dominican Republic indicated that Ciba-Geigy products containing amidopyrine were available there and in other Central American countries.[4] The March 1980 issue of *MIMS* (*Monthly Index of Medical Specialities*) for Africa, information for which is supplied by the drug companies themselves, still listed amidopyrine-containing products from major companies such as Ciba, Hoechst and Sandoz as well as the Polish company Polfa.[5] In late 1979, there is evidence that a Ciba-Geigy sales representative distributed free samples of Cibalgin in Mozambique's capital Maputo.

Replying to journalists, Ciba claimed to have informed Mozambique about the changed formulation and blamed 'long lines of communication' for the delay in taking packages containing amidopyrine off the market.[6]

Others took a jaundiced view. Foo Gaik Sim, of the International Organization of Consumer Unions Asian Office, pointed out that the 'new' Ciba products

have been available for quite some time in Singapore while the amidopyrine ones continue to be available in neighbouring Malaysia. Surely communication lines to Malaysia are not that much longer! Let us face it, the real reason that amidopyrine preparations are no longer sold in Singapore is because its government has banned their sale. In the absence of such affirmative action (and that is sadly the case in many Third World countries for a variety of reasons) pharmaceutical companies occasionally engage in the unconscionable practice of marketing drugs whose safety is questionable, as long as and whenever they can get away with it.[7]

Carol, safely back in England, is lucky. She has been in pain ever since leaving hospital, but in a year or two, her jaw bone will be strong enough to undergo the oral surgery needed to repair the damage. Although the Cibalgin package she bought advised only that the drug might make drivers drowsy, and that it should be kept dry and out of reach of children, it did have a folded paper inside warning, in small print, of the need to have a regular blood count if the drug is taken for any length of time. Who, though, reads such package inserts, particularly when they are couched in terms that only a doctor can understand, for products which everyone knows are sold direct to the consumer? The danger of the drug is that its side-effects are so easily camouflaged. They may kill, but they do so indirectly by reducing a patient's resistance to other infections. In a poor country, with limited diagnostic resources, the true cause of those infections may well elude the hard-pressed health worker.

Good medicines taste bitter

Carol's story is a good illustration of the controversy about the safety of drugs sold to the Third World and provides a concrete example from which to begin our analysis of the pharmaceutical companies. It is important to be clear that what is at issue is not that drugs sometimes cause serious side-effects. 'A good medicine tastes bitter' expresses the folk knowledge of many cultures that effective medicine will occasionally produce undesired results. In a rational world, our aim is to ensure that the positive effects of any drug more than outweigh any harm it may do. Side-effects are thus perfectly acceptable if they occur in reasonable proportion to the threats posed by the illness for which the drug is taken.

Pharmaceutical manufacturers cannot be expected to foresee all the possible situations in which their products may be used. Thus they have a responsibility to give the users sufficient information, and in such a form that they can make a reasoned judgement about the product's risks and benefits. But who are the users? The drug's manufacturer does have the ability to decide which users will be competent to make that judgement. Medicines sold direct to the public must clearly be treated differently to those available only with a doctor's prescription. This is a rich source of confusion, since in many developing countries all medicines are available over the counter, whether or not the law or the manufacturer requires otherwise.

Cibalgin is a case in point. It was an over-the-counter product in Mozambique. Yet the package which Carol bought included, in letters so small as to be almost illegible, the warning (in Spanish) that it was to be sold by prescription. The leaflet's reference to the need for blood tests during prolonged usage did not draw itself to Carol's attention as it might have done to a doctor's. If it had read instead, 'This product can cause dangerous blood disease and should not be used except under a doctor's supervision', events would have taken a different course. That warning would have been in accordance with the available evidence. It would not, however, have helped to promote the sales of the product and this, one must assume, is why it was not given.

This, then, is one example of the kind of double-dealing which has made Third World governments and international agencies take a long, hard look at the activities of the multinational drug companies. One case of unethical practice does not notify an epidemic, however. So what is the evidence for Dr Mahler's statement that drugs not authorized for sale in the country of origin, or those whose use is restricted or which have been withdrawn for reasons of safety, are exported and marketed in developing countries?

The classic case of chloramphenicol

Regrettably, it is a matter of public record. And further, when we examine one of the best known cases, that of chloramphenicol, it is clear that the phenomenon is neither new nor limited to a few, less than ethical operators on the fringe of the industry. The US multinational Parke-Davis isolated and patented this antibiotic from a natural bacteria in 1947 and successfully synthesized it in 1949. Under the brand name of Chloromycetin it was marketed as the drug of choice in the treatment of a wide range of bacterial infections, from tonsillitis to urinary tract infection against which it was—indeed is—extremely effective. It remains the drug of choice in the treatment of typhoid. Unfortunately, as early as 1952 severe problems were noted in its use, the most serious of which was its association with a severe and often fatal blood disease, aplastic anaemia.

The US government Food and Drugs Administration (FDA) decided to allow its continued sale, but only on the grounds that the drug 'should continue to be available for careful use by the medical profession in those serious and sometimes fatal diseases in which its use is necessary'. This intervention had little impact and the amount of chloramphenicol prescribed in the USA continued to grow. In 1961, the FDA required an even stronger warning to be printed on the product label. It read: 'chloramphenicol should not be used when other less potentially dangerous agents will be effective or in the treatment of trivial infections.'

This, together with the publicity now surrounding the drug, cut by half the quantity consumed. In 1967, however, consumption was creeping back towards its 1960 peak of 55 million grams—about 8 million one-week courses—and with it rose the toll of its victims, estimated at around 2000 per year.[8]

By 1968 the government authorities had had enough. An inquiry by the US Senate that year produced such damning evidence against the drug, and gave it such wide publicity, that consumption dropped to just 10 per cent of its peak. Both doctors and manufacturers were now taking its dangers seriously, prompted perhaps by the fact that the families of some of the victims were claiming damages from them in a series of court actions.

When Parke-Davis's patent on the drug had expired in 1966, the company had already sold $45 million-worth in the USA and another $25 million abroad—ample return, it might have been hoped, for its research investment. Far from being satisfied, it carried on actively marketing the drug, neglecting, in much of its promotion outside the USA, to inform doctors and patients that it could have fatal side-effects. Indeed, the company encouraged its use in a wide variety of conditions specifically forbidden in their home country.

This had already been remarked upon in the 1968 hearings. Dr Dameshek of the prestigious Mount Sinai Hospital testified: 'In some areas of the world, notably in the less developed countries as in the Orient, Chloromycetin is used almost as freely as aspirin . . . and without the cautionary recommendations required in this country.'

A Parke-Davis director, Dr Leslie Lueck, claimed that his company 'always met all the requirements of whatever country we distributed our products in and we have met the necessity of the medical profession in that country'. His own words were turned against him by Senator Gaylord Nelson:

What the witness says is we will meet the standards of the country where the drug is sold. That means of course that there is not a single underdeveloped country in the world that has any defence against the exploitation of their people for profit by an American corporation who does not warn them of the serious, mightily serious, possibly fatal consequences here.

Concern at this blatant disregard for the well-being of the company's foreign consumers was clearly not limited to any of the 'vocal minorities' to which such sentiments are usually attributed. In 1970 the US State Department, in an almost unprecedented step, told its embassies in Latin America to contact local health authorities and warn them that Chloromycetin was being sold 'with labelling which is believed to constitute a hazard to health'.

But where were the corpses? Some Latin American doctors discounted the idea that chloramphenical was dangerous, saying that it was being widely used 'without the inevitable occurrence of aplastic anaemia'.[9] The response was damning. One Colombian doctor reported thirty-five cases between 1961 and 1965.

Diseases supposedly 'rare' in South America and common in other countries, usually make their appearance as soon as somebody starts looking for them. Colombians, unfortunately, are not immune to the toxic effects of chloramphenicol.[10]

Another reinforced his finding:

It is agreed by all Colombian hematologists that as soon as chloramphenicol became freely available in this country, the expected occurred—that is, aplastic anaemia became a dreadfully common disease. In fact, I saw forty cases during the two years after the introduction of chloramphenicol as an inexpensive drug.[11]

The adverse effects of chloramphenicol—as with the amidopyrine in the Cibalgin Carol took—may be disguised from the careless or hard-pressed health worker since, by reducing resistance to infection, the drug can paradoxically promote the infection which it is being used to treat.

The proven deaths of consumers did not change the information which Parke-Davis gave out about the product. A working group which in 1972 studied the problem for the International Organisation of Consumer Unions (IOCU) reported that: 'At the time of our survey there was also a wide variation in the indications listed for Parke-Davis's Chloromycetin as found in the various countries.' (They examined twenty-one.) 'Parke-Davis have told us that they are introducing more standardized instructions.'[12]

The company showed little sense of urgency about this. The 1973 editions of the standard Latin American drug reference manuals, compiled with information supplied by the manufacturer, showed that in Central American countries chloramphenicol was still being recommended for sore throats, ear infections, abscesses and pneumonia. While encouraging its use for the widest of indications, Parke-Davis continued to omit reference to adverse reactions, contra-indications or warnings.

A pathological state

We began with Cibalgin's single victim; just one example of the pharmaceutical industry's dangerous dishonesty in its dealings with the Third World. Parke-Davis, operating throughout a whole continent and over a generation, illustrates that the malaise has been general. And when we consider the hearings of Senator Gaylord Nelson's US Monopoly Subcommittee on drug labelling in Latin America, held in 1976, it becomes obvious that the industry as a whole was in a pathological state of making greater claims for the usefulness of its products in the poorest countries where patients were least likely to receive protection or skilled medical care: yet in these same vulnerable countries, it chose to give meagre information, if any at all, about the proven dangers of its products.

A number of testimonies were heard, but it was the evidence of Milton Silverman, pharmacologist and journalist, that demonstrated the systematic nature of the disease afflicting the industry. He had examined in detail the marketing claims made for twenty-eight different drugs sold under a wide variety of brand names by twenty-five leading US and European companies in Latin America. Parke-Davis was not alone in promoting chloramphenicol without any warning of its dangers: three other major companies were doing the same. And it was not just chloramphenicol, he concluded:

It is abundantly clear that there are glaring differences in the ways in which the same multinational pharmaceutical companies describe essentially the same drug products to physicians in the United States and to their medical colleagues in Latin America.

Invariably, the information for Latin America was deficient.

> With few exceptions, the indications included in the reference books are far more extensive, but the listing of hazards are curtailed, glossed over, or totally omitted. In some cases, only trivial side-effects are described, while serious or possibly fatal reactions are not mentioned.[13]

It is important, though, to emphasize that such examples do not come from Latin America alone. Dr John S. Yudkin, formerly teaching at the University of Dar es Salaam School of Medicine in Tanzania, has reported similar findings. He compared the recommendations of the British prescribing guide *MIMS* with the edition for Africa, information for both of which is provided by the drug companies. Hormonal pregnancy tests, banned in Britain in 1974 because of the abnormalities they produced in the children born to women who had used them, were still being promoted by such companies as Schering (Primodos) and Parke-Davis (Norlutin). The powerful drug clonidine, used to treat high blood pressure, was marketed as Catapres by Boehringer Ingelheim without mention of the danger, highlighted in Britain, that sudden cessation of its use could lead to 'rebound effects'—abrupt rises in blood pressure with the very real risk of fatal cerebral haemorrhage. Yet in a country like Tanzania where drug shortages are frequent and patients' compliance less reliable, the danger is even more acute. The company's lack of concern can be gauged by the fact that their promotion campaign included handouts of free samples, sufficient for just two or three weeks' use.[14]

Anabolic steroids were another class of drugs investigated by John Yudkin. They are best known to the European and North American public as a result of the controversy about their use by Olympic shot-putters, wrestlers and weight-lifters as chemical body-builders to put on extra kilograms. These steroids do promote growth, but unless carefully controlled, can also do severe damage, especially in children. This is why their marketing in Britain is limited to the treatment of certain cancers and dangerous anaemias. Through the medium of African *MIMS*, however, major companies like Winthrop, Ciba-Geigy and Schering were promoting these steroids as 'treatment' for malnutrition, as appetite stimulants, or for 'excessive fatiguability' in school children. Their uncontested side-effects include the irreversible masculinization of girls, the stunting of child growth through the premature closing off of the bones, and the promotion of liver tumours.

Problems with anabolic steroids have not been restricted to Africa. Bill Breckon, a BBC journalist, reported in 1979 on the way in which Winthrop's Winstrol (stanozolol) was being promoted in Sri Lanka:

> Its four-page promotional leaflet recommends its use in a number of conditions but under 'demonstrated beneficial effects' it concentrates solely on a trial of Winstrol's use in promoting growth in convalescing children aged between one and a half and six and a half years. No other trial is quoted.

Of particular concern was the fact that while the medical profession was getting one message—that Winstrol was specially prepared in syrup form for children—the company claimed, in the words of its agent's general manager, 'We do not generally indicate, promote it for children.'

In 1979 Winstrol paediatric syrups were finally banned by the Sri Lankan government after Sterling-Winthrop failed to explain why they were marketed in Sri Lanka but not in the USA.[15] The promotion of Winstrol for children has been widely reported: 'Latin American physicians are told that the drug is indicated when an increase in weight and strength is desired or when there is a need for an increase in appetite,' reported Milton Silverman. The promotion of a drug which so blatantly exploits parents' concern for their children—claiming it helps them to put on weight in countries where undernutrition and/or infection are invariably responsible for a failure to thrive—is one of the least creditable of all the examples of dangerous promotion.

Self-regulation—the best medicine?

How has the industry defended its actions? Its common voice, IFPMA (the International Federation of Pharmaceutical Manufacturers' Associations) is less than satisfactory on the subject:

> The communication of misleading or inaccurate data about a drug is self-defeating and therefore self-limiting. As misleading or inaccurate promotion is as harmful to competing manufacturers as it is to doctors and patients, competing manufacturers can be

relied upon to detect it quickly and object to it strongly. Accordingly, self-regulation within the industry is usually the cheapest and most effective method of detecting and eliminating instances of misleading or inaccurate promotion.[16]

Too often, though, manufacturers have a common interest in staying silent about known adverse effects, as is the case with anabolic steroids. For one to raise the question would only reduce the total market for all. Self-regulation has also failed to meet the test of experience. Chloramphenicol's promotion was gravely misleading for many years and was only corrected through outside pressure. As a result, the drug is still used unnecessarily widely in many Third World countries.[17]

The responses of the individual companies tend to be more down to earth. At the Nelson Subcommittee hearings, Parke-Davis claimed to obey the laws of the countries concerned. This is a defence often used, frequently without foundation. Silverman put the countries of Latin America into three categories in this respect:

(1) those where disclosure of hazards was a legal requirement which the companies did not meet (including Colombia, Panama and El Salvador);

(2) those where it was up to the government authorities to insist on full disclosure of the hazards in each case;

(3) those where the companies were absolutely correct in saying that they broke no laws because no laws covering drug promotion were in existence.[18]

Dr Bernard Haines, a technical director of E. R. Squibb in the USA, expressed the difference in graphic form. He drew a map of the world, coloured according to the degree of government regulation imposed on drug marketing. Africa, the Middle East, South-East Asia and parts of Latin America are shown untinted by red tape as areas where there is either minimal or little effective regulation.[19]

There is no law against giving too much information rather than too little. The companies have of course looked for exceptions to this general rule, but they appear to be few. E. J. Ledder of Abbott Laboratories claimed in front of Senator Edward Kennedy's US Senate Health Subcommittee in May 1979 that 'some countries do not even permit a package insert for products sold through pharmacies' and gave the examples of Canada, Guatemala, Colombia and Mexico. His sources of information, presumably within his company, were clearly not very familiar with the technicalities of selling drugs in these, their markets. Two weeks later, Mr Ledder was obliged to apologize to the Subcommittee and inform it that his statement had been misleading:

> In Guatemala, there is neither a requirement for, nor a prohibition against, use of drug package inserts. A manufacturer is free to use inserts with its products. Drug regulations in Mexico require package inserts, intended to be read by the patient, for three antibiotics, anticancer drugs and digoxin. For all other drug products package inserts are optional.[20]

The industry would like us to believe that the problem is one of different approaches in different countries. 'Disagreement among national regulatory authorities regarding the legal requirements for the labelling of prescription drugs has been a source of much irritation,' complained Max Tiefenbacher, then president of IFPMA and a director of Hoechst, the giant German chemical and pharmaceutical company.[21] There are certainly differences of approach, not just on labelling but also on other aspects of drug control. In the USA registration of a new drug takes longer than in Britain where there is more reliance on post-marketing surveillance than on pre-marketing experiments to demonstrate efficacy and detect side-effects. Such differences of approach between rich countries have nothing to do with the weak or non-existent controls in the poor world. There, it is a straight question of the haves and the have-nots—those who have the resources to vet all drugs coming on to the market and to control their promotion, and those who do not.

I have a vivid memory of the desk of a senior health ministry official in Swaziland, loaded down with files on subjects ranging from a WHO treatise on narcotics control to hospital and health centre budgets—was he supposed to be a one-man FDA too? There are the countries in which government service is poorly paid and without motivation, where corruption is the norm—fed, even if only literally in the form of free meals at big hotels, by the multinational drug industry. It is commonplace in some countries for expensive antibiotics to be present on hospital pharmacy shelves but not aspirin, because no aspirin salesman ever took the pharmacist out to lunch. There is no need to ask how those antibiotics got on the hospital buying list in the first place, or why no warning was given of their side-effects.

Even when the marketing practices of a multinational are called into question, non-medical issues will often resolve the argument. When two doctors from Tanzania's medical school circulated a paper outlining the case against Avafortan, an amidopyrine-containing painkiller marketed there by the German company Asta Werke, they were told by the German embassy, in no uncertain terms, to keep quiet. One of the reasons given, they later explained, was that the paper

> criticized the West German pharmaceutical industry for marketing a drug in Africa which was banned in the UK and USA on grounds of safety. We are told that a copy of the paper reached the West German embassy which then approached the university and hinted that such criticism was inappropriate at a time when the university was receiving West German aid in building the new engineering faculty.[22]

Where the relations of a poor country to the institutions of a rich one are concerned, there is rarely an appropriate time for the weaker party to make criticisms.

Bad medicine, but good marketing

For a while, adverse effects, correctly managed, can even help to sell drugs. Dr Oliver de S. Pinto of Ciba-Geigy quoted an example of this kind to a meeting of managers from his company's subsidiaries:

> Not long ago, a woman in Malaysia developed a severe haemorrhagic disease that was closely associated with taking Cibalgin, and her physician regarded this as a drug-induced blood dyscrasia [a range of diseases which includes agranulocytosis]. Our local marketing director was provided with full information and asked to suggest further investigation of the illness which would not otherwise have been carried out. The girl turned out to have an infection called Dengue fever. We had told the physician that her disease was quite probably due to Cibalgin and blood dyscrasia, he proved us wrong and his final comment in a letter thanking us for our help was that whenever possible he would always in the future prescribe Ciba-Geigy drugs.
>
> That, ladies and gentlemen, was both good medicine and good marketing.[23]

The approach has its limitations. Dr Pinto emphasized to his managers that adverse effect reports should always be followed up. His colleagues, out there in the real world away from head office, may be interested to know how his principles were followed by that very head office which laid them down. For in Carol's case, the technical competence of the Johannesburg team's diagnosis could not be challenged. Perhaps because of this, when her doctor in Mozambique wrote a letter to Ciba's head office about her case, the follow-up was a 'We thank you for your interest in our product' reply. Only when the case was reported in the British journals *The Lancet* and *New Scientist*, and the possibility of legal action ahead came into sight, did Dr Pinto try to find out more.

Yet there has been a change in the policy of the pharmaceutical industry over the issue of drug hazards, and it has not been just cosmetic. It was expressed in principle by the resolution sponsored by the US companies, and passed by the IFPMA Council in 1977, which said that 'particular care should be taken that essential information as to the medical product's safety, contra-indications and side-effects is appropriately communicated.' Quite what this has meant in practice is less clear, and IFPMA did not respond to a request for information on the degree of compliance by its members. But it is an advance on the old position of 'we supply the information required by law and have no further responsibility.' Why the change?

It is, in part, due to the fear of legal action by drug victims, a fear which is already very real in the rich world markets. While the pharmaceutical companies complain vociferously about excessive government drug regulations, they welcome the protection they offer against legal action for damage done by the marketing of dangerous drugs. Otto Nowotny of Hoffmann-La Roche puts the point well:

> The more enlightened people in the industry are certainly looking at the regulatory agencies in the long run as our protecting angels because with product liability coming up and knowing how much it can cost, we want these kinds of controls.[24]

It was because of potential damage claims that Dr Pinto wanted to know about adverse effects produced by any Ciba drug in any market:

> If any preparation, in any form (even as just pure substance) comes from Basle or if permission to market any preparation comes from Basle, then in law Basle has a potential product liability as well as your own Group Company . . . the proper use of information about adverse reaction reports depends on past experience, the continuing and critical appraisal of present information and the presentation of information with suggestions that will *protect our future*.[25] (My italics.)

Legal threats from their victims are not the only incentive to the companies to make a fuller disclosure of their products' hazards. At a time when they are launching their counter-offensive against their United Nations/Third World critics, they must be aware that easily visible double standards do little to help their strategy. Thus Charles Medawar, a director of the London-based pressure group Social Audit, can leaf through various international issues of *MIMS* and highlight the differences between the information available in Britain and that supplied to doctors in Africa, the Middle East and Asia. Since, as I have already indicated, the information about each drug is supplied and checked by the manufacturing company, the comparisons can be devastating.[26]

In the future, the pharmaceutical companies will want to choose their fields of battle more carefully, and for them to accept more exacting standards in their giving out of information about adverse effects would seem a sensible tactical move. Full information need not have a great impact on drug sales—there is a consensus that the provision of very detailed information has minimal impact since no one bothers to read it. The package insert for Bayer's Resochin (chloroquine) has three lines about indications, but thirty-three on the side-effects. Some of these are extremely serious—the drug can cause irreversible eye damage as well as a host of less permanent but very unpleasant responses such as nausea, distorted vision, 'nervous symptoms' and, although rarely, muscular debility. Nevertheless Resochin is among the most widely used of drugs in those regions of Africa and Asia where non-resistant malaria occurs. There is little evidence that information about—as opposed to experience of—the side-effects has significantly reduced consumption. Now that clear recommendations for all users to have regular eye check-ups 'before, during and after long-term prophylaxis with Resochin' have been included, Bayer's legal representatives are presumably sleeping easier.

Depo-Provera—a matter for debate

A more open and honest approach will stand the industry in good stead when there are real controversies to be resolved. The US companies are, for example, bound by a law which prohibits them from exporting drugs from the USA if they are not licensed for sale there. As true multinationals, they circumvent this without difficulty by arranging for other group companies to do the business. But they find it irksome, inconvenient and sometimes expensive, and are

pressing to have the law changed. The test case for its amendment is
Depo-Provera (medroxyprogesterone acetate), the now infamous,
long-acting injectable contraceptive. Its use has been attacked
because of its unpleasant short-term side-effects and because suspicion has fallen on it of possibly provoking potentially fatal cancers as
much as twenty years after first use. Because of these doubts, its
manufacturers, the Upjohn company, cannot market it as a contraceptive in the USA. However, the FDA, which made this ruling,
informed the company:

> We recognize that the benefit/risk considerations may be different
> in other nations, where alternative methods of contraception may
> be less available or less acceptable . . . Our evaluation was based
> only upon benefit/risk considerations in the US.[27]

In Tanzania, the local family planning organization UMATI
stopped using Depo-Provera in 1973 because of the controversy
about its safety. Press comment at the time was vitriolic. An article
in the main government newspaper protested:

> That in countries where this drug is manufactured it is still being
> experimented on rats, mice and rabbits is, to say the least, a
> terrible blow to the Tanzanian women who were misled into using
> it by the Family Planning Association of Tanzania. No one knows
> the number of these victims. No one can tell their future. What
> can be said is that they are suffering from all sorts of dislocations
> and abnormalities. What a pity! There are still various elements in
> our society. One of them is the reactionary petty bourgeoisie. This
> is the most dangerous element in our midst today. As long as
> international capitalist organizations are prepared, directly or
> indirectly, to bribe this element with money, or to offer it the
> niceties of air travels here and there, this particular parasitic and
> opportunistic element will champion even a road to the very death
> of its sisters and brothers![28]

The issue provided a handy weapon with which to attack all
methods, indeed the whole idea, of family planning, in the crudest
terms:

> A mother of three said that since she started taking the pills her
> hair went grey and loose. Her eyelashes have also gone grey. The
> mother, who is twenty-four, claimed: 'Before I was trapped I was
> so nice looking that my husband used to feel proud of me. Now
> neighbours, who know my secret, laugh at me. They no longer
> call me "Stella". They call me "Bony".'[29]

On the day that article appeared, an editorial in the same paper drew attention to the deteriorating situation in Dar es Salaam's Ocean Road maternity hospital. Under the headline 'A human furnace', it described how fatalities among mothers were rising year by year—one mother in 300 admitted during the first half of 1973 had died during or immediately after delivery. Conditions were 'enough to drive the most "modern" woman back to her grand-mother for midwifery services and risk death rather than go to this place'.[30]

There, in essence, is the case for using Depo-Provera in Tanzania but not in the USA. Risks have to be balanced against benefits, and the consequences of pregnancy—wanted or not—for women in the poor world are far more dangerous than they are for their rich sisters. Extend such crude calculations to other methods of con-traception in rich and poor communities and they show contracep-tion's risk to be tiny in comparison with that of pregnancy (Table 1). The adverse effects of Depo-Provera would thus have to be extremely serious to outweigh those of childbearing.

Table 1 **Risks of pregnancy versus risks of contraception**
(Deaths per million women per year)

METHOD	RICH COUNTRY *Deaths due to:*		POOR COUNTRY *Deaths due to:*	
	Method	Method + Pregnancy	Method	Method + Pregnancy
Pill	30	35	30	160
IUD	10	19	10	120
Others	0	38	0	560
			0	
None		*150*		*2000*

Notes:
1. Rich World = health care with maternal mortality 250/million. Poor World = health care with maternal mortality 5000/million. (Ocean Road mortality 1973 = 3300/million).
2. Deaths due to method and pregnancy include those for deaths due to pregnancy where the contraception has failed.
3. 'Others' include condoms, spermicides and diaphragms.

Until the results from new animal studies became available, the case against Depo-Provera on the grounds of safety was not as strong as its critics would have it. But based on past experience, there was a healthy mistrust of corporate motives—a mistrust which may now turn out to have been justified—which consistently thwarted Upjohn's attempts to turn an average drug into a real money-spinner.

Depo-Provera serves, however, to show how a drug's safety cannot be assessed in isolation from its benefits, nor, therefore, in isolation from the community in which it will be used. Similarly, criticism of the widespread marketing of amidopyrine products is also related to its benefits for, while the drug is an effective painkiller, there are many others as cheap, so its benefits are by no means unique. Chloramphenicol, on the other hand, because of its wide action, is still recommended and used in the treatment of diseases for which, in the rich world, it would be considered wildly inappropriate.[31] In some cases, though, those using it are conscious of its dangers and consider them more than outweighed by the fact that infections trivial in an essentially healthy person may be life-threatening in one who is undernourished and already suffering from other disease. Further, chloramphenicol is one of the cheapest antibiotics—a week's course costs less than most penicillins and even less than some of the old sulpha drugs. So it is less expensive to keep a stock on the pharmacy shelf until needed.

The accusation that the pharmaceutical companies sell 'dangerous drugs' to the Third World must thus be suitably qualified. Charles Medawar has put it well:

In themselves, drugs are more or less *toxic* rather than more or less dangerous. As a rule, drugs become dangerous only when those who prescribe or dispense or use them do not appreciate how or when they should be used. . . . One of the most important things in determining how dangerous a drug is—or how safe and effective it can be—is the quality and the completeness of information available about it. For this information to be useful, clearly it has to reach those who prescribe or use those products.[32]

Information comes in many forms, and in pharmaceuticals—more so perhaps than in most fields—the form is often as important as the content. The evidence presented in this chapter has been concerned mainly with two of the more objective forms of information—the written information included with the product (the package insert), or the prescribing guide supplied to the doctor (international issues of *MIMS* in particular). On the basis of this alone, criticisms of the multinational companies hold since, as we have seen, they have often failed to give vital information essential for the safe use of their drugs.

It has been convenient to my purpose to use this question of drug safety to introduce, in an anecdotal way, an analysis of the contribution made by the pharmaceutical industry to Third World health. But it should be said that adverse effects occur relatively rarely and calls of foul play on grounds of safety alone are somewhat peripheral to my central concern. The marketing package, and the resulting pattern of drug use as a whole, have to be examined and related to something abstract called the health needs of each community. If the beneficial effects of drugs and the ways they are assessed and communicated are to be analysed on this basis it will be necessary to take an approach that is considerably more rigorous.

Three: Efficacy

Depo-Provera, chloramphenicol and amidopyrine have something in common besides their potentially dangerous side-effects. They do what they are claimed to do. Depo-Provera prevents pregnancy. Chloramphenicol combats many infections, particularly in communities where misuse has not induced resistance to it. Amidopyrine is a strong painkiller which rapidly brings down fever.

It is indefensible to sell these drugs, with their known dangers, without due warnings, especially for trivial complaints where safer alternatives exist. But the multinational pharmaceutical industry has done worse. It has sold dangerous drugs which are not even effective, and has encouraged their widest possible use.

Easy though it is to dramatize these activities, to do so is to miss the point. The fundamental criticism of the multinational pharmaceutical companies is not that they sell dangerous and ineffective drugs but that, in so doing, they have gravely distorted medical practice and deprived many people, particularly in developing countries, of the health care they need. This can be demonstrated very clearly by an examination of the way in which that universal illness, diarrhoea, is treated in the rich and poor worlds respectively.

But first, some definitions are needed. What, for instance, is an 'effective' drug? The English language is imperfect here, and the various definitions available are contradictory. It is helpful instead to use a different word to describe one of the range of situations actually encountered in the use of drugs. For the purpose of this book, three may be defined:
(1) effective drugs: those capable of producing results;
(2) efficacious drugs: those which actually produce desired results;
(3) efficient drugs: those capable of producing desired results economically.
(It should be added that it is usual to accept as efficacious or effective only those drugs whose results can be achieved without unacceptable risk.)

The *effectiveness* of a drug is easy to measure in laboratories or through clinical trials, controlled experiments using actual patients. These provide ideal conditions. But just as the safety of Depo-Provera had to be assessed in terms of the health profile of the community in which it was used, so the *efficacy* of a drug depends on how, where and why it is actually used. An effective drug not taken in the right dose or at the right time will not be efficacious; nor will it be efficacious if the result which it produces is not in fact a desired result. The Third World, in which the majority of people live, is by definition a poor world. Here, the value of a drug has to be measured in terms of its cost as well as its efficacy. One drug may be slightly less efficacious than another. But if it is much cheaper, it will allow more people to be successfully treated and will be the more *efficient* of the two.

To judge by its reception, the latter idea was little short of revolutionary in health care. But before turning to efficiency, and before examing in detail those allegations that Halfdan Mahler put before the World Health Assembly in 1975 that drugs banned for lack of efficacy, or with indications not allowed in their countries of origin, were being sold to the Third World, a brief diversion to the rich world may help to clarify the discussion.

The sale of inefficacious drugs has by no means been restricted to the developing world, as a few events selected at random from the past few years show. First, there was the French revolution, the pharmaceutical revolution, of 1979. New regulations were introduced obliging the drug companies to prove the claims that they made for the effectiveness of their products. Should they be unable to do so consumers had to be told that it had never been proven that the drug actually did what it was claimed to do. An estimated 75 per cent of all drugs on the market had to carry such warnings, although it was hoped that in some cases clinical trials would later prove their effectiveness.[1] Meanwhile, in Germany, a court ruling made it clear that government permission to sell new drugs should not imply that they were effective.[2] And in the USA, the health authorities were pondering the problem of how to stop state-funded health schemes from paying for treatment with drugs whose effectiveness has never been proven.[3] The onus was on the government to show that the drugs were not effective rather than on the pharmaceutical companies to prove the contrary, insisted the US Pharmaceutical Manufacturers' Association.[4]

It took American lawyers to reach the limits of absurdity. Two big US companies entered into expensive legal battle in the US Federal Court over the right to produce and sell the drug isoxsuprine, a 'vasodilator' which was claimed to have beneficial effects in certain diseases of the circulation. The Premo company was disregarding Mead Johnson's patent for the drug, arguing that its 'invention' was a chemical modification of an existing drug so trivial that it did not deserve to be protected by patents. As it happened, the judge agreed, but the technicalities are unimportant. What was astonishing was the fact that the US government's Food and Drugs Administration (FDA) had already decided that the drug was ineffective and had ordered its withdrawal from the market. 'My sensibilities are disturbed', said Judge Lee Sarokin, 'by the spectre of two pharmaceutical giants struggling over the right to control and sell a product which is claimed to be ineffective for the purposes indicated.'[5]

Ineffective products are sold in some cases because they are 'grandfather drugs' which have been around for so long that no one has bothered, or thought it commercially worthwhile, to prove their efficacy. Others have clear clinical effects which should, theoretically, be beneficial in the treatment of disease but which in practice are inefficacious. Isoxsuprine is a good example here. It causes healthy arteries to relax and expand, which suggested to researchers and marketing men that it and similar products might be helpful in cases of atherosclerosis, in which the blood flow is reduced by diseased arteries. 'Attractive as this possibility was, these drugs have not proved useful clinically in peripheral vascular disease.'[6] That conclusion did not prevent Mead Johnson, Premo and other companies from marketing their products very profitably.

More potent if you're poor

These examples show that the sale of ineffective drugs is by no means limited to the Third World. The first criticism levelled against the companies is that they systematically claim more effects, more potency and more value for their products in the poor world than they feel able to do in the more careful and sceptical countries of Europe and North America. To do this they have consistently misrepresented the evidence, or even invented it. As with safety, the examples are legion and Milton Silverman has catalogued a large number. For instance:

— *phenylbutazone* (Butazolidin: Ciba-Geigy)
   (an anti-inflammatory painkiller)
   USA: indicated for 8 specific types of arthritis and gout only.

Central America: 20 different indications including such catch-alls as 'miscellaneous processes with pain and fever'.
— *indomethacin* (Indocid: Merck Sharp and Dohme)
(another painkiller)
USA: 4 specific pain-relieving indications, heavily qualified.
Latin America: 10 indications including the broad category 'pain in dental ailments'.
— *chlorpromazine* (Largactil: Rhône-Poulenc in Latin America)
(Thorazine: Smith Kline and French in the USA)
(a powerful major tranquillizer)
USA: 7 specific indications, mainly for psychotic conditions.
Latin America: 43 diverse indications including such unlikely complaints as pernicious malarial attacks, hypertension, psychosomatic disorders, dysmenorrhea, etc.[7]

The disclosure of drug dangers may have become markedly more uniform since the publication of Silverman's book but the same cannot be said for claims of efficacy. Thus Squibb can market its new drug captopril in Guatemala, Brazil and Honduras not only for all kinds of hypertension but also for all forms of congestive heart failure. Yet in the USA, the company's own experts told a press conference that it was only effective in perhaps 40 per cent of cases of hypertension. The American FDA for its part has said that captopril (known as Capoten or Lopirin) may only be marketed for use by hypertensive patients who have failed to respond satisfactorily to existing drugs. Similar conditions have been imposed in Germany where the authorities insist that patients only be started on the drug in hospital, although they do allow its use for patients with heart failure where other drugs have proven ineffective.[8]

Systematic corporate attempts to exaggerate drug efficacy have been documented by Brazilian doctor Cesar Victora. He found that companies used false statistics, or simply bad science, to boost the image—and the sale—of their products. With drugs of proven efficacy, they exaggerated their effectiveness in relation to competitors. Wellcome promoted its Espectrin (co-trimoxazole), a valuable antibiotic, as 'superior to the tetracyclines' (which are equally valuable) and illustrated their advertising leaflets with pie charts purporting to prove this claim. Unfortunately they don't, since statistical analysis reveals that the difference between the two products is not significant.

To promote drugs which are not particularly effective, the companies simply chose their comparisons more carefully, as in the

case of Parke-Davis's Ponstan 500 (mefenamic acid). Promoting this
for use in the treatment of arthritis and rheumatism, the company
claimed it to be more effective than acetaminophen or codeine,
which it almost certainly is. But, as Victora points out,

> the comparisons make little sense as the problems invol-
> ved require anti-inflammatory as well as analgesic action and
> Ponstan 500—which has both properties—has been compared
> to two carefully selected analgesics devoid of anti-inflammatory
> action.

Aspirin, on the other hand, is at least as effective.

The companies' claims that their advertising and promotion of
drugs really provide an information service for doctors are clearly
contradicted by the poor standards of their scientific and medical
content. Beecham, to name one example, compared the blood
concentration of its drug ampicillin, necessary to kill bacteria, with
that of another antibiotic, erythromycin. The fact that the lethal
ampicillin concentration is lower is totally irrelevant, says Victora.
The two drugs belong to two different pharmacological groups. It
would be as logical to declare that 1000 grams of bronze are worth
more than 500 grams of gold. Nevertheless, the idea that the
smaller the quantity of drug needed the more effective it is appears
to have spread from one company to another. Hoechst used just this
comparison to promote its Daonil (glibenclamide), an anti-diabetic
agent, claiming it to be 50 to 200 times more active than its
competitors. 'This sounds somewhat like owning a car which can
reach 200km/hr in a country where the maximum speed limit is
strictly set at 80km/hr,' says Victora. Since treatment of diabetes
involves establishing balanced blood-sugar levels, too much of an
anti-diabetic drug can produce effects as serious as the condition
which it is used to treat. A highly potent drug may therefore be less
efficacious than a somewhat weaker one which leaves more margin
for error. Victora states:

> It might be argued that the fallacies shown above are the results of
> incompetence rather than ill intent. Actually, it is not easy to say
> which assumption would be less offensive to the departments of
> advertising of these powerful corporations. After reviewing hun-
> dreds of promotional materials, I have not found a single example
> of a statistical or methodological fallacy which would make the
> promoted product seem any the worse.[9]

More than a matter of convenience

After a while, these catalogues of corporate exaggeration and dishonesty begin to pall. Yes, advertising men are hucksters and pharmaceutical companies are run by 'businessmen not bishops'[10] whose job it is to sell as much of their products as possible. As long as this is recognized, does it matter how they try to delude the doctors?

It matters if their propaganda serves to institute the inefficient use of medicine. Developing countries cannot afford to waste what little money they manage to set aside for health care. It matters if inefficacious remedies are used when better ones are available. In the rich world, you can usually count on a second opinion if your first doctor prescribes something silly. In the poor world, you're lucky to have that first chance at all. So the next criticism of the companies is that, through their marketing, they systematically distort medical practice at the expense of efficacious health care.

The varied approaches to the treatment of diarrhoea illustrate the impact which the promotion of ineffective or inefficacious drugs has on the way medicine is practised in the Third World, where diarrhoea is among the more common illnesses and also a leading cause of death, particularly among young children. For them, the loss of large quantities of fluid leads very quickly to dehydration which, if not promptly treated, can be fatal. The discussion of diarrhoea and its treatment leads us to the case of Lomotil.

Lomotil (diphenoxylate) is a drug of convenience: like its relatives codeine and morphine, it relieves the symptoms of diarrhoea by virtually paralysing the gut, although Searle, its manufacturers, prefer to say that it 'reduces gut motility'. However you choose to describe it, the effect is easy to visualize. The gut stops pushing its contents along, so you don't have to be for ever dashing to the lavatory. That's important if you're on a crowded plane or in an all-day meeting. It is of little consequence, though, for Third World children. What matters for them is that the body fluids they lose are replaced.

There is fertile ground for confusion here and Searle have not been slow to sow its seeds. Lomotil does not stop diarrhoea, it only stops diarrhoea from getting out. If a businessman in a hurry takes it, it is not only effective but efficacious too. If given to a young dehydrated child, it may appear effective but it is completely inefficacious. Once that child's body fluids are in its gut, they are as good as lost. They cannot maintain the volume of the blood. Nor can they perform any of their other bodily functions. They might as well be in a bag around the child's neck.

This is not obvious but, where diarrhoea is a matter of life and death, it is crucial that health workers understand it. They need to know what is efficacious in the management of the disease and what is worthless. Searle's contribution to this understanding is distinctly unimpressive. My interest was aroused when I found their drug being sold over the counter in the Sudan in attractive display packs picturing a relieved astronaut, with the sales line: 'Lomotil stops diarrhoea fast: used by astronauts during Gemini and Apollo space flights'. (In most developed countries Lomotil is available only on prescription because it presents certain clear dangers.) Then, in the Philippines, in the children's emergency room of a general hospital in Manila, where dozens of infants are admitted every week with dehydration, I found the young doctors routinely using bottles of Lomotil that had been left as samples by the Searle salesman.

From Kenya, Dr Colin Forbes, a paediatrician, then Professor of Community Health at Nairobi University Medical School, reported that Lomotil was being sold without prescription all over the country. He was concerned about the dangers of accidental poisoning—in children, the fatal dose can be uncomfortably close to the recommended one. He also explained concisely why Lomotil was an inappropriate medicine for children:

> I have seen children poisoned by Lomotil and there are many documented cases. The use of Lomotil in a child is bad (and dangerous) medicine. It paralyses the gut and so pools the noxious secretions in an inert 'third space', when all this fluid is best shat out of the body. Diarrhoea doesn't kill children, dehydration does, and Lomotil does not stop dehydration, it can allow the child to die of respiratory depression and dehydration![11]

When these criticisms appeared in print, Searle's reaction was swift, if not public. In a circular to sales staff, intended to guide them should the issue be raised by doctors, they spelled out their marketing philosophy. Yes, dehydration was the main concern with diarrhoea in children in the Third World and rehydration was always indicated.

> However, to prevent further water loss in most cases, it is also useful to give an anti-diarrhoeal, such as Lomotil, as well. By its action to restore normal gut action, Lomotil aids reabsorption of water and helps prevent dehydration. Therefore Lomotil *does*

have an important role to play in the treatment of such diarrhoeas, to help prevent dehydration.[12]

When pressed, Dr Daniel Azarnoff, president of Searle Research and Development, took a very different public stance:

> We would like to emphasize that Searle does not promote Lomotil as therapy for dehydration but rather as treatment for diarrhoea.[13]

If Lomotil was used for rehydration, that was the *doctors'* decision he implied, neatly sidestepping any criticism of Searle's role:

> Diphenoxylate slows gastrointestinal propulsion, and thus decreases the passage of stools containing water. By increasing intestinal transit time, it also provides a better chance for fluids to be absorbed. For these reasons, under certain conditions, *physicians may prescribe* diphenoxylate as an adjunct to rehydration therapy.

This, he said, is principally the case in developing countries because there it can take a long time to get a child to hospital.

> In these countries, the use of a highly effective anti-diarrhoeal like Lomotil *is considered valuable by many paediatricians* as adjunctive therapy to the administration of fluids. (My italics.)

A dangerous kind of deceit

The manoeuvre is a classic one. The company cannot, at this level, make claims for their products which run contrary to the evidence they have. So they put their words into the mouths of doctors, then hawk them around as third-party opinions. Colin Forbes had a simple solution for this deceitful kind of marketing, and for its agents: 'I used to drive them out of the coffee room in the Kenyatta Hospital when I found them baffling my interns with pseudo-science about diphenoxylate, and with ballpoint pens, letter openers, to support.' For every Colin Forbes however, there will be two doctors who keep their doubts to themselves and another ten who will be taken in.

There is, as far as I know, no scientific evidence to support the view that Lomotil is of any value in preventing dehydration or assisting rehydration in the infectious diarrhoeas which predominate in the Third World. Searle have certainly not supplied any, despite my repeated requests. In fact, among the papers they did supply was one which stated quite categorically that opiate-type anti-diarrhoeals like Lomotil do not help promote rehydration. They work 'because of reduced propulsion (increased retention of fluid within the gut) rather than increased absorption'.[14]

The point is not just that the company encourages its salesmen to promote its product for uses in which it is not efficacious. It is that by so doing, Searle has systematically encouraged a false understanding about the problems of diarrhoea and an incorrect approach to its treatment in communities where it is a matter of life and death to get it right. Almost incidentally, it has also promoted a dangerous complacency about the safety of its product.

It does this first and foremost by encouraging and sponsoring doctors to do new studies of the 'usefulness' of Lomotil in diarrhoea. If these 'studies' really advanced medical science's understanding of the way Lomotil works, that would be entirely acceptable. But Searle somehow contrives to avoid any that might throw some light on such controversial issues as the drug's role in dehydration. In fact, it appears that the African and Asian doctors with whom it has collaborated have not even been told of Searle's official view of the drug.

So among the study reports the company sent me to demonstrate the role of Lomotil in child diarrhoeas are conclusions that the drug is a 'safe agent', 'safe and effective in malnourished infants', that 'there need not be undue restraint on the use of this drug' or that there is 'negligible incidence of side-effects'. Searle helped to set up these studies. But none of the doctors involved seemed to know that the company, which has a far more extensive knowledge of its product, feels obliged to warn that 'Lomotil should be used with special caution in young children because of the variability of response in this age group.'[15]

Searle collaborates too in 'trials' by doctors whose understanding of the diarrhoea process seems limited to the idea that it is necessary 'to reduce the frequency of stools rapidly in order to prevent the dreaded complication of dehydration'.[16] The company did not bother to enlighten them. Such clinical trials are now generally recognized to be more a matter of marketing than of medicine. So we should not expect Searle to point out their technical flaws, particularly if they will ensure that Lomotil is used routinely, if unnecessarily, in one more hospital. The company's first responsibility is after all to its shareholders, not to health.

This distortion of the truth, and subsequent distortion of medical practice, is not an isolated case. It certainly matches Searle's corporate record. The company achieved some notoriety in the USA as a supplier of ineffective drugs: 'Less than half of Searle's drugs are effective in treating even one of the ailments for which they are prescribed,' reported a study of fifteen major US drug companies in which Searle's record, on this count, was worst.[17] Internal documents leaked to the press in 1976 revealed just how the company operated in the Third World. They do not serve to give confidence in the objectivity of any scientific evidence which Searle supplies about its drugs. In India, the company spent $45,000 organizing 'independent' scientific conferences. Of the biggest it said:

> We arranged it and supported it—but remained completely in the background as we didn't wish the already biased Minister of Health to be able to say that any of the papers that were being presented were in any way influenced by commercial considerations, so it appeared to be a completely independent symposium put on by the All-India Gynecological Society.[18]

In Iran, a free visit to England was arranged for the sister of the health official who ordered Searle products. In the Lebanon, Searle supported a medical magazine: 'The magazine recommends "impartially" products to the public for specific common illnesses,' wrote sales executive Derek Evans. Some years later, Mr Evans appeared in Nairobi, paving the way for Dr H. M. Lal, Searle's Medical Director for Africa and Asia, to set up yet another 'clinical trial' for Lomotil, this time at the Kenyatta National Hospital.[19]

As with all examples of corporate malpractice, criticism of deceitful drug promotion is not restricted to an individual company. Lomotil is not the only drug with powerful effects which, used inappropriately, is dangerous as well as inefficacious. And Searle is not the only company which allows its drugs to be misused in this way. Lasix (furosemide) is a powerful diuretic which has precisely the opposite effect to Lomotil. It 'squeezes out' (chemically) excess water from the body. In conditions like hypertension, this helps to bring down dangerously high blood pressure, and this is its main indication. In developing countries, however, it has found another application. Here, kwashiorkor is a common cause of bloated, puffy swelling. In the last stage of this form of childhood malnutrition, the victim's body swells up as its biochemistry goes out of control. Lasix can reduce this swelling almost instantly, but it only serves to bring death closer. Nevertheless, in some poor countries, Lasix, originally made by the German Hoechst company, is used for this purpose. Worse, some drug salesmen actually promote diuretics like Lasix for kwashiorkor, although there is no evidence that salesmen from Hoechst were involved. A health worker in Bangladesh recounted one incident to a BBC reporter:

> the drug rep was trying to persuade this rather young doctor that furosemide . . . was a very good drug to use for children who had kwashiorkor or marasmus. These are deficiency diseases which produce swelling all over the body and the rep was suggesting that this drug was very good at reducing this oedema . . . When it was pointed out that the swelling might go down but the child would be killed . . . the drug representative said, 'Well, the child is going to die anyway.'[20]

Partly because of this kind of promotion, and partly because good information about the drug's correct use was lacking, doctors, pharmacy owners and parents were encouraged to use the drug in cases like these and children did die, as Martin Schweiger, another health worker in Bangladesh, explained:

> We've certainly come across quite a few children who've died as a result . . . well, to say they've died as a result of the Lasix is something I can't prove, but they've died very soon after being given Lasix in cases where I would have expected the patient to survive.

Clioquinol—dangerous, and inefficacious too

In their place, Lasix and Lomotil are both effective and efficacious, and it is only when their effects are misunderstood that they are inefficacious and dangerous. It is another diarrhoea remedy which serves as the classic illustration of how an eminently respectable pharmaceutical corporation can promote the consumption of a drug that is almost completely ineffective for its claimed indication.

There is still much to be learnt about diarrhoea. Medical scientists have identified many organisms which cause it. But present them with a patient suffering from diarrhoea and, until very recently, in only 20 per cent of cases could they name the culprit.[21] The reason lies precisely in the multiplicity of suspects. There are the well-known ones, the potentially fatal infections of cholera and typhoid, the less potent members of the *Salmonella* family which are the commonest cause of food poisoning, and the dysenteries, most of which are familiar. But there are many others. Normally harmless *E. coli* has relatives which can, in people not used to living with them, cause serious illness. There are, too, whole tribes of viruses which can still not be detected as a matter of routine in developing countries but are believed to cause a significant proportion of childhood diarrhoeas occurring there. For these Third World children, other illnesses such as measles and malaria are also often associated with diarrhoea, while universally, simple physiological mechanisms—a change of diet or a good fright—can provoke a bout of diarrhoea.[22]

It is obvious that no single drug is going to *prevent* diarrhoea arising from more than a handful of these causes. Yet a generation of travellers was brought up to believe that if they took their Entero-Vioform (clioquinol) regularly, they would escape Montezuma's Revenge, Delhi Belly, the Rangoon Runs or Mexican *turista*.

The long march of Entero-Vioform's crippled, blinded and deformed victims, starting out in the Japanese courtrooms, has now passed across the world's television screens and the pages of its newspapers to bring home, in human terms, the consequences of that particular medical nonsense. At least 10,000 people are believed to have suffered from SMON, serious damage to the nervous system caused by the drug. They took it, as suggested by manufacturers, to prevent diarrhoea and other stomach complaints. It is little consolation for them to learn now that, on the best available evidence, clioquinol is ineffective. It is a useful treatment for amoebic dysentery and may also be effective in other types of dysentery. But nowhere are these the most important causes of diarrhoea. So the drug's value for prevention or cure of unspecific diarrhoea is minimal. There is even evidence that, like Lomotil, it can make some gut infections worse.

The clioquinol disaster reflects, in part, the history of the drug industry:

> Clioquinol came into use long before good clinical trials were performed on most new drugs (1934) and in this respect resembles traditional folk medicines. Its general use can perhaps be accepted on similar terms, but its commercial promotion, in the absence of clear evidence of efficacy, whether for the prophylaxis or treatment of non-specific diarrhoea, seems undesirable.[23]

Its sequel was, as always, to leave the developing countries exposed to the last to the hazards of the ineffective drug. The Japanese SMON victims began their legal battle for compensation in 1971. By 1977 the terms of a settlement were agreed. Ciba-Geigy and the two Japanese companies involved accepted that clioquinol caused SMON. Ciba-Geigy apologized profusely, as required: 'In view of the fact that medical products manufactured and sold by us have been responsible for the occurrence of this tragedy in Japan, we extend our apologies, frankly and without reservation, to the plaintiffs and their families.' They extended considerably more than this. Their accountants allowed for compensation payments to the order of $150 million.[24]

Corporate concern beyond Japan was another matter. In 1975 the International Organization of Consumer Unions (IOCU) had already reported the vast differences in the recommendations for the use of clioquinol in samples collected from thirty-five countries. Among the twenty-nine samples of Entero-Vioform collected in twenty-eight countries many were recommended for use in various vague forms of summer, traveller's or unspecified diarrhoeas. In twenty-two of them, Ciba also gave recommendations for preventive use. The IOCU highlighted the need for more accurate information.[25] Their advice was powerfully supported by the Japanese court ruling of 1978 which said specifically that the company should have 'warned against the internal use of the medicaments for the treatment of ailments other than amoebic dysentery'.[26] Nevertheless, in 1980 the IOCU Regional Office for the Pacific reported that Entero-Vioform was still being sold by Ciba in Malaysia for preventing diarrhoea and for the treatment of mild, unspecific diarrhoeas. In Thailand, another Ciba product, Mexaform, was being sold for similar indications.[27]

In Kenya, too, Ciba were still selling Mexaform with leaflets recommending it for non-specific diarrhoeas. Given that $150 million provision (more than 10 per cent of the company's 1978 drug sales)[28] it is difficult to accept Regional Manager Klaus Leisinger's professed ignorance: 'I would have sworn that this could not happen. We will have to check it. We will send our working force to all pharmacies to take out all the Mexaform packages, control the leaflets, and if the old leaflets are in we will substitute them.'[29] Kenya, hosting as it does Ciba's regional headquarters, is not, it should be emphasized, a forgotten backwater for the company.

The evidence on which Ciba based its original claims for clioquinol as a prophylactic agent against diarrhoea is so flimsy as to be almost invisible. By 1976, they had already admitted that it was inefficacious against most causes of diarrhoea. In a standard twenty-eight-page 'Dear Doctor' letter used in Europe, they say, 'it is not indicated in infections caused by *Salmonellae* or by *coliform* bacteria'; the possibility of effectiveness against viral causes of diarrhoea is not even mentioned; and they record the consensus that the product is ineffective for 'traveller's diarrhoea'. The best basis they have for claiming activity against anything other than amoebic and bacillary dysentery is that 'there are some 796 publications on Entero-Vioform and Mexaform . . . . the vast majority refer to or give details about efficacy, only a small minority comment on apparent lack of efficacy.'[30]

This might have been acceptable in 1934. Today it is simply laughable. But why would a reputable drug company tarnish its image by marketing a product with no better proof of efficacy than this? The answer is clear. Few people suffer from amoebic dysentery in relation to the many who want to avoid diarrhoea. So when Ciba's Dr J. A. Sobotkiewicz asks, 'Do you think that a big multinational company would continue sales of a compound, of a product, if this would mean a danger to human lives?'[31] the answer, based on the evidence from the developing countries must be 'yes'. Since all effective drugs can have adverse effects, and clioquinol is no exception, to encourage its use for purposes for which there is no evidence of efficacy puts patients at risk with no possibility of benefit. In my opinion that is just what Ciba have done.

An efficacious solution for diarrhoea

There is an effective, efficacious and above all efficient remedy which can ensure that diarrhoea victims do not die of dehydration. This is what matters in the poor world. But while Ciba-Geigy and Searle were actively confusing the medical profession about the mysterious movements of the body's fluids, this most effective of therapies was left ignored. They would have needed no great research resources to find it. Nor was it waiting for some mighty leap forward in scientific knowledge. Its production does not depend on the sophistication of the chemical industry. The remedy was there, waiting to be used. And that, perhaps, is why no one, bar a handful of curious or dedicated medical workers, had bothered to investigate how best to prevent dehydration in patients with diarrhoea. The solution is simple. Sugar and salt in water is the basic mix. This, given in the correct proportions to a patient with diarrhoea, will normally prevent dehydration as long as the patient is well enough to drink.

The traditional treatment for dehydration was to insert a needle into a vein and drip-feed the fluids the patient needed. So what is the advance? First, there ought to be reservations about the routine use of intravenous therapy. Like drugs, all medical procedures have their risks, and putting needles into veins is no exception. More important, it is a therapy that requires a certain minimum of equipment and supplies. It can certainly not be categorized as a home remedy, and is least accessible to those communities likely to need it most. Last, it is expensive. The contents of those bags and bottles may be mainly water, but it is water that has been sterilized, quality-controlled, transported long distances and handled many times before it arrives at the bedside.

Oral rehydration was not promoted before because no one had been particularly interested in the diarrhoea process before the patient reached hospital—except to sell trivial or worthless remedies. Water alone does not help to prevent dehydration since the salts that have been lost leave the chemical balance of the body disturbed. Just adding salt is also not enough because, particularly in severe diarrhoea, it is often not absorbed. The secret of oral therapy appears to lie in the interaction between the components of the mixture. Diarrhoea is the gut's response to irritation, the bowel wall's weeping. The problem is to reverse the process and the answer is to add sugar. Scientists have shown that even in the violent diarrhoea of cholera, the body's salts will, in the presence of sugar—or, better, glucose—travel against the current, back through the gut wall. The sugar, as well as feeding the patient with a minimum of calories, apparently also carries the salts piggy-back. Once through the gut wall, they in their turn encourage the absorption of water.

The actual processes are still not completely understood. But the technicalities are not essential. The proponents of oral rehydration as a form of medical care which can be made available to just about everyone who needs it, talk in terms of leaky pots. A child dehydrated is a pot from which the water has leaked out; to prevent dehydration, you have to keep filling the pot up, to make good the losses. The oral rehydration mix meets one important requirement of efficacious medicine in the Third World—it is easy for people to understand its correct use.

The next advantage is that, in its simplest form, it is a remedy which can be made at home to recipes such as a three-finger pinch of salt, a four-finger scoop of sugar, plus the juice of an orange, in half a litre of water. Alternatively, plastic spoons have been devised to ensure more accurate measures of sugar and salt.

The mixture can be improved to take better account of the body's biochemistry. If prepared in a health centre pharmacy, the potassium needed can be added in controlled amounts rather than incidentally in the juice of the orange; glucose can be used instead of sugar, and the acidity of the mix can be reduced by using sodium bicarbonate. Such improvements have been made in part as a response to the doubts expressed about the consistency of solutions made up by parents at home (doubts which are somehow in conflict with the common practice of giving tablets for children which have to be carved into unlikely proportions, or syrups which have to be measured to the nearest millilitre to get the right dose). But silver foil sachets of rehydration mix with attractive labels take on the aura of a 'real medicine', which may be important if patients are to take it seriously and use it correctly.

The final advantage is fundamental for developing countries——that of cost. Here, there is no comparison. Sudan's National Health Programme estimated the cost of oral rehydration fluids needed for 1984 at £S29,800. The cost for an equal volume of intravenous fluids was a massive £S3.3 million.[32] One estimate suggests that the cost of providing sufficient rehydration mix for treating all cases of diarrhoea in the world's 1000 million children under five years old would be $300 million.[33] This may seem high but it is scarcely half of 1 per cent of the world's spending on pharmaceuticals.

It is difficult to imagine a more efficient medicine, nor one that has waited so long to be found. In the end, it was necessity that mothered the invention:

> Treatment by oral rehydration therapy (ORT) was first used on a large scale among refugees from the 1971 India-Pakistan war. In the camps, the mortality rate dropped from 30 per cent to 1 per cent. Since then, ORT has been used with great success. The Infectious Diseases Hospital in Calcutta and the Hospital of the International Centre for Diarrhoeal Diseases Research in Bangladesh now use only 20 per cent of the amount of intravenous fluid previously used for diarrhoeal diseases treatment. Controlled studies in Indonesia, Pakistan, Costa Rica and the Philippines have all shown major reductions in diarrhoea-related deaths.[34]

A huge leap has to be made between developing an efficient, efficacious remedy and seeing it applied where it is needed. Oral rehydration mix is no exception. One problem, particularly for those who want to see the mix used by parents at home rather than dispensed by health workers in clinics (where children often arrive too late to be helped) is that parents in poor communities do not regard diarrhoea as anything abnormal. But there are others who see the drug-and-intravenous-needle-oriented education of the doctors who decide policy on these matters as the main obstacle to its use. In too many communities, oral rehydration mix is just one more remedy competing in the market with Lomotil and Entero-Vioform and the rest. It will be tough competition because no one stands to gain by selling the mix. No one—except those 1000 million children

A year after he launched his attack on the pharmaceutical industry, Halfdan Mahler returned to develop the theme. There were, he said in 1976, three kinds of drug technologies: those fundamental to solving health problems, those which are simply placebos, and those which are merely palliatives, 'a vast array of half-measures'.[35]

The drugs highlighted in this chapter illustrate his classification well. Rehydration mixes are surely a fundamental health technology. Lomotil is a classic palliative. Entero-Vioform may best be thought of as a placebo. Even in the rich world, said Mahler, there is often not enough money to buy all these for everybody: we have to choose which health methods to apply. 'For the vast majority of the world's population, this choice is very restricted, if it exists at all. They surely have a right to know what technology is really fundamental for health development.' That right is one which the multinationals have tried to deny.

Four: Research

Hazen 'Rich' Richardson was until recently president of the US drug company Parke-Davis, part of the Warner-Lambert group. 'While working at that job, he helped redirect the efforts of the R & D department,' reported the industry magazine *Chemical Week*. '"50 per cent of the research at Parke-Davis during that time was focused on exotic Third World diseases," Richardson recalls. "I steered it into more commercial applications."'[1]

The drug companies make no secret of the fact that they have rapidly been abandoning research into the health problems of the Third World. By so doing, they have put in question the nature of their contribution to this world's needs. So it is of interest to investigate the phenomenon more closely.

Start in the long queue outside the busy health centre in Munhava, Beira's biggest *bairro precária*. Just about any day you choose to pass you will find little Josefina, or a child like her, sitting there with her mother. She's four years old but looks hardly two, and she's sick. She has violent diarrhoea and fever and has just come out in a rash that looks like that of measles. Her mother is worried. So too are the health workers. The prospects for an undernourished child, with measles on top of malaria and various other parasitic infections, are not good. For the research-based pharmaceutical companies, she scarcely merits a passing glance. This is not to say that she could not benefit from their help. But she lives in Mozambique where the drugs budget is only $20 million per year, $1.60 per head.

Far more alluring in the view of the research managers of the multinationals is seventy-nine-year-old Joe Josephs who spends his days in the geriatric ward of a London hospital. He is rarely coherent (senile dementia, say the doctors), suffers from severe rheumatism and is incontinent. But the point is that he lives in a country where his medical care is free, and access to drugs virtually unrestricted. Sales of anti-rheumatic and related medicines alone amounted to more than £100 million in Britain in 1980, £1.70 per head. Unlike

Josefina, who only needs medicine occasionally, old Joe will keep on taking the tablets until he dies.

The logic of the market place

The way in which the multinationals' research priorities are defined is very simple. And the best people to explain it come not from the medical profession, nor even from the ranks of the companies, or their critics. They belong to that skilled and exclusive profession, the stockbrokers' analysts—those who are concerned with the pharmaceutical industry. These financial experts have both the resources and the vested interest to follow the fortunes of the industry, so that they may advise their clients where to invest to back the winners and when to dump the shares of the losers.

So Richard Emmitt, of US brokers F. Eberstadt and Co., explains to his non-specialist audience that a new cephalosporin antibiotic, produced by researchers at the US-based multinational Eli Lilly, will only find markets in the USA if it displaces similar but older antibiotics. Some of those displaced will be the company's own products. This will still be very much in the company's interest since the new product will cost at least half as much again as the existing ones and can thus be guaranteed to boost company earnings.[2]

Consider the broker who investigated the market for anti-cancer drugs and found that they were generating new interest in the laboratories of the big companies. This was not, said Mr Paul Brooke of brokers Cyrus Lawrence, because there were great prospects of new drug breakthroughs. Rather, it was the recognition that the market for anti-cancer drugs was 'demand-inelastic with respect to price' or, put simply, that people dying from cancer, and their families, are willing to spend as much money as they have on any drug which may help. What lent emphasis to this point, said Mr Brooke, was the fact that the largest market for anti-cancer drugs in the world was Japan (which accounted for 54 per cent of total world sales in this category in 1978), not because the Japanese are vastly more vulnerable to the disease but because Japanese doctors, under their payment schemes, boost their earnings by prescribing expensive drugs—and cancer drugs are among the most expensive.[3]

Brooke's is no maverick assessment. It was confirmed by Dr Kiro Shinamoto, director of Takeda Chemical Industries, Japan's biggest pharmaceutical company, who told the 9th Assembly of the IFPMA: 'Research activity in the development of anti-cancer drugs is particularly high in Japan because of the possible assessment of a high price which will ensure high profitability.'[4] Meanwhile, Paul Brooke estimates that the world market for anti-cancer drugs will be worth £2000 million by 1986, more than three times its 1978 value.

The language of the brokers is often elliptical. A team from Kidder Peabody explained how new hypertensives will have to be introduced to the market place in these terms:

> It is our conviction that the universe of hypertensives has been largely penetrated by drug therapy, which implies that future sales growth will have to come more from changes in configuration of market sales than from an expansion of the patient population.[5]

Translated, this reads that everyone with high blood pressure is now being treated for it, so any company which wants to introduce new products will somehow have to displace the existing ones. Whether they need to be replaced is another question, a secondary one in view of the value of the market for hypertensives which, it is predicted, will rise from $1400 million in 1980 to $2500 million in 1988.

The issue as far as the analysts are concerned is not whether the need for a new drug exists but whether it can be generated. The factor that particularly impressed Mr Emmitt of Eberstadt about the new Lilly antibiotic, for example, was not that it was a real improvement over existing products but that the company's promotion had 'created credibility' for it. (See note 2.)

Trivial and wasteful

Much criticism of the multinationals has been aroused by this approach to pharmaceutical research. Sanjaya Lall of UNCTAD, concentrating on the straight economics of the matter, has attacked what he saw as the misallocation of research and development funds to which the developing countries have contributed significantly.

> The nature of commercial pharmaceutical research aiming at patentable and marketable drugs leads to a considerable waste of research expenditures because a large part goes into imitative R & D and molecule manipulation, adding to existing products new ones that are only slightly different in terms of their effect but that cost considerably more.[6]

Halfdan Mahler of WHO took a similar line, but pointed out the consequences of existing R & D orientation for the sick of the poor world:

The expected financial return is one of the prime determinants of priorities in industrial research efforts and in marketing and pricing. For example, the development and marketing of a non-essential product for the symptomatic relief of a trivial condition may take precedence because it is likely to yield higher returns than a new, essential drug for the control of a serious disease affecting millions of people in the least developed countries.[7]

The UN Center on Transnational Corporations, for its part, criticizes the research approach of the industry because it keeps prices high and draws attention away from cost—from drug efficiency—to focus on the supposed superior performance of the latest products. Stressing the amount of money wasted on 'trivial product changes', it quotes the former research director of the Squibb company as saying that only 25 per cent of his company's projects were 'worthwhile', whereas the rest were devoted to 'me-too' products and the development of therapeutically unimportant combination products.[8]

There are thus three interlinked criticisms of the research done by the multinationals:

(1) research resources are not allocated to the development of drugs for diseases predominant in the poor world;

(2) resources are directed instead to the production of 'me-too' drugs, similar to existing products;

(3) drugs are developed not to improve health care but to boost a company's market share and the prices it can charge for its products.

On the first count, there is general accord. Lewis Sarrett, putting the case of the US pharmaceutical industry in 1979, admitted:

WHO can say with very little fear of contradiction that only 3 per cent of the funding for biological research throughout the world is directed to diseases that afflict the poor nations of the tropics .... the programmes of the American pharmaceutical industry directed to the health problems of the developing world are of long standing. At the same time and in their totality, they are only a small component—almost certainly less than 5 per cent—of the overall R & D effort of the industry.[9]

The European companies reported a similar situation. In 1976 they devoted only $20 million to research directed towards the specific health problems of the developing countries[10]—a figure which should be set against the industry's estimated research expenditures of the order of $2000 million.

The number of drugs produced for conditions specifically relevant to the developing countries matches the share of resources allocated to them. Of 339 substances introduced between 1973 and 1977, only nine (2.7 per cent) were anti-parasitics, the category classically regarded as drugs for tropical diseases. Even accepting a broader classification—assuming, for instance, that the three new anti-tuberculosis drugs will be used principally in the developing countries—the proportion is still only 3.5 per cent. Drugs for rich world diseases vastly outweigh this. Thirty (8.8 per cent) of the new drugs produced in this period were for the treatment of rheumatism; twenty-four (7.2 per cent) were anti-depressants and minor tranquillizers; nineteen (5.9 per cent) were anti-cancer drugs.[11] To put these figures in context, it is sufficient to point out that the value of drugs sold to the developing countries accounts for between 15 and 25 per cent of the world's total drug sales.[12]

The industry's research is funded by the profits made on drug sales and this is allowed for when the companies fix their prices. Every time a consumer buys a bottle of medicine, part of the price he pays is effectively a company-imposed research tax. By that reckoning, it is reasonable to assume that the Third World's contribution to the world's pool of research funds is at least 15 per cent. It is getting back a far from fair return on its investment.

Cutting back the Third World

What began to cause wide concern during the 1970s was not just that a tiny proportion of research resources was devoted to the needs of the poor world but that evidently the sum was actually shrinking. Again, this was not disputed.

> As for research specifically targeted to the Third World's particular health problems, it is very clear that the magnitude of the effort has been decreasing over the past decade. Projects have been dropped or cut back in most, if not all, of the laboratories whose directors provided me with information.[13]

By the end of the decade, there had been a recovery of sorts, boosted by the WHO's initiative in launching its Special Programme for Research and Training in Tropical Diseases. The European companies claimed to have doubled their research contribution to $40 million. Under similar aegis, new projects have got underway in the USA as well. How large an injection of company resources this represents is not clear. In the case of the German and Swiss companies, there appears to have been a substantial government contribution. Certainly, at Parke-Davis in the USA, external funding has taken over where the company has lost interest, as one account explained:

> Since the company has some over-capacity in its R & D lab, it has done $1.1 million of contract work for the Agency for International Development (AID) and other agencies on malaria, measles and some vaccines for the period 1976–1977, to which it contributed $0.4 million as part of overhead cost.[14]

Is it unreasonable to look only at the specifically tropical diseases as a measure of the industry's contribution to the health needs of the poor world? Lewis Sarrett thought so:

> In fairness, the work that is being done in tropical medicine *per se* should be seen as 'in addition to' all the work that has application both to the tropics and to the temperate zones. I am not trying to absolve industry from the role in tropical medicine research that its unique expertise imposes. What I am saying is that, as things now stand, the score is *not* 97 to 3.[15]

It is an argument which would have more credibility were the research resources applied differently. But not only is most research directed at areas of little interest to the Third World, but its products are, in any terms, of marginal value. Of the 1087 drugs under investigation in the USA in 1980, the US FDA believed that only 2.4 per cent represented a possible 'important therapeutic gain', another 8.4 per cent 'moderate therapeutic gains'. The vast majority, nine out of ten, was regarded as being of 'little or no therapeutic gain'.[16] This is the second focus for criticism. Too much research appears to be simply imitative, each company trying to make its own version of already successful drugs in high-value markets. 'Molecular roulette' the process has been called, its aim being to produce 'me-too' drugs.

'A straw man,' said Richard Crout, former director of the US FDA when the issue of the industry's concentration on 'me-too' drugs was raised.[17] There is certainly scope for confusion here. One way in which the pharmaceutical companies find new drugs is by screening all new chemical substances to which they have access (for those which form part of the large chemical conglomerates, this is a very large number) to see whether they have any pharmacological activity. There is another approach, which sometimes follows from the identification of a compound with promising activity, but is also a starting point in itself. This is the modification of the chemical structure of an active compound to produce a similar substance with slightly different properties. What is sought in the variants may be a stronger positive effect, or it may be a reduction in side-effects. Lomotil is a good example. Diphenoxylate belongs to the same opiate class of drugs as morphine and codeine, although its closest relative is the anaesthetic pethidine. It was developed in a conscious effort to find a drug with the desired effect on the gastro-intestinal tract but without narcotic or anaesthetic properties.[18]

Molecular manipulation of this kind is an entirely legitimate technique for developing new drugs and it has benefited not only the rich world. Those in the industry who wish to hold high the banner of 'me-too' research need look no further than chloroquine, the best of twenty-five variants of quinine, the ancient but problematic remedy for malaria, and for nearly forty years, the most valuable anti-malarial we have. The propagandists choose to ignore it because it was not developed in an industry laboratory.[19]

It is not the research technique that is in question. At issue is not *how* new drugs are developed but *why*. As Halfdan Mahler charged—and those stock-market analysts confirmed—companies direct their research funds on economic rather than on medical or scientific grounds. Their object is to develop the most profitable products rather than to find those which present economically viable solutions to health problems. Their researchers manipulate existing good drugs, not to improve them, but simply to develop products similar to those already in use. If they turn out to be better, the marketing department will obviously be pleased. But even if the new version is not quite as good as the original, a company with a strong sales force can still use it to capture a share of the market.

The process is not entirely wasteful, since it will generate marginal improvements in available drugs. 'In this sense, supposed overlappings or multiplicities should not be considered as waste,' suggests an OECD report on the pharmaceutical industry. 'They could however be regarded as a process of technology deepening rather than widening.'[20] The companies' priority is precisely to deepen technology. This inevitably conflicts with the priorities of the developing countries which would like to see a widening of research so that more is devoted to their needs. They have contributed to the industry's research funds and they are confronted with overwhelming health problems. So it is hardly surprising that they should complain the loudest about the inanity of pouring research resources into the development of slightly better but invariably more expensive drugs for conditions in which good treatment is already available, while for so many diseases prevalent in the poor world, efficient drugs are urgently needed.

Effective drugs should not be discarded

Drugs and methods of treatment established as effective should not be discarded and rejected like some outlived fashion, just because they have been in use for some time and because they are not as easy to apply as might be conceivable in an ideal world.

Quite right, the critics would say. Except that the comment was made by Bayer researcher Dietrich Wegner and he was attacking not the research orientation of his company but the developing countries for having the effrontery to bang on Bayer's door asking for more.[21] He has held persistently to his theme:

Pharmaceutical companies that have invested time, money and effort in discovering new drugs of proven efficacy for the treatment of tropical diseases are concerned that in many cases, their products go unused, probably due to the lack of funds in the country concerned as well as to the inadequate development of delivery systems and related measures of sanitation.[22]

As it happens, Dietrich Wegner understands very well why the poor countries need new drugs for diseases against which some remedies already exist. His current area of interest, schistosomiasis, the parasitic disease prevalent in the tropics, demonstrates the need well.

It was the sudden hostility of a normally friendly family doctor which, at the beginning of the 1970s, made me aware of the difficulties posed by the drugs available for treating this disease. I had made the mistake of asking him who I should talk to about schistosomiasis control in his small African country. It was a sore point, I learned later, because a young patient of his had recently died, not as a result of the disease which, if fatal, only kills after many years, but as a result of the treatment itself. Hycanthone, the drug responsible, was known to be dangerous. The information provided by Winthrop, who sold it as Etrenol, was in this case clear and explicit: 'All patients should be examined before the administration of Etrenol, whether they are treated individually or in public health treatment programmes,' states the product leaflet.[23] Close medical supervision is recommended for anyone suffering from a tender liver or various other symptoms common in the Third World. 'All patients should be carefully observed after treatment with Etrenol, with follow-up examination on at least the second and third days after the injection.'

Immediately, this drug—which may be useful to doctors in hospitals or in private practice—becomes virtually impossible to use in the rural areas of developing countries where the disease is most prevalent. Doctors here are few and patients cannot realistically be expected to come back twice just for checkups. In such communities, hycanthone is simply not an efficacious drug, however effective it may be in individuals. This is recognized by Dr Wegner: 'It goes without saying that some of the existing drugs are not really appropriate for such a form of therapy requiring medical observation of the individual patient which is almost impossible in large-scale treatment.'

Bayer's discovery of the problems of drug use in developing countries, and Dr Wegner's interest in schistosomiasis, came about by happy accident. The German company E. Merck were looking for (yet more) new tranquillizers. Most of the substances they synthesized proved useless. But, as Dr Wegner later explained to me, they were then sent to Bayer under a long-standing contract between the companies, to be screened for parasitological activity, in which Bayer's veterinary medicine division has an interest. This time they struck lucky. One of the new substances, praziquantel, turned out to be highly effective against liver fluke, an important cattle disease. It has already been marketed for this application. It may also prove to have been a lucky strike for the 200 million people in the Third World believed to be suffering from schistosomiasis. The liver fluke of cattle is a close relative to the human schistosomes. Preliminary testing suggests that not only is praziquantel effective against the three most important forms of human schistosomiasis, but it can be given as a one-shot treatment, by mouth, without any apparent side-effects. 'Praziquantel may prove to be the ideal schistosomicide,' concluded the *British Medical Journal*,[24] although full confidence about its lack of adverse effects must await some years of wide usage.

To a great extent, the Third World had become dependent on such chance advances in other areas for the drugs it needed. The dependence on progress in animal health was spelled out very plainly by a report from the Royal Society of Tropical Medicine, which noted that 'Medical and veterinary research workers from the Universities of Khartoum, London and Glasgow are collaborating to develop vaccines for the control of cattle schistosomiasis and, if this is successful, it is hoped that this will stimulate further work on the development of a vaccine to prevent the disease in man.'[25] The reasons are obvious. 'Parasitic diseases are as well the most economically important group of animal diseases worldwide, producing estimated global losses of over $250 billion a year in livestock production.'[26]

The Third World also 'benefits' from the aggressive intents of some of the rich countries which fund research into the diseases that might affect the efficiency of their soldiers. This is not limited to obvious diseases like malaria. Even unlikely ailments, fungus infections for example, preoccupy the generals of today's armies, although it is hard to accept the claim of Dr W. R. Mackenzie, that 'ringworm infections, the commonest of all mycoses, caused a greater loss of combat hours among US troops in Vietnam than all other causes put together.'[27]

Until the recent initiatives by the WHO (dealt with in more detail in Part 2) it seemed that the Third World was going to have to wait for the rich world's cast-offs and the chance by-products of veterinary and military medicine to meet its needs. The companies implied that the developing countries should be grateful for what they got and be left to get on with their work. 'Experience has shown that only the research-based pharmaceutical industry has the financial and technical resources to develop and make available in adequate quantities effective new drugs for the treatment of parasitic and tropical diseases.'[28] The meddling of developing countries in other aspects of pharmaceutical policy was only likely to make things worse. It could lead to a complete drying up of research in areas of interest to them, warned Dr Wegner.[29]

The industry and its allies are prone to exaggeration, both about their unique research capabilities, and about the unprofitability of research in tropical diseases. However, there is evidence that the Third World could be better served without bankrupting the companies.

Wellcome: 'A reasonable risk'

The Wellcome Foundation is not one of the biggest drug companies, but it is financially healthy and continues to make valuable contributions to medicine. For historical reasons, it has always been oriented towards preventive medicine. It is one of the few companies to have continued a programme of work in tropical disease throughout the period in which the other companies were retreating from the field. So it is interesting to note what industry apologist Professor Jack Behrman had to say about the company and, in particular, its efforts to develop a vaccine against malaria:

> The Wellcome Laboratories have worked in the area of vaccines for several years and have developed some which are effective for varying time periods against viral and bacterial infection. The company considers its work on immunology to be an act of faith, likely to lead to considerable financial losses even if a vaccine is found. Commercial losses will occur because the vaccines can be readily duplicated and are not easily patentable because they are biological rather than chemical entities. Tropical countries would try to force the prices down for mass use, making production too unprofitable to recover development costs.[30]

When I put that traditional pessimistic view to Dr Allan Beale, director of biological research at Wellcome's British laboratories near London, he disagreed on just about every point. He certainly does not accept that there is no commercial future for a malaria vaccine, or for the production of other vaccines. 'Plainly we believe it is an important research area and we have an opportunity to do something about it,' he told me. What about the financial losses, the 'act of faith'? No research project can ever be sure of producing a saleable product, he agrees. Nevertheless, he is optimistic. 'We are working on the assumption that we will be able to commercialize it,' he says. 'I think it is a reasonable risk.' Nor is he particularly worried that attempts would be made to force the price down. 'I'm not convinced about that argument. A vaccine is likely to be a cheap way of controlling a disease situation even if it is expensive.'

The key to his confidence lies in the new technologies developed recently (and independently of the drug industry it should be noted) which make possible the production of very pure cell products; in this case, of the antigens which stimulate the formation of the immunity-giving antibodies in the human body. Since these will be produced in a very pure form, argues Beale, they will be chemical products rather than the crude mixtures of biological components which characterize today's vaccines. If they are chemically identifiable, they may well be patentable, in the rich world at least. Patents do not give as much protection as is sometimes believed, particularly not in the case of pharmaceuticals for developing countries which have been forced to ignore them because of their high cost. What will guarantee the profitability of the new generation of vaccines, Dr

Beale believes, is the production process itself. Professor Behrman believes that vaccines can be 'readily duplicated'. 'I think that's putting it a bit high,' says Dr Beale, who points out that the new products will require a degree of purity hitherto undreamed of. 'I think that is going to take a higher technology than a classic vaccine needs.'

Perhaps because Wellcome has always been in the business of prevention, it seems to see business in the Third World where other companies say there is none. Dr Beale does not shy away from the parallels with veterinary medicine; indeed, he believes they are relevant to the kind of medicine which is needed in the Third World. 'All our parasitological work has got veterinary and medical components.' There is traditionally an important difference between veterinary and human medicine—the former aims to improve the health of the whole community and has to prove itself to be economic, while the latter is focused on individuals. Yet the community focus is one which is of vital importance to the developing countries which have to make the most efficient possible use of their medicines. (It could arguably be applied with benefit to medicine in the rich world too.) 'We are heavily involved in the veterinary and agricultural business. As a result of that, one gets involved in animal health care programmes for countries,' Beale expands. The way in which vaccines are used 'is more analogous to that than to Western-style medicine'.

The disagreements between Behrman and Beale serve to emphasize that it is not necessarily uneconomic to do research on Third World health problems if it is directed at preventive medicine to be used on a community-wide basis. Secondly, if industry research does have a unique role to play, it is not necessarily in finding new drugs or in conducting the prerequisite basic research, but in developing the means of producing new drugs economically. Penicillin, chloroquine, polio vaccine and now the new generation of vaccines, all truly fundamental drugs, were discovered, not by pharmaceutical companies, but by academic or other publicly-funded research bodies. It was for their large-scale production that the pharmaceutical industry became invaluable.

The WHO programmes for research in tropical diseases are showing that the industry's role in the experimental trial of drugs is also limited. Company researchers admit that WHO and government health authorities are better placed to conduct the extensive clinical trials needed to prove the efficacy of a drug which is going to be used on a community scale. The companies can play a valuable role in the routine pre-clinical animal and toxicology trials, although for these, even the biggest research-based companies have at times resorted to outside contractors, proving that they are not indispensable.

Nevertheless, the pharmaceutical companies can contribute to the development of new drugs for tropical disease. Perhaps, since they have proved so clearly reluctant to enter the field on their own initiative, they would best be treated as subcontractors. The problem is that, while they are willing to do only part of the work, they still expect to collect their 'research tax' and leave to other agencies the funding and execution of those components of research to which they are unwilling to contribute. This being so, the pharmaceutical multinationals' research will continue to be the focus for criticism —for just so long as they continue to collect the taxes, while denying their Third World consumers any representation in determining how these are spent.

Five: Market Power

A picture of President Ferdinand Marcos showed prominently in the office of Gregorio Z. Sycip, marketing director, vice-president and assistant general manager of Mead-Johnson's Philippines' subsidiary when I visited him. In itself, that was not unusual. Third World walls are often thus ornamented. What was different in this case was the evident conviviality of the presidential group, and the fact that one of the members appeared to be none other than my host, looking sleek and self-important.

In the rat-race of the Philippines' drug industry, it is helpful to have friends in high, preferably the highest, places. I went to see Mr Sycip about the way he sold his firm's products to the medical profession. His methods would not have gone down well with ethical committees in the USA, home of Mead-Johnson and its parent company Bristol-Myers, but the Philippine authorities had taken no interest. Apart from the huge volume of free samples, distributed discriminately to those doctors who prescribed the company's products, private hospitals received substantial gifts of equipment—since they specialize in paediatrics, Mead-Johnson had been known to equip an entire hospital nursery. Doctors received gifts such as air conditioners for their consulting rooms as tokens of appreciation for their loyalty to company lines. 'It's so corrupting to be aware that you could have almost anything you asked for,' one hospital administrator told me.[1]

The corruption was the least of it, except perhaps as far as it illustrates the highest stage of an industry governed or inspired by nothing other than the profit motive. More fundamental was the burden imposed on the Filipino people and the industry's failure, by virtue of its very structure, to meet their health needs. The pre-sales side of Mead-Johnson's business is a good example. In January 1976 Bristol-Mead imported some bulk ampicillin from its parent company. The price, $177 per kilogram, was more than double that paid for the same product bought at the same time on the world market. The transaction had obvious advantages for the company, as a

Filipino research group explained: 'The higher the price fixed, the better for both subsidiary and mother company, which are one and the same, for they can justify higher selling prices for the product or bigger tax deductible expenses for tax return purposes.'[2]

The subsidiary had in previous years declared substantial losses. It was quite happy to stay in the market, though. Its profits were made by the parent company on those highly priced bulk drug sales. Not only were they tax free, but they were also safely out of the country.

The company's sales methods also imposed high costs on sick Filipinos. The Bristol-Mead group, as one of the country's four top drug companies, spent an estimated 33 per cent of its sales income ($6.5 million in 1979[3]) on marketing and promotion. By this time, even the companies which had initiated some of the more dubious forms of sales promotion agreed that they had got out of hand, and welcomed moves by a new health minister to control them.[4] For many doctors, their appetites whetted by their substantial extra income from the sale of free samples, it was now literally a case of free lunch after free lunch. Since there is, when accounts are closed, no such thing, the costs were passed straight on to the unfortunate Filipino consumers. Most of them could not pay the bill.

'The Philippines has the dubious distinction of holding on to one of the world's highest tuberculosis infection rates,' wrote Sister Mary Grenough in the embattled church newspaper *Signs of the Times.*[5]

> The tuberculosis infection rate is a reliable indicator of the general status of public health and delivery of health services in any country. . . . Leading health problems continue to be common respiratory ailments, tuberculosis, gastro-enteritis and parasitism abetted and complicated by malnutrition. These diseases constitute a life and death struggle for the general population, 90 per cent of whom fall below the poverty line. A recent government study admits that only 30 per cent of the people in rural areas have potable water. The same study describes the health and medical services as sadly inadequate.

Sister Mary focused too on the shameful part the local drug industry has to play in this woeful scene:

> The cost of manufactured medicines is beyond the reach of most Filipinos. Even the government tuberculosis control programme backed by WHO/UNICEF is unable to provide medicines for more than a third of active cases . . . There is a need for drug

research and marketing to make available at lowest possible cost these medicines needed by the majority of people for the prevention and treatment of common problems . . . there are more than 200 companies marketing medicines for tuberculosis under more then 800 brand names. The sale price is at least ten times the actual production cost.

Through their behaviour in markets such as the Philippines, it was the multinationals themselves which created much of the hostility and distrust that surfaced in the 1970s, as critical analyses of their contribution to Third World health strove to explain the discrepancy between health needs and company offerings.

The structure of the multinationals

'The leading drug companies possess an exceedingly high degree of market power,' wrote Sanjaya Lall in that 1975 UNCTAD document which marked a turning point in the debate.[6] This market power has high costs for developing countries, he said.

The direct costs include essentially the excessive profits earned by the transnational drug companies that result in a transfer of scarce foreign exchange resources from the developing countries to the home countries of these companies. The burden on the poor segment in developing countries is particularly heavy. The huge marketing and R & D expenditures incurred by the transnational companies world-wide are borne by all consumers, including the poor ones in the developing countries, although such expenditures contribute little to the real health needs of the vast majority of the developing world.

The indirect social and economic costs include the introduction and promotion of drugs that are inappropriate in terms of price and therapeutic effects, the suppression of local competition, and the stifling of local pharmaceutical research and development that would enable the provision of drugs to a larger segment of the population and would correspond better to real local health needs.

It has been possible to consider the safety and efficacy of drugs without reference to the structure of the industry which supplied them. The analysis of pharmaceutical company research priorities, the divergence between health needs and potential markets, has given a hint of corporate structure. Now that the discussion has moved to allegations of high prices, excess profits and suppression of competition, it is necessary to outline briefly the characteristics of the multinational industry. One commentator writes:

> The pharmaceutical industry is not a single industry. It covers instead a highly heterogenous range of industrial and trade activities. . . . In short, references to the 'pharmaceutical industry' are as imprecise and meaningless as are references to 'pharmaceuticals', 'drugs', 'medicines', etc.[7]

This is a statement at once true and highly misleading.

World pharmaceutical production, as measured by manufacturers' sales, was estimated to have passed $50,000 million by the end of the 1970s. Of that, just twenty-five companies accounted for nearly half. There can be no exact figures because company data are not standardized and are often incomplete. But there is no doubt about the general picture.

Companies like Hoffmann-La Roche are familiar, while American Home Products sounds as though it ought to be the household name which Bayer certainly is. Fewer people will have heard of Merck which, in 1977, was second only to the German Hoechst in sales size, perhaps because, unlike Bayer, Beecham and Johnson and Johnson, it has not promoted its name as widely through a range of popular over-the-counter remedies. Often the size and scope of the major corporations are concealed by the apparently independent lives led by their subsidiaries. Johnson and Johnson, for instance, owns the well-known Belgian company Jannssen, the American companies Ortho and McNeil and the German Cilag-Chemie.

While they dominate the pharmaceutical market, and have sales greater than the gross national product of many developing countries, most of these companies are relative dwarfs beside the giant corporations which command the Western world's economy—except for those such as Bayer and Hoechst, for whom pharmaceuticals are only a small part of total sales, and for the Swiss companies, whose sales account for a significant proportion of their country's GNP: 'Only one pharmaceutical firm was listed among the 100 largest American companies in 1975,' commented a report of the OECD. 'Insofar as comparison is possible, the same is true of the European companies. No pharmaceutical firm has the economic weight of, say, ICI; indeed, the national importance of any one firm is relatively trivial.'[9]

Their roots . . .

The major companies, almost without exception, can trace their

Table 2: **The Thirty Top Multinational Pharmaceutical Companies**

(1977)[8]

RANK	COMPANY	PHARMACEUTICAL SALES (US$ million)	PERCENTAGE OF TOTAL SALES
1.	Hoechst	1573	16
2.	Merck & Co	1446	84
3.	Bayer	1273	13
4.	Ciba-Geigy	1150	28
5.	Hoffmann-La Roche	1145	51
6.	American Home Products	1116	39
7.	Warner-Lambert	1025	40
8.	Pfizer	1016	50
9.	Sandoz	935	48
10.	Eli Lilly	911	53
11.	Upjohn	744	66
12.	Boehringer Ingelheim	735	77
13.	Squibb	668	50
14.	Bristol-Myers	666	30
15.	Takeda	646	65
16.	Rhône-Poulenc	614	13
17.	Schering-Plough	606	63
18.	Glaxo	594	72
19.	Abbott Laboratories	581	47
20.	Beecham	524	36
21.	Johnson and Johnson	518	18
22.	Montedison	487	8
23.	Cyanamid	484	20
24.	Schering	456	51
25.	AKZO	442	11
26.	ICI	414	5
27.	Smith Kline	411	53
28.	Wellcome	385	65
29.	G D Searle	382	51
30.	Baxter Travenol	355	42

origins back to the nineteenth century or earlier—further back in fact
than the political independence of most countries of the Third
World. Much is made of their scientific roots. Among the intellec-
tual contributions of Paul Ehrlich, a founding father of the modern
industry, was his observation that some bacteria were selectively
coloured by certain dyes and thus rendered visible for microscopic
examination. If they could be selectively coloured, they could be
selectively killed, he argued. And very much on this basis, the dye
and related fine chemical businesses proved to be one nucleus of the
development of the modern drug industry. It was by no means the
most important, although many of today's major companies would
be happier with such a science-based origin. The fact is that at least
half of today's twenty-five top companies were always primarily
suppliers of drugs. As such, they started business in an age when
most commercially available medicines were of dubious value, if not
downright dangerous. The companies grew by selling cure-alls—as,
fifty years ago, the Wyeth company was happily selling amidopyrine
as a cure for tuberculosis.[10] This background proved no impediment
when they later moved into a new era of more scientifically based
medicine.

There are clear regional differences in this picture. It tended to be
the European companies, principally in Germany and Switzerland,
for whom the chemical industry was the base for entry into the
business of pharmaceuticals. The American companies, on the other
hand, were the patent medicine makers. They acquired the necessary skills as the industry became more scientific and, if some of
them are today as diversified in other fields as their European
counterparts, it is because they put to work in the development of
household chemicals, cosmetics and other consumer goods the
marketing methods which had served them so well in the patent
medicine market of the Wild West.

These are the roots from which the major companies evolved in
their home countries. They do not serve to explain, however, why
the pharmaceutical companies have grown to be among the most
multinational of the world's enterprises. They have good reasons to
want to sell their products abroad. While the demand for medicines
is large, it is also highly specialized and divided into numerous
therapeutic subgroups. Sales for all but the most commonly used
drugs are relatively small. Thus the value of the 1200 tons of
chloroquine produced in the world was estimated as only $42
million; that for the 2840 tons of ampicillin only $215 million.[11] To
gain the maximum profit from their products, and to permit

economies of scale in their production, the companies must sell to
the widest possible markets.

. . . and their branches

This still does not imply a multinational operation. By definition, a
multinational company is one which owns or controls production or
service facilities outside the country in which it is based.[12] Drugs are
high-value, low-volume products which are eminently transportable.
There are thus no pressing economic reasons to produce them close
to their consumers. In some industries which are very labour
intensive—electronics assembly is the best-known example—there
has been a tendency for companies to shift production from high-
wage countries to the Third World where wages are low. For so
doing, they are criticized by trade unions for exporting jobs, and by
others for exploiting cheap Third World labour with the backing of
repressive regimes.[13] Mr Raeto Schett, a former general manager of
Hoffmann-La Roche, was in the process of establishing a manufacturing subsidiary in Indonesia when he raised this point with me. He
wanted to emphasize that cheap labour was no incentive. The only
reason to begin producing drugs in Indonesia was that the government had made it clear that this was a prerequisite for firms which
wanted to carry on doing business there.[14] With its 150 million
inhabitants, Indonesia would one day be an important market, so
Roche was complying. But any local savings in labour costs would be
significantly offset by the costly difficulties of conducting relatively
high-technology manufacture without the supporting local infrastructure. Switzerland would have been a far more convenient locale
in every way.

There is little reason to doubt this. There is precedent for the
pharmaceutical industry voluntarily to locate new production plants
in areas of relatively low labour costs—Ireland and Puerto Rico
being the two main sites. But the US colony of Puerto Rico shows
that cheap labour is not the predominant attraction. Wage rates in
the island's pharmaceutical industry were just two-thirds of their US
equivalents, according to the state's Economic Development
Administration.[15] It can be calculated that by locating their factories
and employing a total of 10,000 workers in the island, the companies
saved themselves perhaps $50 million in wages every year. But the
real incentive that Puerto Rico offered was its liberal tax laws, together
with the fact that, as a US colony, earnings are free of US income tax
and are subject to only a small 'tollgate' tax when repatriated.

'You still keep more of your net profit than anywhere else in the US,' boast the Puerto Rican authorities. Thirty-four US companies have set up manufacturing plants to supply the US market, and the USA was the destination for 80 per cent of the state's $900 million pharmaceutical exports in 1979. To put the labour savings into perspective, it is estimated that they will have also exported $700 million in accumulated tax savings in 1980.[16]

Financial inducements, host government pressure, and the many specialized sub-markets are three important factors which encourage the large pharmaceutical companies to operate on a multinational basis. There are others. Some degree of decentralization of production and trade is essential to avoid a risky dependence on one factory's output, one currency's stability or one country's political future. There are also obvious incentives for companies to control the marketing of their products. Few pharmaceutical specialities sell themselves. Agents cannot be guaranteed to promote the product with the desired vigour—and there is always the danger that good ones will go into business on their own account. Visiting salesmen won't do, either: 'Effective selling is only possible when national peculiarities are identified and exploited. The sales force is invariably composed of natives of the country, and is given a large measure of independence.'[17]

A local subsidiary can be counted on to put its sales pitch at a level appropriate to its market. So, in the Philippines, where, according to a former senior US State Department official, good business is reserved for friends of the president's family, Mead-Johnson employs Gregorio Sycip.[18]

Given these pressures, it is almost inevitable that a large pharmaceutical company is a multinational. The multinational spread is however variable. The US companies have a relatively low proportion of total sales abroad—40 per cent—a reflection of the high value of their domestic market.[19] The major German companies also have a strong home market but tend to be more internationally oriented, with 60 per cent of their total sales abroad.[20] The Swiss go to the extreme and export 90 per cent of all national pharmaceutical production, while foreign *sales* of the three major companies account for more than 95 per cent of their total.

It is customary to break down pharmaceutical industry activities into at least four basic categories—marketing; formulation and packaging of finished drugs; manufacture of bulk pharmaceutical chemicals; and research and development. Table 3 shows the multinationality of some of the major companies.

Table 3: **Major Pharmaceutical Companies: number of countries in which they had operations in 1974**[21]

Company	Marketing	Manufacture	Type of Operation Packaging	Research (major)
Hoffmann-La Roche	32	16	30	6
Hoechst	130	14	37	7
Ciba-Geigy	50	14	41	5
American Home Products	80	5	25	3
Merck & Co.	60	28	28	2
Sandoz	46	8	22	3
Bayer	48	12	19	3
Warner Lambert	50	10	35	3
Eli Lilly	28	5	12	2
Pfizer	75	10	45	3
Boehringer Ingelheim	46	5	10	1
Takeda	12	4	3	1
Schering-Plough	60	5	25	2

Note: 'Marketing' does not include those countries where agents are used: 76 for Roche, 100 for Merck, 117 for Lilly and 75 for Pfizer.

Not indicated is the degree to which the subsidiaries have been established in developing countries. The pattern of expansion depends on the company's home country. The weaker companies of Britain and France have many foreign affiliates in their former colonies, although these have seldom proved to be the most profitable of markets—in Britain's case, Nigeria, whose UK imports were worth $60 million (10 per cent of Britain's total exports) in 1980 is an important exception, as is Algeria for the French.[22] The European companies have the longest history of expansion. Ten had established themselves in Brazil by 1940, whereas only three US companies were then active in that important market.[23] For the US companies, international expansion has been relatively recent. A sample survey showed that before the Second World War, none had manufacturing subsidiaries in Black Africa or Asia, less than 20 per cent had Latin American subsidiaries, and less than a third European subsidiaries. By the beginning of the 1970s half had established subsidiaries in Africa or Asia, and a third in Latin America.[24]

To plan is to choose

Just as the financial analysts help us to understand how the major pharmaceutical companies decide their research directions, so too do the market researchers—for all the many failings of their craft—provide a key to understanding the significance of the Third World to the multinationals. Hans-Georg Gareis, head of Hoechst's pharmaceutical division, says:

> The pharmaceutical industry is an industry which lives from planning, since what we invent today can be sold at the earliest in ten years' time, or even later. Market researchers who can only tell how the market has developed to date are of little use to us.[25]

These captains of industry, manoeuvring their great ships into the most profitable line of battle on that ten- or twenty-year distant horizon, need to have a very definite idea of what they are likely to find there, and the business of helping them form that idea is a very lucrative one. The methods the market researchers use are sometimes so crude as to be laughable, but from sources of every kind, the same message emerges. The Third World is the market of the future.

Thus Information Research Limited in its report *Opportunities for Pharmaceuticals in the Developing World over the Next Twenty Years*,[26] predicts that drug consumption in Africa will grow nearly twelve-fold over 1980 values, to reach $13,000 million by the year 2000. Latin American consumption will grow almost eight-fold to $55,000 million, while the Asian market, buoyed up by the swelling population of the world's most populous countries, will quadruple to $9,770 million. According to these estimates, the share of the world's drugs consumed by the developing countries will double, to reach 29 per cent.

Estimates from the OECD use a different method but arrive at the same conclusion. They suggest that by the year 2000 the Third

World could account for as much as 40 per cent of the world pharmaceutical market, consuming a total of $72,000 million worth of drugs.[27]

The importance of the Third World as a pharmaceutical market is not just that its consumption is growing most rapidly—for the rich countries will still remain the largest consumers. But it is a market that will, for the foreseeable future, be supplied mainly by imports, which—for the multinationals—means the opportunity to produce on a larger scale at home; and means, too, that they will avoid the political and economic risks which local factories must run. It will be easier, as well, for them to transfer their profits out of the country. The point has not been lost on advisers to the industry: 'The LDC market is one which has a net trade deficit in pharmaceuticals and as such may be much more important than is shown by the share of the world pharmaceutical market,' say brokers Hoenig and Strock.[28]

'To plan is to choose,' said Tanzanian president Julius Nyerere. We may assume that the companies will not choose to ignore their fastest growing potential markets. So an examination of the current sources of their market power also reveals the base from which they will plan a strategy to secure their share of this future business.

The market power which Lall attributes to the pharmaceutical multinationals is not just a matter of brute size and long tentacles. Nor is it simply that they enjoy monopolies or, as one OECD document called them, in an unusually perspicacious bit of jargon, 'transient oligopolies' (markets shared by sufficiently few companies with common interests which serve to deny 'normal' competition —but transient because the discovery of new drugs may suddenly and radically alter the market structure).[29] When accusations of undue concentration of power in the hands of too few companies are made, the industry can put its hand on its collective heart and say, in the words of the US Pharmaceutical Manufacturers' Association (PMA): 'The largest drug firm in the free world has a total market share of less than 5 per cent. The average large firm has a world market share of only 2 per cent.'[30]

Barber-shop chairs

While the major companies are relatively few, the market is certainly shared between a greater number than in, say, the world oil or car industry. There are no equivalents of General Motors or Royal Dutch Shell in the pharmaceutical business. Nor is there any company that can boast a 20 per cent share of its world market, as does the British American Tobacco company. Yet this goes no way to disprove the allegation that too much of the drug business is controlled by too few companies.

The major drug sub-markets—twenty-six, according to the broad classification used by the WHO[31]—are so diverse that no single company has much incentive to develop, produce and sell all the drugs needed for all purposes. Instead, they tend to specialize in drugs for the treatment of a number of different diseases, sub-markets in which they have developed special expertise. Roche concentrates on vitamins, sedatives and anti-depressants; Eli Lilly has its strength in antibiotics and prescription painkillers; at Ciba-Geigy, anti-rheumatics, cardio-vascular drugs, 'neuroleptics' and two antibiotics account for 75 per cent of all sales.[32]

This is quite different to other industries. One company's car, despite differences in chrome trim and engine power, performs essentially the same functions as those of its competitors; it can certainly use the petrol from the pumps of any one of the competing oil companies. But while smokers are switched from one company's brand of cigarette to another by the efforts of the advertising industry, Roche's Valium does not compete with Lilly's Keflex (cephalexin) nor with Ciba's Butazolidin (phenylbutazone). In this lies the opportunity for monopoly. The PMA's own analogy makes the point perfectly. Of the many hundreds of chair-makers in the USA only two make barber-shop chairs, they report.[33] The prospective barber is faced with an effective monopoly. If he wants to buy his chairs in a market where price is determined by competition rather than by supplier's whim, he would have to go into the restaurant business.

In individual countries, the existence of monopolies in the various sub-markets is obvious and not denied by the companies themselves. On an international level, the picture is more confused. In a few cases, one company's product dominates worldwide, as was the case with Valium and Librium from Roche and will be the case with Smith Kline's ulcer remedy Tagamet (cimetidine). More commonly, markets may be shared between a few companies, either through licensing agreements, or where there is a dispute about the ownership of a patent, or where close copies of an original drug have been made. The market for ampicillin was in the early years shared between the originator, Beecham, and licensee Bristol-Myers although later both licensed its sale by many other companies. There are also products like insulin which only a few companies have thought it worthwhile to make the necessary investment to produce.

In Third World countries, what little data there is suggests that market shares are determined mainly by recent history. In countries whose political independence is relatively new, multinationals from the old colonial power tend to predominate. The respective 31 and 19 per cent shares held in the Tanzanian pharmaceutical market by companies from Britain and Germany, the former colonial powers, is typical.[34] In former French Africa, the French companies are disproportionately strong. Similarly, where a few companies have established local drug formulating plants, and these enjoy trade preference, their products will enjoy an obvious monopoly.

However, the fact is that, in comparison with Europe and the USA, the pharmaceutical markets of the Third World tend to be less obviously monopolized by the multinationals. Indeed, the first impression in many countries, especially those which, by virtue of their population or wealth, are regarded as important future markets, is one of a chaotic excess of competition with too many products fighting for tiny shares of the market, rather than one of domination by a few large foreign companies. The picture is confused by the wide gulf between countries like India and Brazil, which support large, self-sufficient drug-manufacturing industries, and the poorer countries like those of sub-Saharan Africa, many of which do not even have the capacity to make tablets. At each intermediate stage, between total dependence on outside suppliers to the partial independence in the production of basic pharmaceutical chemicals, which is the best that even most rich countries can hope for, the characteristics of the national drug market appear to be very different.

The bald facts of market power

In medicine, diseases are usually first defined in terms of their symptoms, and only later are the underlying physical processes explained. So, too, rather than look for the source of corporate market power, it would be sensible first to look for its symptoms. What are they? You have market power if you can sell more than your competitors, even though your price is consistently higher. You have market power if you can persuade your consumers that they want what you make, even when their needs are clearly otherwise.

The issue of prices is the most clear-cut. Why, I asked John Carrington of Beecham's head office in London, did his company reduce by 80 per cent, from one year to the next, the price it charged Sri Lanka for ampicillin?[35] 'If I were you,' he replied, 'I'd put it as a bald statement and leave it at that.' And it is a bald fact that the price of drugs on the world market varies as immensely and arbitrarily as that.

The Algerian Committee Against Tuberculosis, in a survey carried out in 1976, found that the prices quoted by a Swiss company for the supply of isoniazid was nine times higher than that asked by a French company. Streptomycin bought from France cost four and a half times more than the same drug bought from Mexico. El Salvador was paying $126 per 1000 tablets of ethambutol. It was available elsewhere in Latin America for $20.[36]

A more recent study made in the Caribbean revealed staggering differences in prices quoted for the supply of the same drugs (Table 4). These were world market prices, uncomplicated by the different import duties, taxes, wholesale and retail mark-ups which are applied in each country as the products pass down the distribution chain. What is significant is not just the huge variations between the quotations of different companies, but the fact that the same companies asked prices which varied by up to 400 per cent from one country to another.

Table 4 **Differences in prices quoted for the same drug**[37]
(By different companies and by the same company)

| DRUG | PRICE (US$) | | | |
| | All companies | | Same company | |
	Highest	Lowest	Highest	Lowest
Tetracycline (1000 250mg caps)	44.28	9.32	37.68	17.77
Chlorpropamide (1000 250mg tabs)	69.90	7.33	54.28	13.00
Furosemide (1000 40mg tabs)	150.76	8.07	150.76	36.60
Diazepam (1000 5mg tabs)	48.66	2.74	48.66	15.02

This confirms the experience of Sri Lanka, where the introduction of new pharmaceutical policies provided a fascinating demonstration of just how arbitrary the multinationals' prices are. When a State Pharmaceutical Corporation was established to buy drugs by open competition on the world market, former suppliers, principally the multinationals, slashed their prices. Among them was Beecham:

> Beecham was able to charge an independent local firm extremely high prices for cloxacillin and ampicillin. Yet when faced by the prospect of competition where its brand name did not matter and where the buyer had information on alternatives, it was quite prepared to cut its prices by about 80 per cent in each case.[38]

Market power and its sources

The arbitrary prices charged by multinationals support the diagnosis of excessive market power. Its sources are not in simple monopoly but in a series of closely linked phenomena which individually have limited impact but as a system work to give the companies immense influence. They include:

—*Promotion:* The major multinationals spend at least 20 per cent of their sales revenue on promotion, to sell both products and their corporate image.

—*Innovation:* The real, marginal or non-existent improvements claimed for the new products of company research give to their marketing divisions the material with which to encourage prescribers to abandon existing products.

—*Trade names:* Brand names rather than scientific names are promoted to avoid creating a market in which other companies can sell the same drugs as 'generics' at cheaper prices.

—*Patents:* These nominally protect inventors by preventing others from using their methods to make new products. They are in fact used by the multinationals to obstruct competitors which might undercut their prices.

—*Technology:* The know-how about the manufacture of pharmaceuticals is traded not just at its fair economic value but usually for concessions which enable them to keep their share of the market.

—*Raw materials:* The companies can use their control of certain pharmaceutical raw materials to obstruct the development of competitive nationally owned companies in the developing countries.

—*Regulations:* In countries where pharmaceutical affairs are governed by regulation rather than by state intervention in the industry, the multinationals, with their greater technical and financial resources, benefit from the bureaucratic devices imposed to control malpractices which smaller competitors may find too complex or expensive to comply with.

In considering the price of drugs, it was their cost to the country rather than to the consumer that was considered. This is, for governments and consumers alike, the most important issue. Most developing countries cannot afford to buy all the goods they would wish to from abroad. In many cases, the value of their exports has not kept pace with the price rises of manufactured goods from the rich countries. Big investments intended to promote industrial growth mean less funds to import, not just consumer luxuries, but also commodities like medicine. Oil price rises have thrown many economies completely out of balance. Where money is short, high prices mean that fewer medicines are available—for rich and poor alike.

The result is that in most developing countries, financial controls over drug imports are far more stringent than regulations about their quality, safety, efficacy and efficiency. Bangladesh pharmaceutical policy aims to reduce the foreign exchange cost of drugs by 50 per cent.[39] Tanzania's foreign exchange difficulties caused such serious drug shortages in 1981 that the government was forced to appeal for emergency assistance.[40] Relatively rich Brazil found itself obliged in the same year to curb licences for the import of pharmaceutical raw material to conserve foreign exchange.[41] Even at the Beira Water Company, we have felt the pinch when chemicals essential for water treatment were held up because finance officials thought that pharmaceutical imports merited higher priority.

If the cost of drugs to the country is the primary concern, the cost of drugs to consumers is related more to what stage of development the national pharmaceutical industry in their country has reached. Where consumer prices are relatively low, what looks like healthy competition often turns out to be the last round of an ill-fated struggle for survival by small local companies and the final consolidation of the power of the multinationals.

The practical exercise of multinational market power and its consequences can be compared in three countries. Nigeria, the Philippines and Brazil are all at very different stages along the road to economic and political development. Their pharmaceutical industries match this. But the evolution of the drug supply business in each, taken together, illustrates the process which is occurring worldwide.

Wild West medicine in Nigeria

'Many Nigerians die daily because they run away from private hospitals since they cannot afford to pay exorbitant hospital fees and the high costs of drugs and medicines prescribed by doctors,' alleged Mr D. C. Ugaru, Nigeria's Minister of Health, saying that drug companies should reduce their prices.[42]

Nigeria, with a population of 75 million, is the largest country in Africa. It is an oil producer and has thus escaped the worst economic stringencies of the 1970s. With its wealth and its population, it is expected to become one of the ten top pharmaceutical markets of the Third World.[43] But since both its independence and prosperity are recent, its pharmaceutical industry is as yet in its infancy.

When Senator Ayo Fanasmi, former president of the Nigeria Pharmaceutical Society, called for the elaboration of a national pharmaceutical policy, he drew attention to the fact that over 90 per cent of the country's drug requirements were still imported.[44] Many companies are represented in Nigeria, but it is only recently that the major multinationals have begun to expand their subsidiaries there and to set up simple local manufacture, restricted almost entirely to drug formulation. While pharmaceutical trade was confined to importing and distribution, much was controlled by Nigerian-based concerns. Now the foundations for multinational dominance have been laid. Beyond the warehouse door, pharmaceutical supply is still far from satisfactory. Shortages are common, even in the private market where prices are very high—the cost to the patient is frequently anywhere between 250 and 400 per cent of the import price. The way drugs are dispensed also leaves much to be desired. Pharmacist Bode Ladejobi has documented the habit of 'counter prescribing' in Nigerian pharmacies. In a survey, he found that what Nigerian pharmacists dispensed for twelve common diseases differed markedly from the doctors' prescriptions. 'Retail pharmacists "counter-prescribe" according to their diagnosis of the disease based on what the patients revealed in their discussion with the pharmacist,' he reported.[45]

The undisciplined and irrational use of drugs has been systematically promoted by the multinationals whose first marketing efforts concentrated on the over-the-counter (OTC) patent medicines which accounted for $57 million of the $117 million drug market in 1975. William Connelly of Sandoz has described how these were sold using 'sound trucks, where OTC products are promoted and sold on the spot (similar to the old Wild West medicine shows with just about the same type of product)'. He chooses to illustrate the point with a picture of a Sandoz company sound van promoting a calcium plus vitamin C tablet promising the 'powerful energy you need'.

> Specific claims are not made for any of these products, just vague statements promising power, long life, happiness, vitality, instant relief and contentment. The value of such promotion tactics may be questioned by the educated population but the uneducated Nigerian buys these products on the promises that are made, and frequently continues to use them.[46]

If the Swiss Sandoz can confess to using self-styled Wild West quack medicine techniques in Nigeria, it is not surprising to find a well-known multinational like Pfizer promoting its anti-parasitic Combantrin (pyrantel pamoate) there through a newspaper competition. All you needed to enter, and perhaps win a $3000 prize, was the right number of empty Combantrin packets.[47] Nor is it surprising to find that more potent and valuable drugs than Combantrin are being casually used and abused all over Nigeria to the certain detriment of the country's health.

New regulations on the Philippines' menu

In the Philippines, the multinationals' position has been consolidated. Most drugs on the market are locally formulated, although virtually all the bulk pharmaceuticals are imported. Filipino-owned companies still hold a sizeable share of the market, 43 per cent according to UNCTAD,[48] but this belies the essential weakness of their position. The strongest local concern is the United Laboratories group, which has close connections with the ruling Marcos family. United controls over 50 per cent of the government and institutional market, but only 20 per cent of sales through private pharmacies, which account for three-quarters of all drug sales in the Philippines.[49] Despite United's powerful friends, it is under pressure. Other companies have called for the award of government business to be more 'competitive'. And efforts to establish a common market for pharmaceuticals among the ASEAN countries (Singapore, Malaysia, Thailand, Indonesia and the Philippines), a Filipino initiative seen as an attempt to gain access for United Laboratories to wider markets, have been stalled by opposition from the multinationals which objected to 'imitator' companies being included.[50]

The fierce competition brought to bear on doctors in the private sector is notorious, as the call for promotional restraint by health minister Dr Enrique Garcia indicated. Dr Garcia wanted an end to those free lunches and free samples so that drug prices could be cut. The multinationals' hope was that when samples and other giveaways were curbed, their promotional funds could be channelled into more productive selling activities which would emphasize their superiority over local companies.[51] They were also likely to benefit from another regulatory rationalization which aimed to cut promotional costs by prohibiting one company from selling the same drug under more than one brand name. This brand proliferation is a common practice, designed to accumulate many small market shares in a competitive market. For United Brands, the main practitioner of proliferation, with its ten marketing divisions, it was an essentially defensive strategy.[52]

The end of 'pushtherapy' in Brazil

Important São Paulo laboratory, wants to enter into an understanding with doctors in this capital, to prescribe its products. Absolute confidence and discretion. Great opportunity to increase your earnings. Letters to Box Number 7914.[53]

In the 1940s, local laboratories dominated the Brazilian pharmaceutical market. They imported most of their raw materials and manufactured finished drugs on a small scale. Their sales methods at the time were, as illustrated in the newspaper advertisement quoted above, aimed at encouraging doctors by all means possible to prescribe their products. Their intention was not so much to switch doctors from one medicine to another, but to persuade them to prescribe their products consistently since many establishments offered comparable ranges. It was, for all its defects, a Brazilian enterprise.

Brazil exemplifies one path along which a Third World drug industry can develop. Today, the deadly seriousness underlying such promotional tactics as free samples, brand proliferation, incentives for pharmacists and the like is obvious. What is occurring is a struggle for survival on the part of the Brazilian companies which once sold virtually all the country's drug needs. By the end of the 1970s, in the market for prescription drugs, they had been made completely marginal.

'Such laboratories "run in the promotional space" opened up by the products launched by the big companies,' says Geraldo Giovanni, a student of Brazil's pharmaceutical industry.[54] 'While they may promote their patent medicines through aggressive mass media advertising, when it comes to their ethical copy products, they work basically through a policy of bonusing.' So they sell 'dozens of 24', 'hundreds of 200' or 'one plus one' in the trade jargon. In this way, they boost the profit of the pharmacist to make the practice an attractive one for both buyer and seller.

> The marketing of these laboratories thus dispenses with the direct intervention of doctors and health institutions, needing only to have a similar product on the market being promoted to them and the existence of salespeople in the shops with the ability to suggest that the product prescribed by the doctor could be substituted, or to apply 'pushtherapy' for customers without prescriptions.

(Pushtherapy, notes Giovanni, is the term used in the pharmaceutical trade to describe the practice, common in Brazil, whereby salespeople in pharmacies 'push' the medicines which are most profitable for them.) This competition has not been ignored by the multinationals: 'The pharmacy is the first target which must be attained,' instructed the Sandoz guide to promotional tactics.[55]

> It is in the pharmacy that successful salesmen will collect the precious data which helps them to programme more confidently their work of sales promotion. It is thus indispensable to give, at each visit to a pharmacy, the same presentation given in the doctors' consulting rooms; especially when the presence of the product could generate confusion in the pharmacies . . . .

The position of the local companies is further threatened by attempts, supported by the multinationals, to reduce the sale of 'ethical' drugs without prescription.[56] At this final stage of the multinationals' battle for control, prices to the consumer are relatively low. Under the influence of government price controls, expensive give-away promotional tactics are becoming less and less economic. The multinationals may complain the loudest about the effects of the price squeeze but they are in fact best able to cope with it. It is the small Brazilian companies and the pharmacies themselves which suffer the most—in one year, in the mid-1970s, more than

10 per cent of the 1800 pharmacies in São Paulo went bankrupt.[57]

Brazil has made half-hearted attempts to develop the strong national drug industry which it has the technical and financial base to support. They have foundered on the concerted opposition from the multinationals and their allies. CEME (*Central de Medicamentos*), established in 1971, represented the most important post-war initiative. Its stated objective was

> to encourage the development of a national free enterprise industry, to create incentives for the transfer and adoption of technology, diversify the sources of supply of medicines, give the country an efficient system for the control of pharmaceuticals and establish the conditions for the development of a genuinely Brazilian pharmaceutical industry at all levels from the extraction of raw materials to the finished product.[58]

Under pressure, this concept rapidly gave way to one of an organization 'which does not compete with private industry' but would serve as a 'strategic production reserve' and a 'centre for research and development in pharmaceutical technology and a training ground for specialized personnel.'[59] CEME's most important role today is the respectable but limited one of buying and distributing the drugs used by government health services for the majority of Brazilians who have no other access to health care.

More recent efforts to encourage production of pharmaceutical chemicals in bulk have been largely unsuccessful. Patents are not recognized in Brazil and substantial investment aid is available. Nevertheless, when in 1977 the BNDE (Bank for Industrial Development) offered 800 million cruzeiros (about $50 million) to help new production projects, most of the money remained unused.[60] 'The Bank feels that the pharmaceutical industry has shown almost no support for its program because it is foreign-controlled and it is not in the foreign company's economic interest.'[61] Other sources suggest that the Brazilian companies are already too fragmented to benefit. Those few projects for bulk pharmaceutical production that have gone ahead have been partnerships in which big foreign companies play a major role.

Taking profits at arm's length

A recent UN study points out that the supply of raw materials at artificially inflated prices is used to disguise (and export) the true profits of their enterprises. In 1975, they report, foreign companies paid on average 88 per cent more for their raw materials than Brazilian companies:

At the same time, the foreign firms showed a lower profitability than the local ones. It has been further estimated that if the subsidiaries had imported the raw material at 'arm's-length prices' the rate of return on invested capital would have amounted to 65 per cent instead of 15 per cent as declared.[62]

The Brazilian market is now firmly in the hands of the multinationals. And with their profits, we can return to the question of market power. Sanjaya Lall alleged that the fruits of market power are excessive profits. As the Brazilian example shows, the declared profitability of a pharmaceutical company subsidiary in the Third World has little to do with the true profits the parent company makes from its operations. Only those with access to the books know the true story and they rarely tell it. Many companies which give regional breakdowns of sales and profits take care to mix developing and developed countries in their reports, and there are many other, more subtle ways of disguising the size of profits made in any one country.

It is no secret that the multinationals transfer profits out of developing countries by overpricing their raw material supplies, although few would encourage their managers to be as blatant about it as was Roche marketing manager Peter Schurch who told me: 'Aiming that these countries buy our active substances—this is a prerequisite. In many countries,' (he mentioned India and Pakistan as examples) 'you cannot take profit out but you take it out in active substances.'

What is often neglected is the fact that the multinationals' Third World profits are as often as not made using the Third World's money. Pharmaceutical industry investment has proved so profitable that, once started, perhaps with money borrowed locally, a subsidiary will generate the funds for its own expansion. Glaxo's Indian subsidiary started with a capital of just 150,000 rupees in 1914. By 1971, it was worth 72 million rupees according to the books, of which 54 million rupees' worth was owned by the foreign shareholders. The 300-fold growth had been achieved almost entirely with Indian resources. But it entitled the company to send home in one year 2.4 million rupees in profits as well as 800,000 rupees in royalty payments.[63] Such profits are the fruits of market power.

There are countries—they include India, Egypt and others —where a strong national pharmaceutical industry has been nurtured. In those countries where governments choose not to intervene directly, the dominance of the multinationals appears inevitable. Both in its establishment and its maintenance, this dominance exacts its price, financially and in terms of health. In the divergence between the health needs of Third World communities and the way in which they actually use the drugs made available to them, the costs are clear.

Six: Drug Use

The market power of the multinationals gives them formidable influence over the way drugs are actually used in those Third World countries where they are active. It is on this issue that any critical examination of their contribution must focus. The emphasis on drug safety and drug efficacy is to some extent diversionary. Drugs are not dangerous just because they are labelled dishonestly, but they are when they are *taken* according to dishonest instructions. Nor are drugs inefficacious simply because smooth-talking salesmen recommend them for indications which they are ineffective to treat. It is when *prescribed* for such purposes that they are inefficacious. The promotion of expensive drugs where cheap ones would serve as well costs consumers nothing until their money is actually *paid* over the counter.

In short, the problem is not how drugs are labelled and sold, but how they are used. And the evidence from the Third World, sketchy though it is, suggests that drug misuse squanders a substantial proportion of the scarce resources available for health care.

This implies that, every year, millions of people needlessly risk dangerous drug side-effects; those with limited access to health care miss their one chance for successful treatment; whole continents are denied the use of good cheap drugs because resistance promoted by misuse renders them worthless; and whole communities are denied the drugs they need, because what money there is has been wasted on the purchase of others which are unnecessarily expensive.

Since the multinationals control a substantial part of the pharmaceutical supply system—that nebulous network of connections between laboratory, factory, pharmacy, prescriber and patient —much of the responsibility for this waste lies at their doors. For there is a direct link between corporate market power and the Manila bar girl who showed me a handful of capsules from her purse and told me, 'I take one each time against VD'; as there is, too, between the marketing practices of the multinationals and the fact that 85 per cent of gonorrhoea patients in a Nairobi clinic had infections resistant to both penicillin and tetracycline.[1]

In Bangladesh, a country burdened by disease, 25 per cent of drug expenditure goes on vitamins. In that fertile but poor country, vitamins rate very low on the list of health needs. But—

> Yes, both multi-vitamins and vitamin B12 are popular in Bangladesh. Why they're so popular it's difficult to say, but it's my personal opinion that as we're not a very rich country, people in the villages think that if they are sick, they just go to the chemist shop and ask for a vitamin and they will be healthy. It's a very simple idea. . . .

says Mr Aminur Rahman, managing director of the Bangladesh subsidiary of Glaxo, which has the biggest share of its sales in the country's villages, and a sizable share of the vitamin market.[2]

Bad drug use does not simply go hand in hand with poverty. Rio Grande de Sul is in the wealthy south of Brazil. A survey made there in 1979 found that amidopyrine products accounted for half the painkillers used in hospital wards (aspirin accounted for only 11 per cent). Chloramphenicol was used in 10 per cent of all cases where antibiotics were employed, although there had been no diagnoses of typhoid or meningitis—the two conditions for which it remains the drug of choice. Penicillin was used in only 5 per cent.[3]

Clearly, too, there is something very wrong with the pattern of drug use in a country like Ghana when one admission in every twenty-five to the medical wards of a government hospital is the result of a drug-induced or drug-associated illness, particularly since it is likely that the number of adverse reactions will be much higher than those actually diagnosed.[4] When meningitis resistant to ampicillin, chloramphenicol, rifampicin and minocycline is reported from Thailand[5] the victims of the drug abuse which produced it were not just the three children from the Bangkok orphanage who died in that particular outbreak. They could be anyone, anywhere. Just a few months after publication of the Thai case, a British doctor reported finding a strain of *H. influenzae* (which causes bacterial meningitis) resistant to chloramphenicol, ampicillin, tetracycline, sulphonamides and trimethoprim, and capable of transmitting this resistance to other bacteria.[6]

Confronted with the evidence about how drugs are actually used, much of the pseudo-scientific edifice constructed so carefully by the pharmaceutical industry comes crashing down. It is through studies of drug use in the field that the gulf between their undenied therapeutic potential and their actual impact becomes clear. Which is why, perhaps, the study of drug use is a science still in its infancy. This is true in both rich and poor worlds:

One of the most puzzling features of the world of medicines at the present day is the astonishing, and in some respects disastrous, lack of information about the way in which—and the extent to which—drugs are used and misused . . .

writes Dr M. N. G. Dukes of the Dutch Committee for the Evaluation of Medicines. He contrasts the effort devoted to determining the effects and risks of new drugs to the lackadaisical attitude to their subsequent use:

society has on the whole been remarkably indifferent to the subsequent career of these drugs and to the vast volume of quantifiable information that is needed to indicate what role these products are playing in health care, and what good or harm they are doing.[7]

The who, what and why of drug use

The scientific study of these questions began only twenty years ago[8] and can be attributed to attempts in Europe to match consumption of one particular drug (thalidomide) to the epidemic of deformed babies it provoked. The first researchers found that both doctors and patients were unreliable informants about the drugs they prescribed and used. Next, studies of chloramphenicol (whose dangers had already been widely publicized) revealed that it was still in general use in Great Britain. Not only were doctors unreliable informants about their prescribing patterns but, in their prescribing, they apparently ignored the information available about the drugs they used.

The parlous state of knowledge about drug use in Europe in the 1960s is mirrored in the Third World today. A computer search of world medical literature between 1975 and 1980 brought to light only thirty-five papers that could in any way be regarded as systematic studies of drug use in developing countries. Quantity should never be confused with quality, but by way of comparison, over a period of just three months, 120 papers were published about schistosomiasis, which has been described by the Rockefeller Foundation as one of the 'great neglected diseases of the world'.[9]

Drug utilization is defined by the WHO as: 'The marketing, distribution, prescription and use of drugs in a society, with special emphasis on the resulting medical, social and economic consequences'.[10] O. L. Wade describes its study more succinctly through a series of questions: 'What drugs are prescribed, who prescribes them, for which patients are they prescribed, for what reasons and with what resulting benefits or possibly ill effects?'[11]

These simple questions are, from the first, very difficult to answer. The starting point for studies of drug use in a community is information about the quantity of each drug sold. The data is available in detail. But it is not accessible. Companies routinely refuse to supply it, claiming that it is confidential sales information. This is nonsense:

> The pharmaceutical industry . . . long ago developed techniques with the aid of which any drug manufacturer can, at some considerable expense, determine the turnover of any or all the drugs on the market, including of course, those of his competitors. The figures obtained in this way, from large groups of pharmacists and physicians, are reliable, detailed, and up-to-date. The end result of this process is that any pharmaceutical house worthy of its name has access to all the information it requires, and that the primary (competitive) reason for maintaining confidentiality has, to all intents and purposes, disappeared; the only party that stands to lose is society at large, which is deprived of ready access to a valuable fund of information.[12]

It's money, not medicine

There are obvious vested interests in keeping this information confidential. Were it to be public knowledge, it would greatly facilitate the critical analysis of drug use. More prosaically, IMS Ltd, the biggest market research organization in the field, earned over $100 million (60 per cent of its total sales) in 1980 from its surveys of the drug trade.[13]

> A few governments purchase portions of this information, but, with the exception of the United Kingdom and the Scandinavian countries, governments generally do not have a data base that compares with that available to the leading pharmaceutical multi-national companies.[14]

In consequence, neither in the developed nor in the developing worlds is the basic data for assessing the costs and benefits of drug use available. 'Even the simplest of descriptive information is missing or inadequate,' writes one research group.

We had presumed that most nations would have available statistics on the per capita consumption of prescription and OTC compounds, their cost to manufacturers, health systems and consumers, and the correlations between at least major compounds' use and (diagnosed) disease prevalence. This is not so.[15]

It is a reflection of the industry's priorities that much of what information is available is of limited use because it is expressed in terms of money rather than medicine. So entrenched is this habit that the authors of a recent UNIDO study found it necessary, in an apologetic preface, to explain that

a large number of statements on production and consumption of pharmaceuticals [is] in terms of weight of bulk drugs inasmuch as it has been thought that weight is a more precise indicator than value in assessing the growth of the industry or the drug requirements of developing countries.[16]

In those developing countries where governments take an active interest in the pharmaceutical industry, some information about the total quantity of drugs is in circulation. But when it comes to determining how individual doctors prescribe, it is only in those few developed countries with centrally funded health services paying for all prescriptions that this information is routinely available.

Blind marksmen and dumb bullets

In this information vacuum, we have to proceed by hypothesis, anecdote and chance observation to begin to build up a picture of the way drugs are actually used in the Third World.

First, the hypothesis.[17] In graphic terms, if we describe a community's health problems as a target, the bull's-eye comprises that limited set of conditions in which drug treatment is useful. In an ideal world, all prescribers would be marksmen and would hit the bull's-eye every time. Realistically, there will always be a little spread outside it. In rich countries what is actually happening is that while most people needing drug treatment eventually get it, drugs are grossly overused for conditions in which they are not appropriate or where no disease exists at all. In the developing countries, it is worse. Many people who need drug treatment do not get it. A substantial proportion of drugs is used for conditions in which they will be of no benefit. And in some countries, the only comparison can be with the marksmanship of a drunk shooting in the dark.

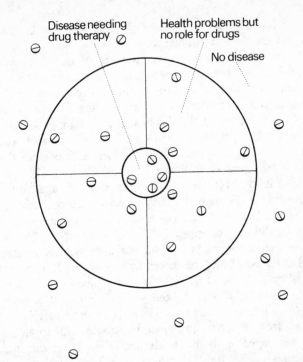

Drug utilization in developing countries: blind marksmen and dumb bullets

Lest it appear that the thesis is that the multinational pharmaceutical companies are responsible for all bad drug use, the first piece of anecdotal information comes from Mozambique in 1980, by which time their influence there was only indirect.

Beira in the hot season can be very unpleasant. Although the temperature rarely rises over 35°C, the humidity is high and oppressive. With everyone's energy sapped and tempers frayed, it is not a productive time of year. Any attempt to beat the heat is thwarted. Air conditioning only makes it worse when you have to emerge outside. The solution is to slow down, but sometimes that is not possible.

At this time of the year, the human body takes its own decisions. I, for one, suffered regular headaches. They were exacerbated every time I did something unreasonably energetic like taking the stairs to the office two at a time and, I noted, were closely correlated with the consumption of life-saving cold beer in the evenings. My colleague Inacio suffered similar complaints. It was like being hit with a hammer at the back of the head, he told me. We each took our own decision. I abandoned my weekday bottle of beer; he went to a *consulta* at his local health centre.

His treatment illustrates one extreme of bad drug use. The prescription he was given contained five items—chloroquine, diazepam, mebendazole (an anti-parasitic), amoxicillin (an expensive broad-spectrum antibiotic) and promethazine (a powerful anti-histamine). Needless to say, his headache did not get better. So he went to another *consulta*. This time he came back with a six-item prescription. More diazepam, co-trimoxazole (a combination anti-biotic), furosemide (the diuretic), potassium chloride (used with frusemide in the treatment of hypertension), aspirin and vitamin B12. As before, he took the tablets and the headaches continued. Only when the rains started and the atmosphere became less oppressive did they disappear.

Those eleven drugs prescribed for a hot-season headache are typical of the way health resources are wasted. And, by coincidence, we saw around the same time the consequences of such waste. Ernesto Vilanculos, who worked 50 kilometres out of town at the water treatment plant, had been diagnosed some months before as suffering from tuberculosis. Since the disease was in an advanced state, he stayed at home while receiving treatment under the supervision of his local health centre. Then, while Inacio was making his round of the *consultas*, we received a message asking whether we could try to find the rifampicin and ethambutol which had been prescribed for him. We tried everywhere, without success. The entire province had run out of these essential but expensive anti-TB drugs.

A colonial heritage?

Prescribing habits do not arise in a vacuum. So I was fortunate to be presented with the opportunity to put these occurrences into their historical context. It arose when the nurse who ran the water company's small health post was knocked off his bicycle by a bus, and died. Before independence, the health post had been restricted to company employees and their families. When medicine was nationalized in 1977, its management had passed to the state. Since there were other clinics nearby, there was no pressing reason to maintain the post, and, with no one to run it, it closed by default.

It fell to me to dispose of its contents. While I was doing this, I came across the prescribing and drug-purchasing records dating back to the early 1970s as well as the nurse's little library of drug package inserts, the only literature available to him on the medicines he dispensed.

Before independence, drug purchases had been controlled by a visiting doctor. Fewer than fifty items were kept in stock. Top of the list in terms of quantity was clioquinol and related products, followed by aspirin, chloroquine, sulphonamides and phenylbutazone. Every month, eighteen ampoules of injectable penicillin were bought. There were absurdities. Considerably more ampoules of vitamin B than penicillin were bought, as well as injectable vitamin C. A range of 'liver protectors', also injectable, was kept in stock. Another regular purchase was Transpneumol, an injectable mixture of quinine, menthol, camphor and eucalyptus extract recommended by its makers for respiratory infections and their prevention.

The most commonly used product, clioquinol, we know to be ineffective for the treatment of non-specific diarrhoeas, which is what it was prescribed for. The vitamins were being used irrationally —vitamin C for anaemia and vitamin B for rheumatism. (The diagnoses are those recorded in the treatment register.) Otherwise, apart from the clearly superfluous products like Transpneumol and the liver protectors, and the excessive use of phenylbutazone for the 10 per cent of patients diagnosed as having rheumatism, the most obvious defect in the pattern of drug use was its excessive reliance on injections. Chloroquine in its injectable form was routinely used, although contemporary conservative authorities recommended its use only 'for critically ill patients with delirium or coma'.[18] The walking-wounded who frequented the health post were never in this category. Similarly, giving vitamins by injection can in no way be justified, if they had any role to play at all.

The issue is not just one of risk. In developing countries, apart from the regular occurrence of infected ulcers, overuse of injections has been suggested as an important mechanism for the transmission of hepatitis and polio. In Mozambique, as in other poor countries, cost is the problem. Injectable chloroquine costs nearly ten times as much as tablets;[19] the differential for other products is similar. Yet perhaps half that health post's treatments were by injection. Since the patients were effectively a captive population, this could not be justified on the grounds that they might not otherwise take their medicines as prescribed.

A year after independence, the position had changed. The flight of the doctors had left the nurse without any supervision, and the drug-purchasing patterns were significantly different. The quantity of antibiotics bought had soared, mostly as various brands of tetracycline capsules. Lomotil in syrup and tablet form made its appearance, as did Cibalgin. Particularly interesting was the fact that these new entries rarely featured in the treatment register. It seems reasonable to assume that they were being diverted for sale and use outside the company, and here there would be a predominant demand for tetracyclines to treat venereal diseases and for drugs like Lomotil and Cibalgin whose potent effects would be best appreciated by those unaware of their drawbacks.

Treatments in this period followed the earlier pattern, although more drugs were used, and this is where we find the link with Inacio's eleven-item prescription. Most Mozambican health workers began employment during the colonial period and, despite retraining, this still shows. Portugal's drugs market in the early 1970s bore all the hallmarks of a relatively rich developing country—chaotic competition spawned by the attempts of the national companies to compete with the increasingly aggressive multinationals—and this was exported to Mozambique. The 1972 *Simposium Terapeutico*, the guide to all drugs on the market, listed 15,000 different products. They included twenty-six brands of chloramphenicol, twelve of tetracycline, fifteen of phenobarbital, more than twenty of the corticosteroid, prednisolone, and its near relatives, with around 150 vitamin B preparations.

There was pressure to use drugs, preferably lots of them. If the nurse at the health post used drugs badly, he was only following the guidance he found in his library of package inserts. Vitamin B for rheumatism would appear quite logical after reading the package insert for Merck's Neurobion. Similarly, if he tried vitamin C as a treatment for anaemia, Merck can also take the credit for promoting its Cebion brand with the advice that 'it is advisable to give Cebion in parallel with the specific medication for the treatment of anaemias.' In some respects, the Mozambican drug market before independence resembled that of Brazil in the 1940s, with its 'pushtherapy' mentality. The Portuguese 'laboratories' tried hard to persuade doctors to prescribe their range of products exclusively. With some, they succeeded. Dr Dias Coelho, who ran a private practice in colonial times and is now director of the Beira Hospital, recounted some of the characteristics of the medicine market of the time.

We knew that with a couple of doctors, all their prescriptions would be for the products of one laboratory, just one or two exceptions perhaps; another, a very good doctor with one of the biggest clienteles in the city, 80 per cent of his prescriptions were products from another laboratory.

It was generally believed that this single-minded prescribing did not go without reward. The multinationals competed by promoting their specialities with the familiar high-powered sales machine. Based in Beira, with its sixty doctors, were nearly twenty salesman with others flying up regularly from the colonial capital of Lourenço Marques. They did not forget the pharmacies either. As in Brazil, companies competed to make their products most profitable to the pharmacists in the knowledge that they would then substitute them for their competitors' brands.

Thus, at independence, Mozambique's heritage was one of pharmaceutical anarchy overlying the total underdevelopment of health services for the majority of the country's population, and aggravated by the mass exodus of most of the doctors who had provided what services there were in the main towns. It has taken time to build on this foundation. But it is perhaps because Mozambique has already lived this particular future that it is taking active steps to develop a coherent pharmaceutical policy.

Drugs: just the ticket

Egypt is another country where the influence of the multinationals has been limited, in this case since 1963, when the government nationalized all but two of the foreign pharmaceutical companies then active, and began to promote the development of a strong national drug industry. In production terms, they have been very successful, 83 per cent of all drugs being produced locally.[20]

Here too, however, the pattern of drug use appears to be little related to health needs, though for different reasons. In a study which deserves to become a classic of its kind, Nawal el Messiri Nadim describes the functioning of two typical village clinics in rural Egypt. The clinics have a set budget for drugs but that is only the beginning of the story.

The doctors of the area commented that the quantity of medicine received depends to a certain extent on the relationship between the doctor and the chemist in charge of the centre's stores. If the relationship is good, the doctor receives more, and more varied, medicine than he or she would otherwise. Thus one centre's ration may consist only of Novalgin (noramidopyrine), sulpha and aspirin, whereas another centre receives antibiotics, vitamins and injectables.[21]

The clinics run a two-tier system of examinations. An ordinary five-piastre 'ticket examination' entitles a villager to a consultation and medicine from the clinic dispensary—usually vitamins, Noval-gin or cough syrup. An extra fee is levied for special examinations. 'This entitles the patient to a physical examination with a stetho-scope and a free dose of medicine selected by the doctor from among the medicines available at the clinic dispensary.' A prescription is thus an integral part of the consultation.

Villagers believe that medicine is the basic tool of the doctor. A health unit is evaluated on the basis of the quantity and quality of medicines in its dispensary. Similarly, the reputation of the doctor is closely related to his or her power in obtaining medicine and generosity in prescribing and distributing it. Very often, the monthly ration of medicine is exhausted before the arrival of the next supply and hardly a villager will approach the health unit.

This arbitrary distribution of drugs, together with the arbitrary decision to consult the doctor only when the clinics have medicine, point to a relation between drug use and health need that is at best tenuous. The study does not go further to investigate for what reasons the drugs were prescribed, for whom and with what result. Nadim is more interested in the role of drugs in helping to establish the health centre as part of its rural community and thus enabling it to gain support for its other, more clearly productive, activities in preventive health care and family planning.

Chloroquine with everything

The last link in the chain comes from Ghana. For reasons of economic and health policy, Ghana was for a while one of the few African countries in which drug shortages were the exception rather than the rule outside the main towns and cities. The surfeit of drugs brought its own particular problems, as the record of drug-related illness already cited shows. Its other consequence—brought to light when a team of researchers went to the countryside to study ways of establishing a new health-care system—was a huge waste of resources from apparently irrational prescribing.[22]

They described one typical clinic where 96 per cent of all outpatient visits resulted in treatment with an injection.

There were only two basic prescribing responses for the majority of symptoms: one involving an anti-malarial injection, and another based on a penicillin injection, with very similar tablets being given in both cases. . . . The commonest tablets were anti-malarials and analgesics. Anti-malarial injections, tablets and syrups were in fact prescribed in 80 per cent of all consultations, although only 51 per cent of the diagnoses were for fever and malaria. An average of 3.9 items were given on each prescription.

It was estimated that pharmaceutical costs could be cut, simply by appropriate prescribing, by 70 per cent. Nationwide, the savings could fund the implementation of a new health care system, the authors concluded.

These examples have deliberately been taken from countries in which the multinational presence is not dominant. They are also examples from the public rather than the private health services. The multinationals would be happy were the focus to remain here, since it is in the public sector that they claim the problems lie.

The myth of private medicine

Willy-nilly, most of the developing nations have evolved a mixed system of health delivery, divided into public and private sectors. The private sector follows the familiar Western pattern of distribution, with physicians providing services in private offices, clinics and hospitals, and themselves dispensing and prescribing drugs to be purchased at retail pharmacies. . . . It must be recognized that the private segment of health care functions reasonably well . . .

claimed Max Tiefenbacher of Hoechst, adding his estimate that these private services account for 75 to 90 per cent of the total drug consumption of developing nations.[23] 'Medicines supplied in the private segment are appropriate to the health needs of the patients,' he summed up.

The poverty of his position is revealed by his own figures. In the four developing countries he cites—Brazil, the Philippines, Venezuela and Pakistan—cough and cold remedies, vitamins and analgesics are the biggest selling classes of drugs, after antibiotics, the preponderance of trivial drugs in these countries being much more marked than in the rich world. Since they carry a heavier burden of disease, this is in itself clear evidence that the private sector functions best for those whose interest is in sales figures rather than health benefits.

Nigeria, where sales of over-the-counter drugs were until recently worth nearly as much as 'ethical' prescription drugs is an extreme case, but one of many. Bangladesh's street sellers hawking their powerful antibiotics for cuts and grazes and any other ill you care to name; multinationals' salesmen promoting diuretics for dying children; pharmacies pushing vitamins, on which they depend for their profits, to hungry villagers—it is for these and for their principals that the private sector functions reasonably well.

This is not for one moment to deny that there are many individual doctors in the private sector who prescribe sensibly to patients who can afford the drugs and will use them correctly. But drug use studies seek out a pattern of use on a community rather than an individual level. And there is no convincing evidence to show that rational drug use accounts for more than a tiny proportion of total use. Concealed behind the screens of thousands of private consulting rooms, consisting as they do of hundreds of thousands of inconspicuous daily transactions in private pharmacies, the gross abuse and misuse of drugs is a less public and more complex phenomenon. But the evidence is strong.

Take Max Tiefenbacher's prototype developing country, Brazil. He claims that the private market caters for 'the emerging urban middle class social stratum of the population—the literate, educated, employed and most productive members of developing societies.'[24] The pioneering studies of drug use in Brazil paint a very different picture. House to house visits in Pelotas, in the (relatively) rich south of the country, found that the number of medicines in use in the peripheral shanty towns and in the best suburbs where the professionals and businessmen lived did not vary much (an average 0.93 per person in the periphery and 1.4 in the 'Class A' suburb). The medicines used by the rich community cost nearly twice as much as those of the poor. So for company directors who think in terms of *money*, it is true that the drug consumption of the poor was only one-third that of the rich. In terms of *medicine* it was twice that.

There was little difference between the types of medicine consumed by the different classes. Although the rich appeared to use more medicine for their digestive and circulatory systems, and the poor more vitamins and analgesics, the consumption of psychotropics and antibiotics was similar. The most important difference between the rich and poor was that the majority of the poor (52 per cent) obtained their medicine without a doctor's prescription, which the rich usually had.[25]

Further analysis confirms that the real difference between rich and poor in Brazil is in their access to the doctors whom Max Tiefenbacher considers an integral part of private sector medicine. Geraldo Giovanni investigated drug use in Rio Claro, a town in the central state of São Paulo. He confirmed that while the difference in health expenditure between rich and poor was substantial (the well-off spent eight times as much on health care as the poorest families) pharmaceutical expenditure was only two and a half times greater.

Table 5 **Monthly medical expenditures (cruzeiros):**
     Rio Claro, July 1977[26]

	Bairro 1	Bairro 2	Bairro 3	Bairro 4
Doctor	0	25	256	400
Farmacia	151	184	408	401
Total	169	275	959	1367
Monthly income	2625	3317	9935	22,833

Note: Total includes dentist and laboratory expenses.

In Rio Claro, the poor community had access of a very limited kind to free medical consultations. What were the reasons for not going to them? '. . . It's a very long way and their prescriptions are expensive.' 'I don't have transport, I can't pay the busfare, so I go to the *farmacia* which is closer.' 'You have to go early to get a *consulta* and where I live there is no bus.' 'Because of the queue. . . .' 'The remedies prescribed by the pharmacist are cheaper than those prescribed by the doctor.' Giovanni concludes: 'This resort to the pharmacy was always explained, by the lowest income group, for economic reasons, because of the distance to centres for free medical care or to previous satisfactory experiences with pharmacists.'

The private medicine idealized by Max Tiefenbacher does not, in practice, exist. In Brazil, as in many countries of the Third World, a substantial proportion of that 75–90 per cent of drugs used in the private sector is dispensed without the benefit of a prescription from physicians in private offices and clinics. This is why such a substantial proportion of the drugs sold in the private sector are trivial products which at best relieve symptoms but most commonly are merely profitable placebos. This is why, as in Giovanni's study, their consumers have only the vaguest knowledge about their correct indications and use. In such communities, if drugs are sold on the understanding that they will only be used under the supervision of a doctor, then they are being sold under false pretences.

In virtually any developing country you choose to look at, the private sector drugs market is grossly deficient in terms of the drugs which are available, those which are not, and the way they are used. 'Part of the drug budget in Ecuador goes on expensive, non-essential, or unsafe proprietary medicines, while many drugs considered necessary in the developed countries are unavailable.' So, in that country, Merck sells its Hydrozet throat lozenges, a cocktail of antibiotics, cortisone and benzocaine, which would be considered unsafe in Britain, over the counter along with its Encefabol (claimed to be a 'neurodynamic' to help phosphate get to the brain). Encefabol can best be described as non-essential. Meanwhile essential drugs such as pethidine, folic acid, the first-choice diuretic hydrochlorothiazide, and the anti-parasitic mebendazole are not available.[27]

Not all private medicine is on the same level as the patent medicine market in Nigeria where the ambition of the multinationals seems to be to supplant traditional remedies based on cow's urine with their own products whose therapeutic benefits are much the same and whose adverse effects, to judge by the number of hospital admissions due to drug poisoning, are just about equal.[28] It is not just the waste of money on products like Sandoz Calcium-C or Parke Davis's Abidec drops that hurts; it is the fact that the marketing of these products is getting priority over drugs which are of value if properly used. From Nigeria's Benin City, Dr C. O. Amah, reporting the problems of his hypertension clinic, notes: 'This was one area that posed the greatest problems as the supply of drugs was unpredictable. Even regular attenders could go without their drugs for some time. Popular brands soon became out of stock, necessitating replacement with less effective drugs.'[29] It hurts that into this market, where fully half of all patients at a well-organized hospital clinic failed to comply with their treatment, Boehringer Ingelheim introduced their clonidine (which can kill those who stop taking it suddenly) with an inadequate written warning about the dangers of abrupt cessation of treatment.

Drug use studies, focusing on the use of drugs in the community rather than in the individual, pose a challenge. It is so easy to select a group of patients all suffering from the same complaint, treat them with a drug under controlled conditions, and show that it is effective. It is quite another thing to launch a drug into a community where there is no control over the quality of the diagnosis, nor of treatment, nor of the patient's ability to buy the drug or take it as instructed.

Evidence from the developed countries is not encouraging in this regard. What studies have been done suggest that doctors' diagnoses are often right only 50 per cent of the time; their prescriptions err similarly; further, less than half their patients take their medicine as instructed.[30] This implies that perhaps only one in eight times is the right person going to get the right medicine at the right time. There is every reason to expect the situation in the developing world to be worse.

Man-made disease

Bad drug use is not just a question of waste. It is also the major cause of the development of infectious diseases resistant to existing drugs. The explosive spread of resistance to antibiotics is common to both the rich and poor world, although the latter, with its more limited resources, feels the loss of good cheap drugs more grievously. But man-made drug resistance has effectively created new diseases in countries where typhoid, meningitis and dysentery had become problems of the past.

The WHO's report on the problem gives the global view:

> Several serious outbreaks of infection with resistant bacteria have occurred in recent years:
> —antibiotic resistant shigellosis in Central America with many thousands of deaths, and in Bangladesh, with very high attack and case-fatality rates;
> —chloramphenicol resistant typhoid fever in several parts of the world—for example, in Mexico in 1972, with many thousands of cases and a death rate similar to that of the pre-antibiotic era;
> —resistant *Salmonella* infections in children's hospitals with many deaths. . . .[31]

Dr Philip Lee helped the USA's Senate Subcommittee on the Drug Industry to see the link between the disease of Latin America and the health of their constituents. He told its members:

> The problem is important to millions of people who live in Latin America, it is also important for the 2.5 million residents of the

United States who travel to Mexico annually. . . . At least one-third of travellers to Mexico and many other Latin American countries are likely to suffer an episode of gastro-enteritis during or following their trip. Although many of these are minor, many are serious and some have proved lethal.[32]

Lest it to be thought that the problem has been exaggerated by critics of the drug industry, Professor von Wasielewski of Hoechst's central research department put the solution of the problem of resistant infections high on his list of 'urgent needs in medicine', pointing out that while 'acute bacterial infections can be controlled quite well with antibiotics, there is often unfortunately no therapeutic solution to resistant bacteria. . . . Much remains to be done in this area.'[33]

The contradiction between corporation and community

There is here a fundamental contradiction between the individual and the community approach to medicine, between the interests of the multinational industry and of society at large. It is a contradiction that confronts me every morning at breakfast. There are a number of drugs that can be used to prevent malaria. Chloroquine is the best known. It is cheap and can thus be widely used. Its disadvantages, apart from its long term toxicity and the occurrence of resistance in some parts of South-East Asia, is that it tastes very bitter and makes some people feel permanently nauseous. The other drugs, Paludrine (proguanil), Daraprim (pyrimethamine), Maloprim and Fansidar (both pyrimethamine with a sulphone) are more expensive. They are, however, virtually free of side-effects and toxic only in huge overdoses. Yet in many countries where malaria is endemic, Mozambique included, you cannot buy them. The problem is that, if used on a community-wide scale where malaria is common, the parasite rapidly develops resistance to them.

My decision was simple. If no one else in Beira takes them, I can take pyrimethamine and my daughter can take proguanil, and they will be effective—as indeed they have so far been. Short-term visitors can also use them safely. People brought up in this heavily infested region usually have some natural immunity to malaria, so tend to take only the occasional curative dose of chloroquine for particularly acute attacks. Those who do not have a natural immunity must keep taking their chloroquine or resign themselves to regular bouts of malaria. That is the present limit of the therapeutic arsenal.

It is not the end of the story, however. While I can, as an individual, make my own decisions about what anti-malarials to use without affecting anyone else, the drug companies cannot. Yet two major multinationals, Roche and Wellcome, are, along with the Hungarian Medimpex and Farmitalia, marketing their brands of pyrimethamine, Fansidar and Maloprim, in African countries where malaria is endemic. This is contrary to current 'gentlemen's agreements'—'No firm is really taking acute care over recommendations in this area,' complained one expert. If continued this will, quite predictably, produce resistance that will render these drugs useless. Yet Roche have even gone so far as to encourage doctors to give such drugs the widest use. 'If not available locally, contact Roche agency,' they suggest in an unusual addition to Fansidar's listing in the African edition of the prescribing guide *MIMS*.[34]

Both Roche and Wellcome stand to benefit considerably from any resistance that they succeed in promoting. Roche has a new anti-malarial under development. By the terms of agreements with co-sponsors WHO and US Walter Reed Institute, it will be kept as a reserve drug and used in malarial regions only when chloroquine resistance becomes a major problem. Roche staff made it clear to me, however, that they see sales in the rich world for travellers destined for malarial countries as a legitimate market from which they intend to recoup their share of development costs. Were resistance to pyrimethamine and proguanil to be reported from popular places of visit like Nigeria and Kenya, this could only boost their sales. Similarly, Wellcome is in the final stages of developing a malaria vaccine for which a similar market can be anticipated.

The research-based pharmaceutical industry has a very clear interest in the promotion of resistance to existing drugs, be they anti-parasitics or antibiotics. Drug resistance is part of their marketing strategy and is explicitly stated to be such by the industry's economists.[35] It is an obvious and important means by which new market opportunities can be created.

Is it fair to lay the blame on the multinationals for the destruction of useful drugs and the creation of new disease—which is what the promotion of drug resistance amounts to? The WHO's experts passed no judgements: 'Control of antibiotic use in man is difficult, but every effort should be made to ensure rational use—mainly by educational means.'[36]

But what is the contribution of the multinationals to that education? Its quality can be gauged from the following advertisement in the *Bangladesh Pharmaceutical Journal*.

'Bactrim' Roche
The broad spectrum anti-infective agent
with the
lowest resistance rate
According to Truffot *et al.* after investigating 10,067 strains from 1970 to 1975, the combination of trimethoprim and sulphamethoxazole is the commonly used 'broad-spectrum' antibiotic to which bacteria are, at present, least resistant.
Conclusion
'Bactrim' offers better prospects of success

This 'conclusion' is backed up by graphs which show on careful analysis that bacterial resistance to Bactrim grew by more than 70 per cent since 1970 when it came into general use. Yet Roche recommended its widest possible application: 'Indications: Infections of the upper and lower respiratory tract, genito-urinary tract, gastro-intestinal tract and of the skin. Infected wounds. Septicemia. Susceptible organisms.'[37] It would be difficult to find a form of words better calculated to promote saturation use. Yet that will certainly destroy a valuable drug years earlier than need be.

The multinationals make by far the largest contribution to the post-qualification 'education' of doctors and pharmacists. They claim to devote 20 per cent of sales, or $5000 million, annually to advertising and scientific information.[38] The pattern of drug use cannot be viewed in isolation from these inputs. The fundamental conflict is between the aims of the industry—which, since it wants to sell more, and more expensive, drugs, has a vested interest in their misuse and overuse—and the needs of society.

Of course, irrational drug use is not solely the product of the companies. There are many irrational forces at work in any country. The Brazilians who live the problem at its worst sum it up best:

It is not enough to accuse this or that group of actors of responsibility for the present situation. It is clearly a more pertinent proposition to say: The companies are to blame for producing anything to make money; the doctors are to blame for prescribing anything to get rid of their clients; the patients are ingenuous for believing in miraculous solutions and blameworthy for asking for them. In fact, the behaviour of each group is perfectly explicable and understandable taking account of the rules of the game which have been imposed on all. It is useless to moralize: it is these rules of the game which must be questioned.[39]

Part II: The 1980s

Seven: Towards Resolution

The chemical factory chimneys which dominate the city of Basle were venting nothing more than a few wisps of steam as I crossed the Rhine one fine spring morning in 1981 on my way to revisit Hoffmann-La Roche. An important sign, perhaps, since this time it was the question of the Third World's contribution to the faltering health of the pharmaceutical industry that I wanted to raise with the company.

There have been problems, serious problems, for the European chemical industry, which the Swiss companies have not escaped. In Germany, Bayer's profits had fallen by 63 per cent in the third Bquarter of 1980 and Hoechst's, by more than 40 per cent; while Bchemical sales generally had fallen by more than 10 per cent. But Bcommentators noted that not all areas of business were so severely hit. 'Some sectors, like pharmaceuticals, have even managed some growth.'[1] Since pharmaceuticals account for 45 per cent of the Bproduction of the Swiss chemical industry, the impact of this recession had been cushioned.[2] But it was sufficient to worry the home-town newspaper of the three biggest companies, Roche, Ciba and Sandoz. Under the headline 'Basle Chemistry at a Turning Point', the *Tages-Anzeiger* reported research centre closures, as well as major reviews of overhead costs, research expenditures and corporate structures aimed at enabling the companies to 'survive the difficulties of the 1980s', as a Sandoz spokesman put it. 'We find ourselves in a critical phase comparable to the introduction of electronics in the watch industry,' elaborated Roche.[3]

The industry's malpractices in the Third World, described in the preceding chapters, may be taken as the basic symptoms of its underlying illness. But the sale of unsafe drugs, the over-promotion of others well beyond the limits of their efficacy, the total lack of interest in whether its products, as actually used, do good or harm, and the diversion of research from pressing 'tropical' health needs to 'more commercial areas', need come as no surprise. They were a logical consequence of corporate organization in which targets are financial rather than medical. As George Squibb, former marketing vice-president of the American company which bears his family name, told the US Senate Monopoly Subcommittee: 'It is customary for the Directors to leave all day-to-day operating procedures to its field management, and then simply to inspect the financial results of such procedure.'[4]

For the industry, the focus on profit is not perceived as an illness but as an essential quality to be fostered and defended. To begin to understand their response to the problems of the Third World, the companies' perception of their own health must be considered. So a diagnosis of 'profit hunger', though justified, is as trivial as a prescription of Valium for the anxiety of the unemployed. Like unemployment, the problem of the pharmaceutical industry today is a structural one. If it can be labelled, it could best be described as a mid-life crisis.

It is a fair description. The modern pharmaceutical industry is hardly forty years old. Many of its senior directors entered it in the halcyon days of the penicillins and the sulphas, 'wonder drugs' which truly transformed medical practice. Good new drugs which bring real benefits to their users continue to be produced, but they are fewer and lack the startling impact in a wide range of diseases that characterized the advent of antibiotics. 'Since the end of the 1960s, drug research has lost its tremendous momentum. Fewer new drugs have reached the market and the number of therapeutic breakthroughs have decreased,' Professor Alfred Pletscher, Director of Research at the University Hospital in Basle, told the IFPMA Congress in 1980.[5]

There are exciting developments waiting in the wings. But the fact remains that for many diseases, the old, tried remedies which account for a substantial portion of the sales of the research-based companies will remain the drugs of choice. The delayed impact of the end of this first golden age of innovation is only now beginning to be felt as the patents on the second- and third-generation improvements to existing drug types run out, and the opportunities for further development that will bring genuine therapeutic advance become more limited. The result is a severe squeeze on company sales and profits.

The development of penicillin and its subsequent improvement is a case in point. The advance represented by penicillin is immeasurable. Not quite in the same class but still an important innovation, was the first major improvement, ampicillin, a synthetic derivative which is effective against a wider range of bacteria and is easier to administer. The research into amoxicillin, the third-generation improvement, achieved the important breakthrough in 1962, shortly after ampicillin, but Beechams (which originated both) did not officially register its discovery until 1968.[6] Each time, though, the improvement is relatively smaller. Bacampicillin, the latest modification launched recently by Pfizer in the USA, has, as major selling points, its reduced incidence of diarrhoea and the convenience of its twice-a-day dosage (ampicillin is normally given four times a day).[7] This picture of diminishing therapeutic returns on innovation is typical within wide areas of disease.

The research-based pharmaceutical companies pay their research expenses (and the high cost of the marketing machine needed to launch their new drugs on the most rapidly rising trajectory) by raising the price of existing products. That is easy while they are patent-protected. The companies try to keep the prices high even when their patents expire and competitors enter the market. But eventually, sales income invariably falls. So long as there are new products in the pipeline, that is acceptable, but when new product development is stagnant in many areas of therapy, trouble lies ahead. That was the situation at the start of the 1980s. The crisis has been compounded by other pressures, as George Squibb told the US Senate:

It is very stupid, indeed, for a well-established, profitable, and progressive industry to endorse or permit practices in its sales promotion areas which can produce only short-term dollar return, and then will lead to restrictive controls which will overreach the abuses with which we are now concerned and go on to other pharmaceutical affairs now left unregulated.'[8]

It was stupid. It was that stupid disregard for the needs and resources of the Third World that accelerated its confrontation with the companies and now threatens to lose them some of their most promising future markets just when they are needed to help cushion the impact of the dearth of new products. Simultaneously, economic recession and soaring health-care costs are forcing rich world governments to economize on health care, so the growth of the pharmaceutical industry's domestic markets is none too healthy.

It would be rash to venture any prescription for the current ills besetting the industry. To do so would, for a start, contradict one basic theme to this book: that many diseases are self-limiting, and that the processes which lead to the resolution of others often owe little to medical intervention. What applies to the human body can equally apply to that corporate body which we call the pharmaceutical industry.

Reekie and Weber note, in another context, that 'health care expectations are a key determinant of the demand for pharmaceuticals.'[9] Apply this to the case of the pharmaceutical industry, and we see that rising expectations, generated in large measure by the industry's own behaviour, have created an environment in which it will have to meet new demands. Just as simple environmental sanitation can transform the health of a poor community, so this new environment carries in itself the seeds of a transformed relationship between the industry and the Third World. It may be characterized by demands for strong medicine to remedy the ills of the drug industry, but it is the rising expectations rather than the specific prescriptions that are the key to the future.

The expectation that medicine will be used rationally and economically is a revolution in itself. So, too, is the expectation that people in developing countries will be given sufficient information about their medicines to use them in this way. It is now expected, albeit optimistically, that poor countries will not be hindered in their attempts to use their limited health resources to best effect, and that a reasonable proportion of the funds that they have contributed to the world research 'pool' will be used to tackle their problems.

The second half of this book investigates the evolving Third World pharmaceutical strategy, looking at the policies proposed as rational attempts to meet these rising expectations rather than as attacks against the multinational corporations. But what will be the implications of these policies for the research-based multinationals in the pharmaceutical business? There is much confusion about this both outside and within the industry. Thus at Roche, Peter Schurch, 'chief of staff' in the marketing division, was adamant that his company could not get involved in the sale of the cheap, out-of-patent, generic drugs that best meet the Third World's health needs. 'There is no way out by the generic road. A research-based company cannot sell generics.' A few miles down the River Rhine, a few days later, Fritz Schneiter, a Ciba-Geigy marketing man who had spent the previous four years establishing a subsidiary company to sell generic drugs, told me: 'We expect to have a sizeable portion of the Third World market.' Needless to say, Ciba-Geigy has no intention of abandoning its research base.

Are corporate dilemmas such as these of any relevance to the Third World? Should developing countries just press on with the implementation of their health policies as best they can? That is certainly the view expressed by some commentators from those countries, but they are wrong.

The multinationals represent a major resource. A Third World which understands their limitations, what they can do and what they cannot, will be able to gain the maximum from pragmatic cooperative ventures which benefit both parties. Of fundamental importance, however, is the fact that the multinationals will remain key actors in the health arena for the foreseeable future. They are, naturally, undertaking a formidable campaign to protect their interests—national and international—and for the developing world, forewarned will be forearmed.

Third World governments should be aware, for instance, that the industry, through the IFPMA, has called for the companies to focus their attentions on national governments 'with special emphasis on your government representatives at these WHO and UNIDO meetings'.[10] It is a matter of public record that just five major American drug companies spent approximately $12 million on 'pay-offs' in connection with what Sterling Drug Inc. described as 'a variety of . . . governmental actions related to increasing the profitability of the foreign business of the corporation's subsidiaries'.[11] So I found it particularly chilling to be told by one company manager that, in his estimation, no more than 250 people decided whether a drug would be successful or not in most developing countries, particularly those where the state bought or distributed most of the drugs.

It does not follow that companies will opt for some of the less legal and more unpleasant methods open to them to maintain their profitability. The existence of more clearly defined and better directed policies on the use of drugs will help to reduce markedly the opportunities for such tactics. Those working towards such policies have no illusions about the difficulties they face. They do not talk of right and wrong.

We speak of 'optimal' and in so doing quickly reach the heart of the matter. Optimal is ideal, and what is ideal depends on what people value; how one defines a good or bad thing, a cost or a benefit. But 'optimal' is also pragmatic; it connotes what can be done. And to know what can be done requires a knowledge of medicines, illnesses, available resources and how people act and are influenced.

People and, one might add, multinational corporations.[12]

To examine the conflicts and compromises inherent in the emerging Third World pharmaceutical policies, and the corporate response to them, it is first necessary to review the new health philosophies of which these policies are part. Which brings me back to Beira.

Eight: Primary Health Care

Batista João swaggered back home like any five-year-old who knows that now he has seen the world. Home was three somewhat ramshackle, thatch-roofed, mud-wall houses close to the river Muda, surrounded by the high maize and millet plants of his grandfather's *machamba* (farm).

The 'world' which Batista João had seen was not a particularly pleasant one. He had suddenly become very ill. Worried by his profuse diarrhoea, his mother had carried him to the office of the state farm, 5 kilometres away. From there, they got a lift on the trailer of a tractor which was going to Inhamatanda, 15 kilometres away. The health centre nurse immediately diagnosed a probable case of cholera. Following explicit instructions, he arranged to have the boy taken to the district hospital in Mafambisse, 60 kilometres away, in the jeep lent by the railways for the health workers to use during the cholera outbreak.

At Mafambisse, Batista João had been kept in the cholera ward—a small treatment room, converted for the emergency. It had five special beds, with holes in the middle and a bucket underneath, for those still in the acute stage of the disease. Outside, less serious cases were housed in tents inside a fenced enclosure. Batista's treatment consisted of intravenous fluids until he was well enough to drink, and tetracycline to limit the infection. Four days later, laboratory results from Beira, another 50 kilometres down the road, confirmed that he had indeed had cholera. By then, he was up and about, as chirpy as only a child who has succeeded in really frightening its parents can be.

And now I was driving him home, through the state farm's sunflower and maize fields, just one week after taking my leave of the multinational pharmaceutical companies in Europe. Batista João was one of a number of new cases of cholera from this district, most of them concentrated in a narrow strip close to the river. The doctor from Mafambisse, who was helping out in his neighbouring district during the epidemic, had asked me to come and have a look at the water supply for the small railway town of Inhamatanda. The 4000 inhabitants were drinking water taken from the river just a few hundred metres downstream from a farm workers' compound where several cases of cholera had been confirmed. Since the river bank was a favourite lavatory for the compound's residents, there was a very real danger of a direct water-borne transmission of the disease.

Batista João was discharged on the day of our visit. It was not out of charity that we took him and his mother home. My medical colleague wanted to find out whether the local health workers had been to Batista's home for the follow-up expected of them. Yes, they had visited, the boy's grandfather confirmed as we sat talking under the ragged eaves, while a passing shower poured down outside. They had given everyone pills and also done that—and he gestured between his legs to show how the visitors had carried out the rectal swabs which would, in the laboratory, reveal whether there was a cholera carrier in the household, someone with no symptoms but capable of transmitting the disease. That was a day or two after the boy had been taken to Inhamatanda, and the *brigada* had also done the same at the other three houses between here and the river. No, no one else in the family or among the neighbours had had diarrhoea like that since the boy was taken ill. Yes, the health workers had said that it would be a good idea to build a latrine to help prevent this kind of disease, but really, with all the space here, who needs it?

We were interested, too, in how the boy had come to catch cholera less than a fortnight after a massive campaign had taken place to treat the entire population of the district with sulfadoxine, a cheap, long-acting drug effective against the disease, with the object of trying to halt its further transmission, sixty or so cases of cholera having already been confirmed. At least ten probable deaths from cholera had been reported from the more remote parts of the district, and it was thought likely that the true figure was at least twice that.

The family had not taken the tablets, it appeared. The boy and his mother had been away visiting his father; the grandparents were among the few in the area who had not heeded the call to go to the farm offices to get their pills. This case, then, was one which had slipped through the net. Since the campaign had successfully reduced the incidence of the disease it was hoped that firefighting preventive medicine would stop the few remaining cases from generating another wide outbreak.

All in a day's health work

A day in the life of Mozambique's health workers, and nothing particularly unusual about it, although it is hoped that cholera will absorb less of their energies in the future. The campaign to control cholera was not a one-off effort, merely an intensification of the normal working methods of the health system. In each district, there is always communication between the curative services whose work is based at the health centres and the preventive medicine services, which occupy an equal place in the organizational hierarchy and usually share the same premises. There is normally a mobile *brigada* which acts on the basis of information from the health centre staff about cases of infectious disease such as measles, polio, hepatitis or cholera, and visits the homes of patients who are suspected of having one of these diseases. They also do the routine vaccinations and environmental health work, reporting on a weekly basis to their district chief. The difference during the cholera epidemic was that the mobile *brigadas* had been enlarged by people brought in temporarily from the community, and their reports-back had been daily. Theoretically, these enlarged *brigadas* should have been formed already at a community level to carry out weekly local checks on the health situation. In Inhamatanda, a district only recently created after an administrative reorganization, cholera had provided the impetus to organize the *brigadas populares*.

No doctors were involved. Batista João's diagnosis and treatment had been carried out entirely by health workers whose maximum formal qualification was six years' schooling followed by a two-year course for *agentes de medicina* or *agentes de medicina preventiva*. Both the treatment and preventive health work was carried out according to guidelines established at national level with resources and guidance from the provincial health directorate. The only intervention by a doctor was the initiative of the medical director from the neighbouring district in calling me to look at the water supply; to diagnose and treat not an individual syndrome but a collective hazard affecting a whole community. In many districts of Mozambique, this responsibility is executed by *tecnicos de medicina*—they have nine years' schooling and three years' general medical training.

This story puts flesh on the bones of a concept that is much talked about but sometimes little understood, that of 'primary health care'. China's 'barefoot doctors' are the best-known example, but too often they are described in terms of the health care they provide, without sufficient reference to the organizational structures and philosophies on which they are based.

The significance of Batista João's story is not just that no doctors were involved. It is that it encapsulates some of the important features of primary health care in Mozambique: first, it reaches past the towns into the rural areas; second, its focus is not on individual cures but on prevention of disease in the community; third, it depends not on highly trained doctors but on sufficiently trained, organized and motivated health workers who do not work alone but as part of a team; fourth, it is supported by, and has access to, more specialized and better-equipped services in cases where this is necessary; fifth, it functions as a joint effort by health workers, political organizations and economic entities, be they state farms, private traders, or even the local water company.

The focus and methods of Mozambican health care did not come about by accident. Nor were they the product of a reform within the existing health services. Arguably the best thing to have happened in Mozambican health care over the past ten years was the flight of the majority of doctors in the years around independence. Some were frightened away simply by the idea of the Mozambican revolution and independence. Others left when their comfortable living standards were threatened by the abolition of private medicine.

The new government could have tried simply to fill the gaps. But Frelimo, the ruling party, had not fought a ten-year war against the colonial power of Portugal just to rebuild the inequality—and ineffectuality—that had existed previously. The white population had enjoyed reasonable access to medical facilities—the distribution of doctors for instance, matched precisely the distribution of the white 2 per cent of Mozambique's population. The health standards of the majority can be gauged from contemporary estimates which put their life expectancy at between twenty-five and thirty-three years.[1]

The end of the old system was celebrated in blunt political terms: 'The nationalization of medicine and the prohibition of its practice for profit put an end to the exploitation of disease in our country,' said Frelimo's Social and Economic Directives in 1977. 'It has opened the way to fight for the elimination of the colonial-capitalist conception of the health services at the level of their structure, working methods and philosophies.' The experience of the war had provided much inspiration: 'In the liberated areas, preventive medicine took priority over curative medicine and the people organized themselves to defend their own health.' So preventive medicine was to remain a priority. Existing health installations were

to be recuperated in the first instance, but they would be organized
on the basis of the new structure in which, as in Inhamatanda,
curative services worked directly with the preventive medicine
services. Expansion of medical services would be directed towards
organized centres of production which, in the rural areas, meant the
newly established communal villages. Health care, said Frelimo,
could only be realized as part of this more general social and
economic development. It could not be delivered to dispersed rural
populations.[2]

Worldwide disenchantment with medical care

This analysis of Mozambique's health problems, and the direction in
which health care ought to be developed, is today by no means
unique to this small corner of the Third World. Indeed, what was at
independence in 1975 still revolutionary, is today mainstream
health ideology. Take the report of the WHO and UNICEF to the
Alma-Ata Conference on Primary Health Care in 1978:

> There is widespread disenchantment with health care throughout
> the world. The reasons are not difficult to discern. Better health
> care could be achieved with the technical knowledge available.
> Unfortunately, in most countries this knowledge is not being put
> to the best advantage for the greatest number. Health resources
> are allocated mainly to sophisticated medical institutions in urban
> areas. Quite apart from the dubious social premise on which this is
> based, the concentration of complex and costly technology on
> limited segments of the population does not even have the
> advantage of improving health.[3]

The failure of health services to meet actual health needs in the
Third World has been just about universal. At its simplest, this is
seen in the distribution of doctors, representing as they do a large
part of national investment in health.

> Three-quarters of the population in most developing countries live
> in rural areas. But three-quarters of the spending on medical care
> is in urban areas where three-quarters of the doctors live.[4]

In many countries, the situation is far worse.

> Honduras, Colombia, Jamaica, the Philippines and Pakistan have
> six or seven times more doctors per head in the cities than in the
> rural areas. Ghana and Senegal have ten times. Haiti has twenty-
> five times. Thailand has thirty-one times.

The gap between town and country is really a gap between rich and poor. It exists equally within the cities, since many of the doctors are private practitioners and, as in Brazil, are inaccessible to much of the population. The maldistribution of doctors would not matter so much, were it not for the parallel maldistribution of all health resources. Care based on hospitals and similar institutions is intrinsically more expensive than community-based care. Hospitals are invariably located in the cities and larger towns and their funds come from the same source as those for the health centres and clinics which serve the rural areas. So there tends to be a ladder of deprivation. The major hospitals of the biggest cities consume the lion's share of health resources. The provincial or district hospitals get less, but their share remains greater than the allocation given to the facilities which, in most developing countries, serve the majority of the population. The situation revealed by the study of health-care provision in Ghana is typical:

> The medical costs of the hospitals represent 57 per cent and 54 per cent of all health expenditures in the two districts. The maldistribution of health resources between Accra and the rest of the country is therefore repeated within each district.

In both cases, the number of patients at the community health centres and clinics was more than double that of the hospitals, and would have been greater had staff and other resources been available.[5]

Imperial Ethiopia had erected great showpieces of irrelevant medicine. My memories of the country are of the flies clustered around the children's eyes, and of the bars and brothels clustered along the main roads on the periphery of every large town or city. Their consequences—preventable blindness and easily treatable gonorrhoea—were epidemic. In the provinces, health care was sparse. Much of it was of the most dubious kind, provided through private 'drug stores' run by dressers whose qualification was to have worked for some years in any kind of health institution. In Wollega province, eighty-four drug stores provided the major source of health care to the few million inhabitants.[6] Meanwhile, in Addis Ababa, the country's capital, the huge Black Lion Hospital stood unused for seven years after it was built while funds were sought to cover its running costs—estimated at two-thirds of the national health budget.[7]

Third World politicians often make campaign promises about

improving health care in the rural areas where the bulk of their constituents live. As everywhere, these usually come to naught. Thus, in Kenya, the 1964 health development plan was formulated in order to provide 'adequate health services to all'. The goal has not been pursued with as much zeal as it might. The distribution of doctors between town and country is among the most extreme in Africa; 57:1 according to one estimate. This is matched by the distribution of other health workers, all concentrated where the lucky minority live.

> For many years past and many years to come, the bulk of Kenya's population—85 to 90 per cent—has been and will be rural. It can be seen that 87 per cent of the registered nurses, 53 per cent of the enrolled nurses, 70 per cent of the enrolled midwives and 45 per cent of the health inspectors serve 10 to 15 per cent of the population . . .

writes Dr F. M. Mburu of Nairobi University's Department of Community Health.

> Clearly, the rhetoric, meant to be heard, and the policy implementation, meant to be achieved, are different.

To highlight what he calls the rhetoric-implementation gap, he cites the expenditures planned in the 1974–8 health development budget, in which no less than 52 per cent was earmarked for hospital development, while the categories of public health and rural health were relegated to 6 per cent and 23 per cent respectively.[8]

The health problems

These few examples of the mismatch between health needs and the allocation of health-care resources in Africa can be repeated many times, in Asia and Latin America too. It is this mismatch which has provoked a re-examination of health care in the poor world. The alternatives now emerging are being promoted, not just by Third World radicals, but also by institutions solidly rooted in the rich world, institutions like the World Bank, which in 1974 adopted a formal health policy for the first time.[9] (The idea that better health would somehow simply 'trickle down' to everyone as a consequence of economic growth has not stood the test of time well.)

The Bank's current health policy paper gives a good technical summary of the Third World's principal health problems, characterizing them in the first instance in terms of short life expectancy.

This, it says, 'can largely be attributed to very high death rates among children'. In Africa, life expectancy is only forty-seven years, and 100 out of every 1000 babies born die in their first year. The picture is similar in many parts of Asia. Life expectancy in Latin America is sixty-one years, halfway between those and the rich world's seventy plus.[10]

But health should not be measured simply in terms of surviving childhood, or of reaching a respectable old age.

> For those in developing countries who reach the age of five, life expectancy is only six to eight years less than in developed countries. However, these people suffer frequently from non-fatal diseases. . . . The few detailed studies that are available suggest that illness disrupts normal activities for roughly one-tenth of people's time in most developing countries. Many of these illnesses are intermittent with recurrent acute episodes; these illnesses disrupt economic activity, often at critical times such as planting and harvesting seasons in the case of malaria. Chronic and debilitating diseases impair people's ability to concentrate, students' ability to learn and adults' productivity.[11]

So which are the critical diseases?

> The most widespread diseases in developing countries are those transmitted by human faeces— the intestinal parasitic and infectious diarrhoeal diseases, but also poliomyelitis, typhoid and cholera. . . . The second major group consists of the airborne diseases. The group includes tuberculosis, pneumonia, diphtheria, bronchitis, whooping cough, meningitis, influenza, measles, smallpox and chickenpox.

The third major cause of death, particularly in children, is malnutrition. Add to this list the parasitic diseases of malaria, sleeping sickness and schistosomiasis and the contact diseases, particularly syphilis and gonorrhoea but also leprosy, and you have accounted for the principal causes of illness and death in most developing countries. Degenerative disease—cancer, cardio-vascular disease—is relatively uncommon, although important among better-off city dwellers.

The means for their solution

There are no insuperable obstacles to prevent most of these diseases from being tackled today:

The health problems of developing countries can be controlled or treated with presently known technologies. Infectious diseases can be reduced through good hygiene, early diagnosis and treatment, and immunization. Improvements in water supply and waste disposal would greatly facilitate control of faecally related diseases, but good personal hygiene, careful preparation of food and the use of safe drinking water are also essential. Immunization against the most common and serious childhood diseases . . . [is] available at moderate cost. Use of better weaning foods and continuation of breast feeding would reduce childhood malnutrition and diminish the seriousness of infectious diseases.

With the exception of tropical diseases such as malaria and schistosomiasis, for which appropriate drug and control methods remain to be developed, much of the developing world's disease is either preventable or curable.[12]

What is technically feasible is not necessarily politically practicable. This is why the WHO is now giving voice to slogans such as 'health for all by the year 2000'. They are challenging governments to take the political decision—and the political risk—implied in diverting health resources to where they are most needed, and where they will have most effect.

Primary health care was defined by Halfdan Mahler of the WHO as 'essential health care made universally accessible to individuals and families in the community by means acceptable to them, through their full participation and at a cost the community and the country can afford'.[13] For most developing countries, that means abandoning attempts to develop health systems based on the doctor-plus-hospital care of the rich world. Such systems could, with available resources, meet only the needs of a small minority. They should instead build systems on a scale which can reach all.

The WHO has, since the Alma-Ata Conference, specified more clearly what it means by primary health care in poor countries:

it will be considered it is available to a whole population with at least the following:

—safe water in the home or within fifteen minutes' walking distance, and adequate sanitary facilities in the home or immediate vicinity;

—immunization against diphtheria, tetanus, whooping cough, measles, poliomyelitis and tuberculosis;

—local health care, including availability of at least twenty drugs, within one hour's walk or travel;

—trained personnel for attending pregnancy and childbirth, and caring for children up to at least one year of age.[14]

From this, it should be clear that primary health care does not mean just a network of cheap semi-trained doctors to diagnose and treat disease at least cost. The new breed of health workers will have to go beyond curative medicine. They will have to tackle the health problems of their communities with the most appropriate weapons available. Their work may lead them as far from medicine as the peasants' fields—better use of available food or increased food production is perhaps the single most important contribution to better health in the poorest communities. They will be involved in the most mundane organizing work—promoting the digging of latrines in a village, perhaps. They will have to encourage parents to bring their children for vaccination to make immunization campaigns a success. They will work with local government and community organizations to tackle pressing problems such as the need for a new water pump.

They will work abetted by management, guidance and support from a radically different kind of health service. The primary health care workers will benefit immensely, not least in the esteem in which they are held in the community, from association with the hospitals and their doctors, even when the functions of these have changed, for their traditional services will continue to be widely desired, perhaps because they have always been out of reach. The primary health workers will be gatekeepers to this level of health care through a disciplined system of referrals. This will not just boost their status, it will also benefit the work of the hospitals since they will no longer be overwhelmed by cases best dealt with at the community level. In their gatekeepers' role, the primary health workers will continue to provide basic medical care, be it first aid for injuries or treatment of common diseases. For this last of their many activities, they will need a supply of a few basic drugs.

A supply of a few basic drugs

Programmes of primary health care cannot be successful unless large segments of the population have access to the most essential drugs and vaccines [says the WHO]. As the front-line health-care coverage of the population is extended and the referral system is

developed, the selection of essential drugs, quality control, supply, distribution, local production and proper use within the
health care system become crucial issues.[15]

The drugs policies currently being elaborated by the WHO and its
sister agencies must be seen squarely in this context. The pharmaceutical industry has not been singled out for attention, as some
of its members would seem to believe; no more so, at least, than
Third World doctors who had hoped for a consultant's job, or than
the architects and builders who had hoped for lucrative contracts to
build big new hospitals. As part of its promotion of primary health
care, the WHO has encouraged member countries to plan systematically the allocation of their health resources. Thus in the Sudan,
WHO advisors provided technical support to a Ministry of Health
committee which identified the country's major health problems and
proposed programmes and projects through which they could be
tackled. These proposals inevitably called for a shift of emphasis
from hospitals in general, and from Khartoum, the capital, in
particular.[16] Some Sudanese doctors no doubt complained that the
WHO was attacking specialist medicine, but its advisors were simply
helping to determine where health resources were most needed and
could best be used.

Similarly, the organization is supporting the International Drinking Water Decade. Specifically, it is taking steps 'with a view to
enhancing the flow of resources to national water supply and
sanitation programmes'.[17] Health ministries, never first in the queue
on budget day, could certainly complain that through these measures, the WHO is siphoning resources away from Health. It is of
course doing nothing of the kind. In most developing countries,
investment in water supply and sanitation is among the most cost-
effective ways of improving health in poor communities.

Pharmaceutical policy is treated in the same way. Given the
unsavoury background outlined in the first part of this book, it
would not be surprising were the WHO to respond with restrictive,
defensive policies. The reverse is the case. Its aims, as outlined in the
current objectives for its drugs division, are the following:

To promote and collaborate with member states in:
—the formulation of national drug policies, including appropriate
legislation and regulatory control, consistent with the Organization's objective of health for all by the year 2000;

—the selection of essential drugs at different levels of the health care services, with particular emphasis on primary health care, and the provision of information on their proper use;

—ensuring the quality, safety and efficacy of prophylactic, diagnostic and therapeutic substances;

—the rationalization of drug procurement (including the promotion of local production of essential drugs), logistics and distribution within the health services through efficient drug management;

—improving the use and standardization of medicinal plants.[18]

Their selection . . .

Of these aims, it is the selection of essential drugs that has proved to be among the most controversial. At first sight, it is not clear why this should be. The use of a limited number of drugs is not new to any medical tradition. Most individual doctors in general practice in Europe and the USA work to an informal list, established through their daily practice, of a few hundred. Hospitals and other institutions have for more than 100 years worked to formularies—drug lists established by consultation which then determine which products will be stocked.[19]

National formularies exist in many countries, rich and poor, governing either the use of drugs in public hospitals, or listing those for which official health insurance schemes will pay. Even Switzerland, home of the free-market drug industry, limits the number of products paid for by health insurance to 7000 out of an estimated total of 36,000 medicaments on the market.

It was, above all, its brevity which made the WHO's model list of less than 200 essential drugs so controversial when it was published in November 1977. Its claim that these were those 'basic, necessary and indispensable for the health needs of the population' was taken as a challenge to the makers of the myriad of other products which were excluded. In one sense, it was. Its express aim was to ensure that the money spent on medicines produced the maximum benefit for the whole community. So its publication did represent a challenge to all who promoted the less-than-optimal use of available medicines.

Many pharmaceutical products are marketed with little concern for the differing health needs and priorities of individual countries. Promotional activities of the manufacturers have created a greater demand than the actual needs. Since up to 40 per cent of the total health care budget in developing countries may be spent on drugs, the result has been an increase in the cost of health care or a reduction in the funds available for other health services. The cost has affected even the affluent nations and their governments are increasingly worried by the rising expenditure on pharmaceutical products . . . . It is clear that for optimal use of limited financial resources, the available drugs must be restricted to those proven to be therapeutically effective, to have acceptable safety and to satisfy the health needs of the population.[20]

That throw-away remark about the problems of the affluent countries was a second source of controversy. This, together with the inclusion of thirty-two non-essential 'complementary' drugs as alternatives if resistance to essential drugs was present, or for the treatment of rare disorders, suggested that the essential drugs list might usefully be applied beyond the frontiers of the poorer developing countries.

. . . and their savings

Putting a limit on the number of drugs available offers cost savings on two obvious fronts. By eliminating the less effective products, waste of resources is avoided. Where two equally effective products are available, it is clearly sensible to choose the cheapest. Beyond these banal but important savings, are other economies to be made all the way along the tortuous route from the chemical factory to the final consumer, the patient. Leave aside for the moment questions of production and sale. A compelling economic argument for limiting the number of drugs in circulation, particularly in a developing country, is simply the high cost of their handling, storage and distribution.

A visit to the spare parts store of any motor car dealer puts the problem in perspective. For any one make of car, many thousands of different parts must be stocked. The cost of keeping that stock is the major overhead for the dealer. Yet, unlike medicines, car parts do not need to be kept in specially cool or dark conditions. They do not expire, or need to be taken off the shelves in any particular order. Their distribution is not difficult. If there is one Volkswagen dealer in a city, potential customers will find their way there. Drugs on the other hand have to be distributed to a series of small outlets. Each transaction generates its own bureaucracy, and each product stocked multiplies that bureaucracy many times. For Third World countries which may have to stock a year's supply of drugs to guarantee that the right patients get the right medicine at the right time, the economic logic of limiting the number of products is obvious. In 1972 Sri Lanka reduced the number of drugs it imported from 2100 to 600. 'Without this significant step, the SPC (State Pharmaceutical Corporation) would not have been able effectively to undertake bulk purchasing and save on foreign exchange.'[21]

There is another factor beyond the cost-saving one. One reason why good drugs are not used effectively is that users, be they prescribers or patients, lack the information to use them correctly. Such information needs increase at a rate out of all proportion to a simple increase in the number of products available. So, too, does the training needed by a health worker who has to decide, in any given situation, which drug would be best. In developing countries, where no more than rudimentary information and education can be delivered to the front-line health workers, the number of drugs to which they have access must be limited accordingly. The same judgement can be applied at other levels of the health system. Can a doctor in private practice, without access to reasonable laboratory facilities, really use effectively any more than the twelve antibiotics listed by the WHO as essential or complementary drugs? Are there really district hospitals with staff who feel the need for more than the eight anti-hypertensives?

The mere process of elaborating a list can help to clarify such issues and put drugs policy on a sound basis. Clioquinol, to take a controversial example, demonstrates the value of a systematic approach. It is included in the Mozambican national formulary, and di-iodohydroxyquin, a close relation, is in the Bangladeshi list of thirty-one drugs for primary health care workers.[22] In both cases, the drug is included for the treatment of amoebic dysentery in full knowledge of its potential risks and its ineffectiveness against other causes of diarrhoea. It was kept on Sri Lanka's lists as well, as Professor Lionel of Colombo University explains:

There are, however, more effective drugs for this purpose, such as diloxanide, but they are generally much more expensive. In Sri Lanka, a course of treatment with diloxanide is ten times more expensive and so clioquinol continues to be used in these countries. . . . In the light of the fact that the alternative more effective drugs are now becoming cheaper, I think that it will be necessary to review the position again in Sri Lanka and other countries because the chief reasons for not banning clioquinol but restricting it to prescription only no longer appear valid.[23]

The drug lists for the primary health worker have been the easiest to draw up. In Bangladesh, those thirty-one products (excluding vaccines) for primary care were complemented by a list of 182 products for use at the next tier, suggested as the procurement list for most government hospitals. No list was established for the country's few teaching and research hospitals where it was pointed out that, while the number of drugs employed might be large, the quantities involved were much smaller.[24] The cost of drug consumption by these centres is not mentioned. It can, however, come to represent a sizeable proportion of a country's pharmaceutical budget. It is significant that in Tanzania, where the battle between the doctors (fighting for their 'right to prescribe') and the health ministry (struggling to contain costs) has been fiercely fought,[25] the compromise has been to allow specialists at the two major hospitals an annual foreign exchange budget to purchase drugs not included in the procurement list from official importers.[26]

Who uses what list?

What is at issue here is less a question of *which* drugs are on *whose* lists than one of *who* has access to *what* list, and whose prescribing is bound by none. The Sri Lanka government, it should be noted, in an early effort to economize, reduced the number of drugs available through the public health care system from 2100 to 590 as long ago as 1959. What provoked controversy in 1972 was the attempt to extend this control to the private sector.[27] Similarly, Brazil's CEME, the state-run Central de Medicamentos, has a restricted list of 347 drugs.

Its target group were those people receiving the official minimum wage or less—in other words, exactly that segment of the population that is normally excluded from the commercial market for medicines. Thus, CEME was not likely to take any customers away from private firms.[28]

Any move to restrict in similar fashion the private section of the Third World's biggest pharmaceutical market (in which 14,681 products were registered between 1966 and 1975) would be quite unthinkable.

The Andean countries of Latin America have announced, as part of their regional cooperation on drugs policy, a limited list of 287 drugs. Only in Ecuador will this be mandatory and there, only in the public sector.[29] Peru, which is party to this cooperation, had already introduced a basic drugs programme as early as 1971. This included the acquisition, through a central agency, of a limited number of essential drugs, again for distribution through the public health sector. A tentative attempt was made to broaden the scheme to enable private pharmacies to take advantage of the lower prices and make the basic drugs more widely available. There was no suggestion, however, that the other products they sold should in any way be limited.[30]

So Mozambique still finds itself in the vanguard. Its initiative is not that it introduced its essential drugs list in January 1977, nearly a year before the publication of the WHO's list. Rather, it is that within the state medical service only the 300-odd products listed in the national formulary may be prescribed. That is no different to many other countries. Since private medical practice has been banned, formulary products will be the only prescription drugs available in the country. This control has been reinforced by the establishment of Medimoc, the state drug-importing company.[31]

'Our list contains all the drugs we think are needed for any Mozambican, be he peasant or university professor,' says Carlos Mazargão, head of the Medical School in Maputo and member of the Therapeutics Commission which formulates Mozambican pharmaceutical policy. So, as well as clioquinol, the Mozambican formulary also includes diphenoxylate (Lomotil). This in no way negates the general critique of its limited applicability in a developing country. Its use is specifically contra-indicated in the case of diarrhoea in children.[32] But anyone who knows the pace of work for the hard-pressed core in the upper echelons of Mozambican politics and government will understand why some symptomatic relief for diarrhoea is considered necessary. Within the list of essential drugs, there are selections which health workers other than doctors can use. Similarly, a number of basic medicines can be sold by country stores where access to them might otherwise be difficult.[33]

The elaboration of essential drugs lists is an obvious response to the pressing problems posed by the promotion of unsafe, inefficacious or overpriced drugs. It provides a mechanism through which disputes can be resolved at policy level rather than through bitter and expensive experience, and regulatory intervention after the event. Indeed, for developing countries which do not have the resources to establish an effective drug regulation authority, the limited drugs list is the only alternative to a total abdication of responsibility.

It is the key, too, to many other of the objectives of drugs policy defined by the WHO and national governments. Local production, better and cheaper buying practices and effective quality control all depend, given the capacities of most developing countries, on some limitation of the products available on their markets. The effective training of health workers at all levels, the efficient distribution of drugs to all levels of the health-care system, will only be possible in many countries once the number of drugs available has been cut. On the other hand, the introduction of an essential drugs list without consideration of these other components of pharmaceutical policy, and of the place of pharmaceuticals within a coherent health policy, is likely to bear little fruit.

Drug safety provided a starting point from which to examine the actual conditions in which drugs are used. From the concept of an essential drugs list, we can now proceed to investigate these other components of the new pharmaceutical supply systems which are emerging in the Third World—and the conflicting forces which are acting to shape them.

Nine: Rational Policies

In a corridor in the WHO's Geneva headquarters, I came upon a
queue of experts, jostling volubly in five languages as they waited
impatiently for their expenses vouchers. The sight jarred somewhat
after Beira, where people frequently have to queue for many hours
for commodities as basic as rice and cooking oil. It is fashionable,
after all, to be rude about the United Nations experts who jet hither
and thither on missions so abstruse that sometimes they themselves
don't seem to know their purpose. And the Geneva *per diem*
allowance would feed a family in Beira for a month.

'Yeah, I know,' said one of my interviewees from the WHO's
Drugs Division. 'All we do is blah blah blah and spend a lot of
money and never do anything. But I'll tell you something. We've
achieved more in drugs policy in the past three or four years than
had been done in the twenty years before.'

'We now realize that the importance of the models or ideas they
propose is not that they are binding legally,' says Dr Burkhard
Wenger, the lawyer from the Ciba-Geigy Pharma Policy Unit
responsible for the international organizations. 'They are more
important as mechanisms; a treasure of ideas falling into the
unconscious of the national legislator. So when he has a problem and
is looking for ideas—"Bloop!"—down it comes from his unconscious as *his* idea.'*

There is a misconception abroad that the WHO and other
members of the United Nations family can take independent action:
'Since reasonable marketing practices have not come about voluntarily, perhaps the World Health Organization should begin to control
the marketing practices used by the pharmaceutical industry in the
Third World,' suggested two doctors in a letter to *The Lancet*.[1] Ciba-
Geigy understands the position of the agencies better. 'In many ways
they are completely helpless,' said Dr Wenger. 'When it comes to

---

* It would be as well to emphasize at this point that the frequency with which Ciba-
Geigy appears in the text reflects their relative willingness to address specific issues. It
is not because their conduct is more open to criticism.

setting out to do anything, they are totally dependent on national governments.' He was only echoing the often-voiced sentiments of the WHO secretariat.

'What do I mean when I say "*we*" must ensure action for health?' asked Halfdan Mahler rhetorically of the delegates to the 1980 World Health Assembly.

By 'we' I mean the Organization as a whole and each of its individual parts. I mean first and foremost Member States both individually and collectively. Of course I mean the Secretariat, but at the risk of boring you I must repeat once more my old refrain of the overriding importance of the action of Member States. The usefulness of WHO in support of Health For All will depend on the single-mindedness and intensity with which you, the Member States, apply nationally as well as internationally the policies and principles you have generated and adopted in WHO.[2]

While the organization is ultimately dependent on its members, it has prodded and challenged them to put their fine conference principles into practice. Mahler went on:

Are you ready to introduce in your own countries health policies in the spirit of those you have adopted collectively in WHO?

Are you ready to base your requests for technical cooperation with WHO on the policies that you have adopted collectively in WHO, and on these policies only?

Are those of you who are in a position to do so ready to provide material support to other countries in the spirit of these policies?

Are you ready to influence other sectors at national and international levels to take action for health development in the light of these policies?

I hope that you *are* ready, because I remain convinced that an affirmative reply to these four questions is the crux of the matter. For you deserve a WHO that not only keeps world health policy relevant to people's needs, but that also foresees these needs and shapes and reshapes its policies accordingly. You deserve a WHO that supports you not only in defining and updating your own health policies in accordance with your peoples' evolving needs but also in realizing these policies through wise interaction between national and international endeavours. But to get what I think you deserve, you must appreciate that this depends on you and you alone.

The policy package

The idea of an essential drugs list did not come originally from the WHO, nor was its model list the first of its kind. The limitation of health workers' access to drugs is not a novel idea either. In its essence, all that the WHO has said, borrowing freely from the experience of others, is that such a list will be a tool of great practical value for meeting the particular health needs of the majority of the world's people in these last two decades of the twentieth century. By itself, though, it is meaningless. Only as part of a package can it be an effective instrument of policy. Its potential economic benefits must be won through new systems of drug buying and by control over the marketing of premium-priced speciality drugs. Since the marketing of those speciality drugs depends heavily on unique brand-name identification in place of their scientific or generic name, the enforcement of the use of generic names will be an important component of any policy package. The scope a list provides for streamlining and simplifying the training of a new generation of health workers can only be exploited if information about the products which constitute it is carefully prepared and widely disseminated. National organizations and institutions will have to be adapted or created to permit its use in the different health-care systems.

The policy proposals in these areas may sound like a series of prescriptions laid down by the international organizations. They are not and, as Dr Mahler has indicated, they cannot be. What the WHO and UNCTAD and similar agencies have done is to provide a forum in which appropriate policies have been distilled from the unique national ferments of their individual members. (They have in the process, demonstrated that in many areas, developing countries would do better to follow the example of their more resourceful fellows rather than imitate slavishly the techniques of the rich world.)

The proposals are conveniently divided into the bare bones of policy and the organizational and institutional flesh and blood needed to implement them. The principal elements of the policy skeleton are: (1) the control of drug buying and/or importing; (2) the use of generic names for drugs; (3) the creation or adaptation of institutions to promote pharmaceutical policy. The ways in which these policies are implemented will vary greatly, according to the nature of each country's health services and its resources. But some organizational issues will be common to all: (1) the problem of disseminating information about the correct use of drugs; (2) their distribution, and control of their quality; (3) the need for cooperation between countries on various aspects of drug supply. (Fundamental throughout the development of these policies is the extent of pharmaceutical manufacture undertaken in each country and its proposed expansion. Somewhat separate is the question of the development of new drugs. Both will be dealt with in the next chapter.)

Meeting market power with combined forces

It has been shown repeatedly that the multinational pharmaceutical companies have a market power which enables them to charge considerably more than their competitors for the same product, and yet win the lion's share of the sales. For developing countries which want to buy their drugs at the most economic price, the obvious answer is to meet market power by applying organized buying forces.

The establishment of a central buying organization either for public sector drug purchases, or for all pharmaceutical imports, or both, is 'most important if countries wish to reap the benefits from an essential drugs policy,' in the words of Dr Nitya Nand, director of India's Central Drug Research Institute. Among the benefits he cites are: an organized market intelligence; the advantages of larger purchases and therefore better bargaining power; easier management of quality control of imported products; easier control of unhealthy trade practices; insurance that local drug manufacturers, including subsidiaries of foreign companies, purchase their raw materials at equitable prices; easier adoption of the use of generic names, and the building of the country's medicare programme around essential drugs.[3]

There is ample evidence of the economic benefits of central purchasing. The Sri Lanka State Pharmaceuticals Corporation saved 40 per cent on its drug purchases in the first six months of its existence compared with the prices paid by private sector importers for the same products in the six months before. That foreign exchange saving for the country was achieved by the simple expedient of buying in larger quantities from a wider range of sources.[4] Brazil's CEME is estimated to have saved 60 per cent, buying drugs on its national market by generic name and requiring only functional packaging.[5] Peru claimed to have cut drug costs by 34 per cent in the first year of its basic drugs scheme[6] while according to Dr Carlos

Mazargão, Mozambique has enjoyed a steady decrease in drug costs since the formation of its drug import company Medimoc, in direct contrast to the experience of most other African countries at the same time.

In Egypt, the benefits of central purchasing have been felt mainly by the consumer. Pharmaceutical prices remained fixed after the establishment of EGOPCA (the Egyptian General Organization for Pharmaceutical, Chemical and Medical Appliances) in 1963, until 1981. Only then did inflationary pressures become irresistible. 'Industry sources have indicated that a 20–30 per cent across-the-board increase is needed to restore profitability,' reported *Scrip*.[7] While central purchasing was by no means the only factor in Egypt's success, and was in any case limited to imports of raw materials and control, through EGOPCA, of purchasing by other agencies, it helped to create the conditions for the development of the country's strong, publicly-owned industry which is today its main source of savings.[8]

The biggest developing countries may be too big to buy all their drugs through a single national organization. Thus in India, imports of key raw materials and essential drugs in bulk are 'canalized' through the state Chemical and Pharmaceuticals Corporation (CPC). To protect consumers from exploitation, India relies on price controls which are complex and universally unpopular. Data from the CPC on raw material costs is used by the government to help fix drug prices. The CPC is also intended to reduce bulk drug prices although its effectiveness in this area is disputed.[9]

If buying organizations serve some parts only of the pharmaceutical industry or the community, so too the savings they make will not necessarily benefit everyone. Governments may not put much priority on effecting savings for the customers of private pharmacies; the finance ministry may be more interested in saving foreign exchange than reducing prices to consumers; or the aim may be to help curb spending by public health services. If, in Egypt, centralized buying helped to keep prices of pharmaceuticals constant for eighteen years, in Sri Lanka, its introduction brought few changes to the private medicine market. Customers at private pharmacies paid the same prices as before, or even more. The savings made by the State Pharmaceutical Corporation were used to reduce the cost of medicines distributed to the public health services. The Sri Lanka Treasury benefited too. Fewer chests of tea had to be exported to buy the same quantity of medicine, releasing the scarce hard-currency earned from tea exports to be used for other purposes.

Calling drugs by their names

Only in the most exceptional circumstances will it be necessary for a national purchasing organization to buy drugs by their brand names. This is vitally important. Commercial brand names are an important source of corporate market power, used for the promotion of an individual company's narrow self-interest. Applied differently, a drug's name can be a useful tool by which to encourage its rational use.

Yet again, the case of Cibalgin helps to make the point. The active ingredient of the old formulation was amidopyrine; or aminopyrine; or aminophenazone; or phenyl-dimethyl-dimethylamine-pyrazolone —four different names for the same substance, the last being its chemical description. The scope for confusion is obvious when the ingredient of the new formulation Cibalgin, noramidopyrine (or propyphenazone; or dipyrone; or metamizol) is considered.

This confusion was overlain by the commercial nomenclature. 'It is probable that several hundred different branded products remain available, and the difficulty of identifying them is compounded by the confusing variety of official names used to describe these two substances,' noted the WHO's *Drug Information* bulletin.[10]

'It is no more a matter for debate that a number of undesirable practices are connected with the brand names of drugs,' asserts Dr Nand.[11] For reasons of economics, UNCTAD strongly supports the use of generic names as a basis for pharmaceutical policy. So, too, does the WHO which has the responsibility for naming chemical substances for medical use. Even the World Bank cites brand names as one reason for the failure of health care to reach the majority of people in the developing countries.[12]

The advantages of using generic names seem clear-cut:

Generic names help prescribers to think more clearly about drugs . . . [they] carry the advantage that they ensure recognition of the identity of prescribed drugs . . . the generic names ampicillin, cloxacillin and carbenicillin indicate that they are all penicillins whereas no such indication is given by their respective brand names Penbritin, Orbenin, Pyopen. Another source of confusion is the existence of many brand names for a single drug so it becomes impossible for a doctor to remember all of them. In Sri Lanka, tetracycline was sold under more than twenty different brand names. . . . It was not uncommon for a doctor to unwittingly switch from one brand name to another for what was the same drug in the belief that they were different drugs. Patients would be inconvenienced by searching for a prescribed brand from pharmacy to pharmacy when alternative brands were available. This has disappeared with the use of generic names.[13]

Yet nowhere is the political complexity of introducing new pharmaceutical policies better demonstrated than in the apparently simple and logical step of calling a drug by its name. Sanjaya Lall wrote in 1975:

> The abolition of brand names appears to be desirable and feasible, but it is not an easy or straightforward task. Its implementation would require very careful and gradual introduction with the full cooperation of the prescribing doctors and pharmacists.[14]

He had the benefit of hindsight. In 1973 Pakistan had introduced, almost overnight, a generic-name policy. Failure to inform and convince the doctors and the public of its benefits, lack of mechanisms to control the quality of the drugs on the market, and concerted opposition from the multinationals rapidly ended the experiment.[15]

Generic names have long been in use in the public sector, without problems. In Sri Lanka, they were made compulsory in the public health services in 1959. With the creation of the State Pharmaceutical Corporation they were introduced to the private sector too, but gradually. Manufacturers had to show the generic name of their products in print twice the size of the brand name, and doctors and pharmacists were provided with cross-reference lists of generic and brand names.

What's in a name?

Opposition to generic-name policies by the industry concentrates, as it did in Sri Lanka, on the problem of guaranteeing the quality of generic-name products.[16] Since the use of generic names in no way prevents the identification of the manufacturer, this is a sizeable red herring. The quality of drugs sold under the brand names of multinationals is, in any case, by no means guaranteed—as was nicely shown in Morocco when two Hoffmann-La Roche executives were jailed for obliterating the expiry dates on a number of products to enable them to be sold after their due date[17] The high prices commanded by brand name drugs has in fact encouraged the sale of adulterated substances or faked imitations.[18]

The real reason for opposition to the policy is purely commercial.

The question is particularly complex in countries where there is already a substantial national pharmaceutical industry, as in Brazil, for here companies survive by promoting imitations of the branded products of the multinationals. Thus in Argentina, the six leading national companies launched, annually, twice as many products as the nine largest multinationals in their market. To introduce a generic-name policy here would be to attack directly the local industry.[19] India too has a strong national drug industry. Yet it is committed to introducing the use of generic names. The pace of change testifies to the difficulties. The original proposal, in 1975, was to begin by abolishing brand names for thirteen drugs. The suggestion was violently opposed by the Organization of Pharmaceutical Producers of India (OPPI) which warned that the market would be flooded with low-quality products. Nevertheless, in 1978, the government accepted the idea in principle, but decided to begin with only five drugs: analgin, aspirin, ferrous sulphate, piperazine, and the tranquillizer chlorpromazine. Hardly a dramatic move, but it took another two years to decide how the change would be introduced. Then it was announced that it would be made over a seven-year period, to coincide with the renewal of brand-name registrations.

More fundamental, and of more concern to the companies, is the proposal to amend the Drugs and Cosmetic Rules to require that all branded drugs should, as in Sri Lanka, have the generic names of their constituents writ large, larger at any rate than the brand name, on product packaging. And, with an eye to the long term, it is proposed that new single-ingredient drugs introduced to India for the first time should be allowed to be sold only under their generic names. The multinationals' response to this rationalism was to threaten that no new drugs would be introduced.[20]

It is not denied by Indian policy-makers that these objectives run contrary to the immediate commercial interests of local drug companies. They are being introduced in an explicit attempt to make them shift its emphasis from supplying medication for the often trivial—but profitable—needs of India's affluent minority to producing the 117 drugs identified as essential for the basic health requirements of the whole population. The judgement is that the national industry is sufficiently well-established (and the competition of the multinationals sufficiently controlled) to make the transformation possible without long-term prejudice to its interests. This reinforces the final advantage of the generic-name policy; that, by reducing the opportunities for the profitable marketing of trivial remedies, it will help to divert pharmaceutical production more certainly towards meeting the basic needs of the majority in the developing countries.[21]

The institution of control

India's attempts to rationalize drug production, relying, in part, on the rules governing the use of brand names, highlight the complexity of the institutions needed to develop and implement pharmaceutical policies in developing countries. 'Institutions' here can mean the law, or the agencies which enforce it—be it the pharmaceuticals department at the Ministry of Health or the National Formulary which governs drug purchases; an instrument as formal as a State Pharmaceutical Corporation or as informal as a Finance Ministry approval procedure requiring a Health Ministry signature for the release of foreign currency to be used for drug imports. What matters is that the institution or procedure is vested with sufficient powers and resources to perform its functions.

Examples of the contrary practice abound throughout the Third World, at all stages of the operation, from drug production to their sale. One India commentator writes:

> Although the Ministry comes in for criticism if any spurious or sub-standard drugs are detected, very few people have realized that the Ministry has no power to license drug manufacturers or suspend or cancel their licences. This Ministry has undertaken responsibilities without concomitant power.[22]

Dr Philip Emafo, Chief Pharmacist in the Nigerian Federal Ministry of Health, explains what is supposed to happen at the other end of the pharmaceutical supply system in his country. 'In Nigeria, many agencies of Government enforce the drugs laws.'[23] His use of the present tense is optimistic. One of those laws, the *Nigerian Pharmacists Act 1964*, defines who pharmacists are and establishes that 'any person, not being a fully registered pharmacist . . . who (a) For, or in expectation of, reward practises or holds himself out as a pharmacist . . . shall be guilty of an offence.' This and other Acts require that most ethical drugs should be sold only under the control of pharmacists on licensed premises. The law runs far ahead of the possibilities of its enforcement: 'At present it is estimated that there are more than 5000 illegal pharmaceutical premises in Lagos State alone. The number of registered pharmaceutical premises in Lagos State was 218 as of 31 December 1979.'[24]

The total disregard for the rules and regulations concerning the sale of drugs is general in the Third World. Thus in Ethiopia, 'a drug shop is a private business but the dresser is permitted only to sell drugs included on an approved list (antibiotics are not included).' Nevertheless, 'it is a well-known fact that a lot of antibiotics are sold in rural drug shops, and this study confirms that sulphonamides and antibiotics constitute a very substantial part of the sales.'[25]

There is an awareness of the need for a control on the movement of pharmaceuticals within Third World countries. 'Kenya deserves the services of a reputable body whose recommendations can be trusted,' writes Dr A. O. K. Obel in an *East African Medical Journal* editorial.[26]

> It is becoming virtually impossible for specialist clinicians to keep abreast with developments in therapeutics. This may be even worse for the general practitioner who may be amenable to persuasive but fallacious claims emanating from drug representatives. The establishment of a drug regulatory authority is long overdue. It is a common sentiment that Kenya is 'on the run' and yet it has not even started crawling in this important regard. We cannot afford to be silent bystanders while perfunctorily studied agents are administered to our people under the guise of cheap remedies, particularly when safer and more effective remedies are available.

Resources before regulation

Unfortunately, effective control is not a question simply of establishing organizations or writing regulations. What must be provided are the resources with which to back them up. Thus the Thai authorities professed themselves happy about the impact of their country's 1967 Drugs Act. Its procedures for the registration of new drugs are not particularly onerous:

> The following is the procedure for drug formula registration: on receipt of a completed Application Form valid under the Drug Act, the official shall consider, according to the law, whether such a drug has been proved to be therapeutically reliable and safe to users, whether it is a true formula and not a formula which has

previously been revoked. The name used for the drug shall not be boastful, impolite or misleading.[27]

Industry observers were not so impressed by the controls:

> Although Thailand's pharmaceutical legislation is observed by the reputable pharmaceutical companies, the small budget of the Food and Drug Control Division (about $175,000 a year) and the shortage of government personnel make it difficult to keep track of 'fly-by-night' companies who initiate products or produce products of sub-standard quality. Furthermore, with the lack of control at the retail level, it is quite easy for pharmacies to substitute local sub-standard copies for the more reputable products.[28]

The drug authorities themselves are usually conscious of their lack of resources. In India, a 1 per cent 'cess' was proposed to pay for drug regulation.[29] In Brazil, health officials estimate that the funds available for the Medicines Directorate DIMED should be increased from half a per cent of national pharmaceutical sales to at least 4 per cent to enable it to execute its functions.[30]

Four per cent of the Brazilian drugs market is worth more than $60 million. For most developing countries, the resources available for drug control are closer to Thailand's $175 thousand. For them, it is vital to prevent a wasteful drug market from developing which it is beyond their capacity to control. This alone is a potent reason for adopting essential drugs lists restricted to well-known, well-tried products (instead of creating impotent, underfunded regulatory authorities); for establishing a central buying agency (rather than attempting to control the activities of a hundred profit-motivated private importers); for using generic names (instead of relying on burgeoning bureaucracies to control the prices of branded drugs). In short, the new policies are designed to reduce to a realistic minimum the regulatory resources needed to assure the supply of those medicines essential to the health of each country's people.

Substituting the salesman

Along with brand names will disappear that venerable figure, the drug company detailman, still found everywhere from Durham to Davao City and Dakar, hovering hopefully outside doctors' surgeries, waiting for his chance to 'make a presentation'. His disappearance will be little missed, except by those accustomed to selling the samples he offers. To judge by the end result, the quality of the information he purveyed has not contributed greatly to the rational use of drugs—but that was never its purpose. Similarly, a staunching of the flow of company-sponsored pharmaceutical literature will not, on balance, be a great loss to the scientific practice of medicine, if the experience of Brazil is anything to go by. What the disappearance of both will highlight, nevertheless, is the continued need for better information about the correct use of drugs, new and old.

At the pinnacle of a new international order devoted to the dissemination of such information, and sitting there uneasily, is Dr John Dunne, senior scientist in the WHO's drugs division. It is difficult to get to see him. Not, I should add, that he is inhospitable. The problem is rather that he is being physically overwhelmed by his job. His small office is being taken over by paper. It was difficult to find space to sit down and, having moved a pile of journals from chair to floor, it was more so to find a space on his desk to rest a notebook. In the end, I kept it on my knee. While we talked, after office hours, two more big bundles of technical papers and journals were brought in from the library and balanced precariously on top of the already over-flowing in-trays. His secretaries had lost most of their office to the filing system. They looked harassed.

Dr Dunne's main job is the compilation of a short newsletter, *Drug Information*, 'devoted to international transfer of information on current drug problems'. It is, potentially, a powerful weapon. Its efficacy has already been proven to the extent that the publication—or to be more precise, the pre-publication circulation to relevant companies for comments—of a series of critical articles on the continued use of amidopyrine closely predated the moves to withdraw it from world markets.[31] In particular, it reports actions taken by national drug regulatory authorities over specific products, giving summaries of the technical issues for those in the Third World who do not have access to the medical literature; it also carries information about new drugs registered in different countries, as well as general reviews of aspects of drug policy. It provides an accurate alternative point of view, for those professionally involved, to that of the pharmaceutical industry on contentious issues.

But the information emanating from Dr Dunne's Geneva office will never reach the leaflet library at the health post of the Beira Water Company, and if it did, there would be no one there to comprehend it. Yet the need for information at this level, and at that of the patient, is desperately acute. 'How intelligible are the warnings shown on drug labels to the common man?' asked the columnist of India's *Eastern Pharmacist*. He pointed to the experience in Britain where studies found that many people did not understand the instructions on medicine containers. 'If understanding of instructions on drugs labels poses a real problem in the UK, the situation in this country must be far worse. Should not something be done to review the labelling requirements laid down in the Drugs and Cosmetics rules?' He went on to call for 'suggestions as to how cautionary notes and warnings on drug labels could be made more direct and intelligible to the common man'.[32]

Telling people what they need to know

At this point, Dr Dunne despairs. 'How do you write information at this level?' he asks. The answer is that you don't. You cannot write for people who cannot read, and the majority perhaps of drug consumers in the Third World are illiterate. At best, you can use pictograms to explain how often medicines should be taken. In communities with people who cannot read, it is either the health worker who dispenses it, or the person who sells the drug who must explain its correct use. To do that, they need accurate accessible information.

Three examples, from different sources, of the giving out of information about the treatment of diarrhoea serve to illustrate the possibilities:

Leodal is effective to treat diarrhoeal diseases of different aetiology. Besides the intestinal effect for dihydrostreptomycin and sulphaguanidine, the absorbable sulphonamides give systemic antibacterial effect.
Indications: Infant diarrhoeas, dysenteries, gastro-enteritis, intestinal amoebiasis and food poisoning.[33]

Infectious diarrhoeas are caused by bacterial infection of the bowel wall. Antibiotics that are not absorbed (like streptomycin or neomycin) do not reach the site of the infection. These drugs have not been shown to help in patients with infective diarrhoea.[34]

In general, it is not correct to prescribe antibiotics for cases of diarrhoea. However, there are three specific situations, relatively rare, which require the use of an antibiotic in diarrhoea (as well as the case of diarrhoeas associated with respiratory infections or otitis where it may also be necessary to use an antibiotic).[35]

The first is the manufacturer's information for Leodal, a combination of streptomycin, four sulpha drugs, kaolin and pectin. The next comes from an impartial source, a manual written by three doctors in Tanzania 'to assist in the rational purchase and use of drugs', and giving as well the relative costs of a week's treatment with different remedies in that country, incidentally showing that the antibiotics of choice for serious dysenteries and infections (tetracycline or chloramphenicol) cost thirty times less than Diapec, a proprietary remedy similar to Leodal.

Books don't prescribe; people do. So the importance of the last example, from the Mozambican guide to the treatment of diarrhoea in children, is that it takes the form of instructions to primary health workers. As such, it carries more weight than a simple recommendation. It is intended to be followed unless there are good reasons to the contrary. The exceptions mentioned are clearly defined (serious food poisoning, cholera and prolonged dysentery) and so is the treatment recommended (chloramphenicol for the first, referral to the next level of health care for the other two). It provides the structure for the effective supervision of drug use. But the importance of combining good information with other elements of the pharmaceutical policy package is shown by the radical change in the way diarrhoea is treated at primary level in Mozambique since the introduction of the guidelines. Doubtless they helped, but more important has been the reduction in supplies of traditional diarrhoea remedies such as clioquinol and the sulpha mixtures, and the distribution of large quantities of Oralyte rehydration mix.

Follow-up, be it called supervision or continued education, is essential and its form will depend on the nature of each country's health system. William Connelly of Sandoz explained that the success of detailmen in Nigeria, apart from their valuable free samples, derived from the isolated situation of doctors there: 'The physician is usually receptive, and very often becomes interested and enthusiastic since this is one of his few intelligent medical conversations of the day with someone who understands what he is talking about.'[36]

Information on drug use is generally available, although the WHO has yet to publish its compendium of standard format information sheets on the products in its model list of essential drugs. What matters is the way in which it is disseminated. One possibility is the preparation of prescriber's journals similar to the US *Medical Letter* and the British *Drugs and Therapeutics Bulletin* which are independently funded and thus able to look critically at drug use. For best effect this would have to be geared to a country's individual needs—as was Sri Lanka's *The Prescriber*—although the Pan American Health Organization made a start in Latin America by circulating a Spanish translation of the *Medical Letter*. Another approach, already adopted in Guyana and under consideration for use in Tanzania, is the employment of state detailmen to visit health workers, as their commercial counterparts formerly did, but in order to dispense less partial information.[37]

The question of quality

If the problem of providing sound information about drugs and their uses cannot be separated from the education and management of the health worker, so, too, the question of drug quality cannot be considered without looking at the way in which pharmaceutical products are distributed through the health care system. In March 1981, Beira health department's hearse driver, who usually drives faster than he should, was speeding in deadly earnest. A measles epidemic was sweeping the city and, at its peak, so many children died that he could not keep up, even though he carried two coffins per journey. The outbreak was particularly tragic because it followed an apparently successful vaccination campaign which had reached the majority of households. A significant proportion of those children who died had been vaccinated. It was by no means a unique experience. In Guatemala, a continued vaccination campaign that had initially reduced measles deaths by 90 per cent appeared to have failed when, in 1976, the death rate returned to its former levels. The potency of measles vaccine is easily destroyed if it is not kept at the correct temperature. The health authorities reported:

> Vaccine was shipped from the health departments to rural health centres in poorly insulated containers that could not adequately protect the vaccine. Kerosene refrigerators in health centres often lacked replacement parts or fuel, and electricity for electric refrigerators was sometimes unreliable. Personnel were inadequately trained in vaccine handling or refrigerator maintenance.[38]

It is probable that similar weaknesses led to the failure of Beira's programme.

So the correct policy, the right products, and the best of intentions can all come to naught when up against the practical problems—intellectually less interesting although in practice more demanding—of delivering the right drugs to the right place in the right conditions. Drug quality has unfortunately become an important competitive tool used both to promote and denigrate pharmaceutical products. Were it otherwise, many of the issues might have been resolved earlier, by determining which products are most vulnerable to deterioration and concentrating attention on their correct handling. Only recently, for instance, has the WHO begun to produce guidelines for the analysis of essential drugs that make it possible to determine, by simple means, whether gross deterioration has taken place.[39] This must be, for the moment, the priority for developing countries. It was a Ciba-Geigy production manager who gave me the most practical perspective. What matters, he told me, is not that people in Africa get 10 per cent more or 10 per cent less chloroquine in every tablet but that they get chloroquine at all.

An essential form of cooperation

One focus defined for the United Nations agencies by their predominantly developing country members is the promotion of technical and economic cooperation between them. It is a strategy intended both to end old colonial ties and the abuses which are part of them and to create the ground for self-sustaining growth and development based on the real needs of the countries themselves. In the field of pharmaceuticals, this strategy is already being implemented. Apart from cooperation in drug production and related trade agreements, some countries which are too small and too poor to be able to afford the minimum of an essential drug scheme alone are joining together to make one possible. The island countries of the South Pacific are the best example. Their South Pacific Pharmaceutical Service is conceived as having four parts: a joint purchasing service; a joint warehouse to facilitate drug distribution; a quality-control programme, including a quality-control laboratory; a drug information service which, in addition to providing information about the drugs distributed by the service, is also required to advise member countries on pharmaceutical policies and to help them to harmonize their laws on pharmaceuticals.[40]

That other more developed archipelago, the Caribbean, is the focus of another attempt to develop cooperative pharmaceutical services. Already a joint drug purchase scheme is in operation, but there is an ambitious plan to expand this further into areas of information, quality control and, eventually, production.[41]

So, from the policy ideas outlined by the WHO and UNCTAD, concrete results are already emerging. This is a triumph in itself.

Surrounded by the opulence of Geneva, it is hard to appreciate that the WHO works on a shoe-string, compared to funds available to the pharmaceutical industry. Dr John Dunne's cramped office gives an accurate image of the constraints under which the Organization has to operate. The $9,875,000 budgeted for the activities of its drugs division in 1982/3 is less than 10 per cent of the market research income of just one company (IMS). Weighed against the multinational companies' information and advertising budgets, estimated at $5000 million, the WHO's 1982/3 regular budget of $484 million is puny.

Irrational medicine—the spectre at the feast

The WHO's efforts at formulating drugs policies are moving towards a set-piece finale in 1982. The Action Programme on Essential Drugs, which it is implementing in collaboration with the United Nations and other agencies, the World Bank in particular, is soon to be unveiled. For a number of poorer developing countries, it will be easier to obtain supplies of drugs on the WHO's essential drugs list, either through cut-price purchase schemes or through more complicated aid arrangements, some of which will be dealt with in the next chapters. With Halfdan Mahler soon due to leave the WHO, it would not be surprising were there to be some celebration of cooperation between rich world and poor, for which he has worked so hard, at the 1982 World Health Assembly in May, or at the next IFPMA Congress in New York in June. But the mere supply of drugs is in fact a secondary issue.

The WHO has consistently refused to be side-tracked down the easy path of providing the drug needs of the poor and ignoring the more general problems of pharmaceutical policy, despite the solicitations of the multinationals. The companies have, with considerable impudence, claimed credit for improving health standards in the poor world and continue to attack the emphasis of the UN organizations. Jay J. Kingham of the American PMA asserts:

In the private sector, the population:doctor ratio, the population:hospital ratio and the per capita drug consumption reach levels that can be considered low but adequate. Health standards have been improving steadily. Average life expectancy in thirty-four poorer countries increased by about eight years between 1960 and 1975. It would be fair to assume that the lion's share of this gain was enjoyed by the populations in the private sector. The public sector on the other hand is woefully in disorder, looked at from any vantage point. . . . it is with the public sector that UN agencies could provide needed assistance.[42]

The WHO has rejected this; 'World health is indivisible,' said Dr Mahler. As important, it has rejected the pessimism of the US Agency for International Development (AID) report which claimed 'rational drug therapy exists nowhere in the world, nor can it ever, and efforts to pursue rational drug therapy as a national goal would hardly be practicable and certainly not cost-effective.'[43] Dr Mahler stated:

> Thirty years ago modern health technology had just awakened and was full of promise. Since then, its expansion has surpassed all dreams, only to become a nightmare. For it has become over-sophisticated and overcostly. It is dictating our health policies unwisely; and what is useful is being applied to too few. Based on these technologies, a huge medical industry has grown up with powerful vested interests of its own. Like the sorcerer's apprentice, we have lost control—social control—over health technology. The slave of our imagination has become the master of our creativity. We must now learn to control it again and use it wisely, in the struggle for health freedom. This struggle is important for all countries; for developing countries it is crucial.[44]

The right of the pharmaceutical industry to continue to promote irrational medicine to any sector of the community, private or not, has never been conceded. And that will be the spectre at the feast.

Ten: Producing What's Needed

In an ever more complex world, there is something intrinsically satisfying about the machines used to make tablets. They click away busily, spitting their products into stainless steel bowls at a pace that is by no means old-worldly. But there is a simplicity about them that is reassuring. Everyone can understand the basic principle of operation—taking a small quantity of powder and compressing it to form a tablet—although the technicians assure us that the latest models are in fact highly engineered precision machines. And it is in the tableting room of CAPS, a pharmaceutical company in Zimbabwe, that one of the essential truths about the pharmaceutical manufacturing process reveals itself. It is, in its later stages at least, a relatively simple business.

This point is highlighted by Dr Michael Burstall, in his report on the production of pharmaceuticals in the developing countries, prepared for the OECD:

> A pharmaceutical industry of a simple kind is not merely desirable; it is within the capacity of almost all countries. The infrastructure required is modest. A developing African state may not be able to build jet fighters, but it can turn bulk drugs into their dosage forms and package them for the local market. The technology involved in the later stages of pharmaceutical production is relatively easy to obtain and apply. A pharmaceutical industry of its own is therefore an attractive and, up to a point, realistic objective for a developing country.[1]

Apart from the fact that it is possible, what makes the establishment of pharmaceutical production so desirable in the eyes of developing-country governments? According to Dr Burstall, the answer is cash, more particularly hard foreign currency. The notion of self-sufficiency, which may be attractive for strategic reasons, is a secondary factor, he says, as is the number of jobs provided by the industry, for these are limited. 'The most common reason for government action,' he concludes, 'has been the need to control imports.'

His thesis is amply supported by the experience of CAPS. Throughout the years of illegal rule by Ian Smith's rebel government in Rhodesia, those tableting machines, ticking away in their dust-proof booths, were saving money and helping to beat the economic sanctions imposed to bring the rebels to heel. Henry Briscoe, technical director of CAPS, explained what the rebellion had meant for his company:

It very quickly became apparent to government that medicines were a strategic kind of good and the government treated us as a very important industry. We were brought under the umbrella of protection. They were constantly watching and asking, 'What would be your situation if you were not able to get supplies; how long could you go on for . . .?'

It became very important from the government point of view to keep this fledgling industry, as it then was, viable. So that what happened very quickly when sanctions began to bite, and they did not begin all that quickly, was the government brought in a regulation that said that if you could make anything locally that was comparable in quality to an overseas product, they would stop the overseas product. So it became called import substitution and that helped the local people a lot.

It was not just the local companies that had to adjust to the exigencies of the siege economy:

The multinationals had their products manufactured locally as well because they could see that there was going to be import control which would not allow them to bring in finished products if there was someone locally who could manufacture. And if it was a product still under patent, they would only get a certain allocation of dollars. That allocation would only bring in so much finished product but if it was manufactured in the country from raw materials, it would be so much more product.

The result was a rare degree of self-sufficiency for a developing country of 7 million people. CAPS, for instance, was selling by 1978 nearly 100 different drugs, each in a variety of forms, including a good proportion of the products on the WHO's Essential Drugs List.[2] And, although there are no figures available, it seems that Rhodesia was producing enough to meet nearly all its basic drug needs.

This apparent success depends, however, on a rather limited

definition of the term 'production'. The Rhodesian industry was confined to making its tablets, capsules, ampoules and lotions from raw materials which were almost exclusively imported. Hardly any of the ingredients for drug manufacture were bought locally, despite the priority given to local production. CAPS was even buying its starch abroad. Nevertheless, the value of that limited element of local production was large. Henry Briscoe says:

> I put it to you this way. If that drug is manufactured by a principal overseas, into that drug goes not only the material price but you are also paying for someone else's labour. You bring just the raw material and it's your labour and it's in your country. The fact is that we're giving 300 people work, so that's money being generated into the economy by wages. All the labels, all the cartons are made in the country so there's a spin-off from that too.

The costs and benefits of self-sufficiency

Dr Burstall has calculated the costs of such Third World self-sufficiency to the rich countries.

> The transfer of pharmaceutical technology has had a modest but adverse effect on the OECD nations. As a group, their 1975 national incomes were probably $2,200 million lower than would otherwise have been the case. Their aggregate balance of payments with the Third World was $3,900 million less favourable.[3]

For 'costs to the rich world' can be read 'benefits to the Third World' and in these lie the attraction of an indigenous pharmaceutical industry.

Zimbabwe's drug industry and its distance from self-sufficiency is typical of the situation in most Third World countries. UNIDO (The UN Industrial Development Organization) has established a breakdown of developing countries into groups broadly classified by the degree of technological development achieved by their pharmaceutical industries. This is shown in Table 6 along with examples of some representative countries in each grouping and a simple illustration, from the manufacture of aspirin, of what is implied in each stage.

Table 6: **Stages of Development of the Pharmaceutical Industry**[4]

GROUP	TYPICAL MEMBERS	LEVEL OF PRODUCTION	EXAMPLE FROM ASPIRIN MANUFACTURE
1	Honduras Mongolia Mozambique Yemen	No manufacturing facilities. Drugs imported in their finished form.	Import aspirin ready-packed for distribution.
2	Guatemala Philippines Sri Lanka Zimbabwe	Re-pack formulated drugs. Process some bulk drugs into finished products.	Import aspirin in crystal form and make tablets.
3	Algeria Ghana Iraq Peru	Manufacture a wide range of finished drugs. Produce some simple bulk drugs from intermediates.	Import salicylic acid and acetic acid. React together and separate acetylsalicylic acid. Purify it.
4	Egypt Argentina Pakistan	Produce many bulk drugs from intermediates; manufacture some intermediates from local raw materials.	Produce salicylic acid from phenol, caustic soda, carbon dioxide and sulphuric acid. Then produce aspirin.
5	Brasil India Mexico	Produce most intermediates needed for pharmaceutical industry. Local R & D of products and processes.	Local raw materials used for synthesis. Process designed to suit available raw materials and by-products of other processes.

UNIDO is to drug production what the WHO is to drug use. And the history of its involvement in pharmaceuticals parallels closely that of its sister agency. Until 1975, its emphasis 'was almost exclusively on production and how to increase it. The international structure of the industry, the proliferation of drugs, the role of patents, all were noted but taken as given: production was to develop within this structure, according to established rules.'[5]

A new order for production

Then the Third World countries decided that it was time the rules were changed. They believed that the old rules were hampering their economic development and diverting it from the real needs of their people. What they called for, through the forum of the United Nations, was nothing less than a new international economic order. In this context, the Second General Conference of UNIDO looked at the problems of promoting an industrialization which would serve the basic needs of the developing countries. For pharmaceuticals, they set an apparently modest target, that by the year 2000, 25 per cent of the world's pharmaceuticals should be produced in these countries.[6] They have a very long way to go. In 1977 the Third World's production accounted for only 11.4 per cent of the total.[7] Since overall world production will continue to grow, the target in volume terms is for the Third World to produce six times more than it presently does.

It is in this area of pharmaceutical production that the conflicts of interest between the developing countries and the multinational industry are most obvious. For most of those countries which do not, as yet, formulate ready-to-use drugs from imported bulk pharmaceuticals, the question is simply one of the pace at which industrialization will take place. It is estimated that any country with at least 3 million consumers (the total population will be larger in those countries where health services are not universally accessible) can support a formulation industry.[8] The points of issue will be the sources and prices of the necessary raw materials.

For the most advanced developing countries, however, the problems are more complex. The multinationals possess a unique resource of expertise in the manufacture of pharmaceutical chemicals from raw materials, expertise which it would be costly and wasteful to duplicate. For the companies, though, this knowledge is the key to their continued control of Third World markets. So a considerable controversy surrounds the terms under which this technology will be made available, a controversy which is central to the goal of a new international economic order. The multinationals, whose directors have on occasion said that the Third World is of marginal interest to them,[9] have proved consistently reluctant to sell to the developing countries pharmaceutical technologies without conditions which guarantee continued access for their companies to these markets.

From 1976 onwards, UNIDO has directed its activities in the

pharmaceutical industry more towards the production of essential drugs. It encouraged the use of generic names for drugs in all its projects and promoted the idea of cooperative production by groups of developing countries.[10] Its consultations clarified the views of the various interest groups and confirmed that the contentious issues for the 1980s will be the price and availability of the bulk drugs and chemical intermediates needed by the less developed national industries and, for the more advanced countries, the terms under which technology will be transferred.[11]

Does collaboration pay?

At the root of both of these issues is the continued dependence of the developing countries on the multinationals. National attitudes towards the companies have varied greatly, from Brazil's open-door welcome to India's grudging acceptance that in certain high-technology areas of the pharmaceutical industry, local technology cannot fill the needs, and the multinationals must be allowed in. Does cooperation pay dividends? To date, the record of the multinationals in promoting industrial development has not been a convincing one.

There is a huge gulf between the pharmaceutical industries of countries in UNIDO's groups 4 and 5 and the small, poor countries of groups 1 and 2 (see Table 6). But apart from gross poverty and obviously limited markets in the case of the smaller countries, there is no obvious connection between the wealth of each country and the degree of development of its pharmaceutical industry. Thus India (GNP $150 per capita) is rated as a group 5 country along with Brazil and Mexico (GNPs $1360 and $1120 respectively). It is in fact widely recognized that the Indian industry is considerably more advanced than that of the other two—one report shows that while India was manufacturing from local raw materials part of its needs for thirty-five out of a list of forty-three essential drugs, Brazil was doing this only in the case of five antibiotics, while Mexico was manufacturing just three antibiotics and aspirin.[12]

Nor is the relative development easily explicable in terms of the availability of skilled manpower, of which the pharmaceutical industry is a greedy consumer. Egypt (GNP $350 per capita, population 41 million) was rated as a group 4 country. Its estimated 590,000 trained scientists, engineers and technicians do not compare favourably with the 1 million claimed by the Philippines. Yet the Philippines lags way behind Egypt in this respect, relegated to the ranks of the group 2 countries. The basic requirements for the development of a strong national pharmaceutical industry would thus seem to be not just a sufficiently large national market, nor the supply of skilled manpower (and the technical infrastructure associated with it). What is crucial is government determination actively to promote the growth of the industry—which typifies Egypt and India—rather than the passive encouragement of multinational investment as in many of the countries which find themselves less advanced in this respect.

Brazil's relative incapacity, for instance, has a long history. It is instructive to look back to see what the multinationals were promising there in the 1960s. Arguing that Brazil should respect patents and cooperate with the foreign companies, Ney Galvão da Silva, production director of Laboterapica Bristol, said:

> What we need to do with foreign patents is to make a selection of those whose application would be of interest in this country; what we must take into account is that patents which come with 'know-how' represent an enrichment of national technology. We need to import technologies at each stage more advanced and train Brazilian technicians to apply them in the country. This is being done by the Brazilian pharmaceutical industry which, through its association with foreign pharmaceutical companies, is introducing into the country advanced techniques and training hundreds of Brazilians in their use. . . . The benefits of this policy are visible in the technological progress of the pharmaceutical industry in Brazil.[13]

Fifteen years later, the benefits are harder to find. Indeed, said Dr Osmar Xavier, talking about the development of a new antibiotic plant, previous governments' policies of recognizing patents had retarded the development of a Brazilian industry because the foreign companies had preferred to maintain their monopoly of technology rather than license it to Brazilian companies.[14] The result of this dependency was shown when Brazil attempted to control the prices of imported raw materials and the multinationals cut back on the production of essential drugs like penicillin and tetracyline in retaliation.[15]

The conflict of interest between the national and the multinational companies came to a head in Latin America when, at the end of 1980, the local companies of ten countries broke away from the multinational dominated regional organization FIFARMA to establish their own regional organization, ALIFAR. In its inaugural statement, ALIFAR highlighted the Latin American industry's dependence on imported bulk chemicals. It called for rules governing the transfer of technology, abolition of patent protection for pharmaceuticals and fair and stable conditions for the supply of raw materials, to prevent in particular 'artificial price fluctuations which affect the local production of basic drugs'.[16]

An industry which responds to needs

While the promotion of national pharmaceutical companies may help to build a manufacturing capacity, it will not necessarily create an industry responsive to the health needs of its country. Indeed, in the Philippines and Brazil it was the parallel existence of national companies and multinationals that often encouraged the former to similar excesses of trivial and over-promoted medicine. It may be appropriate that the Indonesian company Phapros (which is part-owned by the civil servants' health insurance agency) should be chosen to manufacture cimetidine (Tagamet) in that country[17]— indeed unobjectionable since that drug is likely soon to find itself a place on essential drug lists. The more traditional pattern, however, has been, as in Sri Lanka, for local production to concentrate on products of marginal health value but offering maximum immediate profits.

The contradiction was obvious at CAPS in Zimbabwe which, immediately after independence, wanted to concentrate its efforts on the development of its successful 'Strong Boy' range of over-the-counter painkillers and cough medicines, which was boosted by the marketing impetus of the company's highly successful football team. They also wanted to develop more brand name specialities. 'One of the things we have learned is that specialities pay time and time again,' Henry Briscoe told me. The company's R & D unit was being run by the marketing rather than the production division 'to ensure that research and development did not lose its market orientation'.[18] Yet the direction of the new government's health policy is towards a more rational system of drug distribution through an expanded health service where the need would be for cheaper generic products in large volume. This particular contradiction has apparently been resolved since the government's acquisition of a substantial holding in the company, an investment which will permit CAPS to re-equip and expand its installations.[19]

It is relatively easy to turn tablet-making machines to producing different drugs. Chemical plants on the other hand are more difficult to adapt. So when India's Drugs Controller decided to ban amidopyrine, he had to think of the effect of his action on his producers. 'M/s IDPL who are the indigenous manufacturer of this drug have also been asked to gradually stop the production of this drug. This would result in preparations containing Amidopyrine gradually being eased out of the market.'[20] India will have a similar problem when it comes to restrict the sale of clioquinol and similar compounds, of which it was producing over 200 tons in 1980, 70 per cent of total demand according to the Minister for Chemicals.[21]

The rest of the developing world can profit from India's pioneering experience as it moves from tablet-making to the more complex business of producing pharmaceutical chemicals in bulk. If it is to avoid wasting scarce technical resources developing the production of drugs of limited value to health, it would do well to allow its production priorities to be guided by the WHO's essential drug list or similar considerations. There are signs that even in Latin America, where the national companies are traditionally fiercely in favour of free enterprise (the Argentinian companies published a series of advertisements titled 'Freedom for Health' which attacked the concept of limited lists of essential drugs, saying that Argentina 'is not a country of the Third World'[22]), they are beginning to accept that their own development would best be served by cooperating with governments in promoting rational pharmaceutical and health policies rather than trying to out-compete the multinationals in innovation and marketing. So, at the UNIDO consultation in December 1980, ALIFAR called for health policies to take account of their impact on national pharmaceutical companies and for the programmes of international organizations to promote their participation.[23]

Cooperation—the way forward

The smaller developing countries will not be able to go into the production of bulk pharmaceutical chemicals on their own account. For those with the commitment to develop a national industry, the only way forward will be in cooperation with their neighbours, since the multinationals are unlikely, except in special circumstances, to produce these in any but the biggest developing countries. This was recognized by Sanjaya Lall in his 1975 UNCTAD paper where he suggested the formation of COPPTECS (Cooperative Pharmaceutical Production and Technology Centres).[24]

Regional cooperation is less of an ideal than a necessity. Henry

Briscoe, looking at the future for CAPS in an independent Zimbabwe, saw the prospects for his company in these terms:

> It depends very much on what happens in Central Africa. Central Africa is looking towards getting together. It's in its rudiments at the moment, but if this is handled properly, we could be looking at a common trading area—it makes a lot of sense. We should sit down and look at what we're importing from expensive sources . . . very often some of these raw materials are actually grown in the country and sent over 'there' to be processed. It could only come about if the nine or ten nations in Central and Southern Africa got together . . . even though Zimbabwe is comparatively well-off in comparison with the others, even it couldn't keep this company going. If we couldn't export one-third of everything we make in this plant, we couldn't live on Zimbabwe alone.

The cooperative concept appeared set for success in the Middle East, where circumstances appeared particularly favourable. Egypt, and to a lesser extent Iraq, offering large potential markets, had the manufacturing experience and the skilled manpower, while the oil-producing countries could provide their financial reserves and a vital interest in using their oil as the basis for a chemical industry. ACDIMA (the Arab Company for Drug Industry and Medical Appliances) seemed off to a good start when political factors intervened. The Egyptian-Israeli peace agreement caused Egypt to be excluded from the partnership. Nonetheless, the remaining countries have carried on with it, and already three projects have left the drawing board for the construction site—an antibiotics plant in Iraq, a pharmaceutical manufacturing plant in Kuwait and a plant for the production of specialized pharmaceutical glass in Syria.[25]

Political obstacles will continue to be important, yet experience elsewhere suggests that they can be overridden by sheer economic logic. Thus members of the Caribbean Community are still moving towards the establishment of a Caribbean Centre for Pharmaceuticals, despite the political distance between countries like socialist Guyana (which had been chosen by the non-aligned Third World countries to organize a trial pharmaceutical cooperation project in the region[26]) and the new pro-American government of Jamaica. While the Centre's focus will, in the first instance, be on extending existing joint purchasing schemes and promoting common pharmaceutical policies, the next priority will be to reduce the region's dependence on imported drugs. This will mean first the rationalization of existing production plants to use their capacity to the full, and then the expansion of manufacture.[27]

For regions like the Caribbean, access to the relatively simple technology needed for drug formulation and the first stages of bulk chemical manufacture is unlikely to be a problem. The WHO is working out a plan for a model low-cost formulation plant which would, in its first phase, produce perhaps thirty different tablets, capsules, liquids and lotions in quantities sufficient for a market of up to 3 million people.[28] The more advanced developing countries like India, Brazil and Mexico are already in a position to offer both technical advice and the hardware for drug formulation and production, as a glance through the advertisements in India's pharmaceutical industry magazine, the *Eastern Pharmacist*, will show. They are arguably better able to give appropriate advice for small-scale manufacture than the multinationals whose emphasis is on the production of long runs of a small number of their speciality products rather than on small batches of many different products. 'We would have difficulty scaling down to such a level,' Dr Barthel, a Ciba production manager, admitted to me, adding that he would be unhappy trying to make more than twenty different products in the same plant.

This kind of cooperation between developing countries is already well underway. India, for example, is providing technical assistance to Algeria[29] and the United Arab Emirates.[30] Private Indian companies have set up joint ventures in other developing countries—as, for example, the Ranbaxy Laboratories joint venture in Nigeria.[31] Of most importance, perhaps, is a UNIDO-funded project under which Sarabhai Enterprises, India's largest private drug company, is to set up a plant in Cuba to produce, in bulk, fifteen different drugs from raw materials.[32]

The price of packaged technology

It is when it comes to the more complicated production processes that the outlook is less bright. Countries or companies which wish to move into the production of bulk pharmaceutical chemicals from raw materials have either to develop the production processes themselves or acquire the know-how from someone who already has it. Just as a cake cannot be baked from a list of its ingredients alone, so, to make a complex pharmaceutical, other information is essential—the temperature and the time needed for reactions to occur, the type of container to use, the rate at which raw materials are mixed, the purity required to obtain the most economic yield. All this information can be gained through experiment but it is a costly, time-consuming business. And, invariably, for the products which the developing countries want to make, the information already exists.

At issue is the way this production know-how is packaged for sale. Ideally, the Third World would like to be able to buy it for a straight fee, as the state-owned Indian Drugs and Pharmaceuticals Limited has done. In a series of deals with Italian, Swedish and Swiss companies, it purchased the technology to manufacture a number of antibiotics and other drugs for fees ranging from $85,000 for a doxycycline plant to $500,000 for a plant to make semi-synthetic penicillins, and even more for a niacin plant.[33] Under these contracts, the foreign companies produce designs, and accompany construction and the start of production until the required level of efficiency is achieved.

This kind of technology-transfer deal is not particularly attractive to the multinationals which hold a significant proportion of world know-how. They prefer packages based on a combination of patents, licences and participation. *Patents* as a means of transferring know-how are relatively unimportant, providing only the list of ingredients without the essential recipe. Their importance to the multinationals is that they represent ownership of knowledge, either about a product or about a particular method for making it. The companies press for their inclusion as part of a technology-transfer package because, if recognized, they limit the access of other producers to the market and enable high prices to be maintained. The multinationals claim that this is essential to pay for continued research while the developing countries, whose needs have been virtually ignored by such research, have no particular incentive to recognize them. While patents are a crucial item in the negotiations on international policy towards the transfer of technology between the rich and poor worlds, *licensing* is the most common form of technology transfer where specific products and processes are involved. Under a licence agreement, the technology holder will supply his know-how in exchange for payment of royalties, usually fixed as a percentage of sales. Very often, the licence agreement will include restrictions on the use that can be made of the technology, limiting exports perhaps, or tying the user to supplies of raw material from the purchaser.[34] These components of the package are usually negotiable. The last form of transfer is by *direct investment*, either through the establishment of a subsidiary of the foreign company or through joint ventures with local companies.

K. J. Divatla of India's Sarabhai Enterprises has no doubts about the disadvantages of this last method. It is far cheaper for the country to import the technology it needs directly rather than to do so through the direct participation of foreign companies, he says, and claims that, measured by the direct foreign exchange payments involved, the cost to India of technology imported by local companies through licensing or know-how agreements was only half the cost of royalties and profits sent home by foreign investors, as a percentage of sales. An important advantage as well 'is that there is no interference in the management of the enterprise by the collaborator. The Indian entrepreneur is free to import his raw materials from competitive sources and is also able to export his finished products without any constraint.'[35] This is in marked contrast to the situation in Brazil where subsidiaries of the multinationals not only take more money out of the country through their control of raw material imports, but also limit Brazil's pharmaceutical exports so as not to compete with their parent companies.

The case of chloroquine

The problem is that those with the know-how are frequently not prepared to sell it, however compelling the reasons to do so may appear to the developing country concerned. India accounts for one-third of the world's consumption of chloroquine. Yet most of the drug is produced in France, Britain, Germany and Hungary.[36] Some is produced in India, using half-way synthesized intermediates, but this has proved to be less than economic, a situation often encountered by Third World countries which do not have the chemical industry base to produce all the raw materials they need for drug synthesis. In many cases, 'It might be cheaper to import some drugs rather than conjure up a "pseudo-manufacture" from imported intermediates on the basis of foreign technology,' notes one Indian study.[37]

'The drug was of strategic value to the country and the infrastructure required to undertake the basic manufacture of the drug was available within the country,' says a UNIDO account of India's attempt to buy chloroquine technology. Nevertheless, it proved impossible to negotiate an acceptable deal for the supply of technology without an accompanying package of restrictions. A deal with Hungary, which at one stage looked signed and sealed, broke down when the Hungarians insisted that India would have to agree to buy all its chloroquine needs from them while the factory was under construction. 'The transfer was linked to a commercial transaction and was thus unacceptable.'[38] In the end, Indian scientists were put to work to scale-up laboratory methods for industrial application, a long and costly business. Their efforts are claimed to be successful. 'India is in possession of competent technology for the manufacture of chloroquine. . . . Import of technology for the manufacture of anti-malarial drugs from foreign countries is not required,' the Indian Parliament was told at the end of 1980.[39]

Where new drugs will come from

If the most advanced developing countries can now wrest their independence from the rich world in limited areas of technology like this, they are not, for the moment, making any serious attempt to compete in the development of new drugs. In most areas of disease, it would make no sense to do so. The competitive pressures in the rich world are such that as soon as scientific knowledge opens the way to the development of a new series of drugs, the multinationals' researchers rush in. There would be little point in the Third World trying to beat these sprinters to the finishing line. But for those tropical diseases in which the multinationals take no interest, a new approach has had to be found. In the compromise they have reached, through the agency of the WHO, the developing countries may have something to teach the rich world about the rational use of resources.

The WHO's Special Programme for Research and Training in Tropical Diseases was created to fill the gap left by the pharmaceutical industry. It is based on two premises: first, that to tackle the six diseases on which it focuses, the best available skills must be brought to bear; and second, that there is no point in developing remedies outside the countries affected without at the same time creating a technical base within those countries which will enable them to continue the research and, more important, its scientific application to disease-control. So one-fifth of the Special Programme's funds have so far been devoted to strengthening the research capacities in the developing countries themselves.

Both the Programme's methods and its results to date are important, for they show that the multinational pharmaceutical industry is not essential to the development of useful new drugs, although their resources and experience may be of great help. It has already been emphasized that the development of a new drug can rarely be attributed to a single agency. Nevertheless, the Special Programme, in its first major development since it began in 1976, can take the lion's share of the credit for the introduction of mefloquine, 'the first new anti-malaria drug to be developed to clinical trial stage in thirty or more years'.[40] Because of the spread of chloroquine-resistant malaria in South-East Asia, this was an early priority for the Programme. The scientists of the WHO's parasitic diseases division emphasize, almost ritually, that there is no alternative to the multinational industry for the provision of new drugs to the developing world. But the story of mefloquine shows that the contribution of the industry to new drug development need only be a limited one in cases where the lack of a suitable product is truly felt.

Melfloquine was isolated in a screening programme at the Walter Reed Army Institute of Research. Their studies showed that it was effective against chloroquine-resistant malaria and that it did not appear to cause unacceptable side-effects. The WHO's Special Programme took up its development and it was decided to offer the pharmaceutical industry the opportunity to participate. An agreement was reached with Hoffmann-La Roche whereby they would undertake some elements of the work. This could have been done on a straight contract basis but, according to Dr Michel Fernex, the Roche scientist who deals with the research aspects of the project, Roche was reluctant to accept such payments from the WHO. 'It was not accepted by Roche as good policy,' he explained.

The studies could probably have been contracted out to some of the specialized companies which provide similar services to the pharmaceutical companies themselves. But for the WHO, there were obvious advantages in working with a single, self-sufficient organization. The final agreement was that Roche should take responsibility for producing the drug in the quantities required for trials, and re-do some of the early Walter Reed studies on toxicology—they had, for instance, ignored the possible danger of the drug for pregnant women, not apparently a proper concern for military medicine, so reproductive studies had to be started. The WHO, for its part, undertook to arrange the clinical trials needed to assess the drug's efficacy in large-scale use. Here they had a clear advantage. 'They can organize field trials in 60,000 people; we'd be limited to a maximum of 600,' conceded Dr Fernex.

As regards the commercial exploitation of the drug, it was apparently agreed that Roche would accept the WHO's constraints on its marketing to maintain mefloquine as a 'reserve drug' for use only where resistance to chloroquine made it necessary. The company still sees the way open to it to sell it in the rich world. 'We would not sell it in East Africa, but there would be no risk in

Switzerland,' said Dr Fernex. It was probable, he continued, that the company would continue to give the drug away for use in the final trials in South-East Asia until it had been registered for sale in Switzerland. Its price would then be calculated, using, as a basis, the costs of one course of non-effective treatment for chloroquine-resistant malaria in Thailand. Since this involves up to ten days in hospital, with three expensive doses of quinine every day, it is not likely to be cheap, so Roche might yet recoup some of their investment in the project, estimated to be around $5 million up to 1980. Although the product is not protected by patents—it was one of a number of substances offered free for development by the Walter Reed Institute[41]—Roche will have some protection since the ten-stage synthesis used to make mefloquine is quite difficult, as is the formulation of the tablets which have to be accurately compounded since, if they dissolve too fast in the stomach, they cause vomiting.

With new therapy urgently needed in South East Asia—where there were an estimated 400,000 cases of chloroquine-resistant malaria in 1980—the final phase of clinical trials will probably be telescoped into its first general clinical use. The areas threatened by poly-resistant malaria (resistant to all available products) are growing, and it is likely that the WHO will be obliged, by pressure from national health authorities in Thailand, Cambodia and Burma, to release mefloquine for general use there as soon as possible.

Its final development cost will be hard to calculate. The Walter Reed research programme is said to have cost $100 million over ten years, but much of this will have gone into basic science important for the development of other products.[42] Roche's research expenditures may reach $10 million, much more than the Special Programme which has spent a similar amount on mefloquine and 149 other malaria research projects, combined.[43] The total cost will certainly be less than the $70–100 million estimated by some drug companies to be the cost of putting a new drug on the market, despite the specialized clinical testing it has needed.

Mefloquine is the Special Programme's first drug, but there are others under development for the treatment of malaria and river blindness. The groundwork has been laid for the discovery of more candidate compounds for use in other diseases by the establishment of eleven new screening laboratories to fill serious gaps which previously prevented potentially useful compounds from being routinely checked for effectiveness. The Special Programme is also sponsoring research into new methods for administering existing drugs in slow-release formulations which, in the case of malaria, will permit such more effective prevention against the disease. Much of the basic science which will permit the application of new molecular biology techniques to tropical disease is being funded by the Programme. These 'bio-engineering' techniques are important not just for the vaccines whose development they will allow, but also for the development of cheap kits to diagnose tropical diseases. If these were to become generally available, it would in itself be a major contribution to the efficient use of drugs.

Mention of the new bio-engineering techniques, and their multiple applications, brings us back to the question of drug production in the Third World. While public attention has been focused on the interferons and other exciting new products that these technologies will allow, their first application in the pharmaceutical industry will not be in the creation of new drugs, but in the production of old ones. This is of crucial importance to the developing countries and to the debate about the transfer of technology in the pharmaceutical industry.

The threats and promises of new technology

If the focus of the Third World's research effort has to be restricted to the processes by which existing drugs are produced, this is of great interest for the rich world's industry as well. The pharmaceutical multinationals are under pressure to make their production processes more efficient, and not only from their potential competitors in the Third World. A more serious threat for them is the challenge offered by the major world chemical companies which, because of the fearful costs of building new plants for the production of basic industrial chemicals in large volumes, are looking to relatively high-value goods like pharmaceuticals.[44] 'For a long time we have needed to see a larger percentage of our profitability coming from chemical-related high-technology downstream products,' says Paul Oreffice, president of Dow Chemicals, explaining why companies like his are expanding into pharmaceuticals and similar areas.[45]

For the multinationals, any further increase in pharmaceutical production by the developing countries can only aggravate their competitive difficulties. So in drug formulating, they are opposing it by manipulating prices. To discourage countries from entering the business too soon, they have boosted the price of bulk pharmaceutical chemicals and reduced, relatively, the price of their ready-formulated products to the point where, as the director of one small Southern African drug manufacturer complained to me, for some products 'it is cheaper to buy the tablets ready-made than to buy the bulk powder from which to make them.' The market for some bulk pharmaceuticals is supplied by so few producers as to be a near-perfect monopoly.[46] In other areas, such as antibiotics, Third World producers are already competing directly with the multinationals.

There is clearly a period of instability ahead, as the British multinational Glaxo recognized when it reorganized its production companies:

> The management of the new company, Sefton Bulk Pharmaceuticals, is responsible for stimulating and coordinating sales in bulk to third parties in the UK and abroad and ensuring close cooperation with those responsible for production. A comprehensive and stringent review of present and future business in this area is in hand. . . . a rapid response to changes in the pattern of supply in the market for bulk pharmaceuticals will in the future increasingly be the key to profitable operation in this highly competitive activity. The creation of Sefton Bulk Pharmaceuticals Ltd. as a central organization for handling this trade will enable us to deploy our fermentation capacity more flexibly to meet changing demand.[47]

The future: high or low technology?

In technology transfer, the issues are firmly placed within the broader context of the North-South dialogue. The extent to which the rich world is prepared to concede to the poor world's demands probably depends, in pharmaceuticals at least, on their reading of future technological development in the industry. Michael Burstall goes to the heart of the matter:

> In recent years, the rate of innovation has slowed considerably. Existing technology has therefore a longer life. If this trend were to continue or to accelerate, the importance of innovation would be reduced. The nations with a high innovatory capacity would have only a marginal advantage over those with a low capacity. If, however, the rate at which technology changes were to increase, then the ability to innovate would assume a greater importance. Countries well endowed in this respect would enjoy a distinct, perhaps commanding, advantage.

A future in which technical change is slow would also undermine the position of the multinational companies in the developing world. . . . the multinationals are tolerated as a source of new technology. If innovation ceases to be important, their major *raison d'être* will be gone. In economic and still more in political terms they will be left in an exposed position.[48]

A 'high-technology' future does not simply imply the introduction of many new products. As important could be changes in production processes, particularly if these alter costs. The larger and more advanced developing countries are now actively seeking foreign markets for their manufacturing industries, pharmaceuticals included. Their success in the other Third World markets which, in many ways, they can serve better than the multinationals[49] will be dependent on their maintaining competitive prices.

So forget interferon. Bio-engineering is first about making existing products more efficiently. According to the estimates of Dr J. Leslie Glick, president of the Genex corporation, by the year 2000 nearly half of the $11,000 million worth of bulk pharmaceuticals affected by the new technologies will still be products which already exist today.[50] That is why Frank Adams, president of Pfizer's chemical division, is looking to bio-engineering to maintain his profits: 'During the 1960s when inflation was at 3–4 per cent per year, it was easy to make up the difference by improving productivity. But there is no way that can be done now. Now costs must be cut,' he told *Chemical Week*. The article reported:

> One of Adams' more ambitious projects to accomplish that end is to funnel more of the division's R & D dollars into genetic engineering projects to develop more effective micro-organisms for use in fermentation processes. . . . Adams is gambling that Pfizer can come up with either a new substrate [bacterial food, such as sugar] for current micro-organisms or a new organism that can thrive on cheaper raw material.[51]

Similarly, one of Ciba's two bio-engineering projects aims to reduce production costs of their antibiotic rifampicin.[52] The point has not been lost on the developing countries. For ventures into antibiotic production, India's Dr Nitya Nand agrees 'It is best to try to obtain the latest technology with the highest yielding strains and guarantees for them; the economy of this industry is very highly dependent on the technical efficiency of the process.'[53] The question is not so much whether the developing countries will be able to gain access to the new technologies, but whether these will alter the economics of competition sufficiently to restore the ascendancy of the rich world and its companies.

The terms of trade and the pace of change

The countries of the Third World have made it clear that they cannot continue to base their economies on imports of consumables like drugs, for they would need to be able to pay for them through their exports, and experience has shown that earnings from exports to the rich world are unstable and unreliable. So, rather than serve the needs of the rich, both as suppliers of raw materials and as captive customers for consumer goods, they are trying to turn their economic development around to serve the needs of their own peoples, creating internal growth and reducing expensive dependence on imported goods and unstable export markets. Their best medicine is surely the exploitation of local materials for local needs. The Third World may benefit less from the drugs themselves than from the economic development implicit in the bricks and mortar of the factories built to produce them.

UNIDO's efforts to help Third World countries to develop indigenous pharmaceutical industries cannot be separated from the efforts of UNCTAD to negotiate a new international agreement on the terms for the transfer of technology, nor from the work of the WHO to bring about the rational use of existing drugs and to develop those others for which there is a need. Until 1978, these organizations had 'no formal strategy as such. It has never been printed in one document. It has never been announced by the UN Secretary-General or even by one of the UN agency heads.'[54] There is now, it is true, an Action Programme on Essential Drugs, with a proposed formal management structure that will make the WHO the agency responsible for implementation.[55] These activities follow from the formal call by the non-aligned Third World countries for such action, and particularly for cooperation between developing countries themselves to generate the development of self-sufficient drug industries.[56] But the change has a pace of its own and, in this case, it will be determined as much in the laboratories as in the conference halls.

Dr Burstall concludes: 'The pace of technical change will give the advanced nations and the multinational companies a better or worse hand to play. It will not change the nature of the game.'[57]

Eleven: The Corporate Response

The industrialized world, although the smallest [market], obviously offers the brightest business prospects. Yet the Third World is a vast potential market. These countries need health care and they need our pharmaceuticals.

But there are barriers to business in many countries. Business is chilled by negative government policies . . . . Multinational pharmaceutical companies are fatigued by Third World bureaucracies. These countries worship politics. They demean economics.

These are the harsh words of Robert Dee, chairman and chief executive of the US Smith Kline Corporation. His best business is other people's ulcers (Tagamet, his company's ulcer remedy is expected to earn over $1000 million by 1982). Dee has a view of a world in which

an innovative minority conceives the world's technology, raises most of the world's food and produces most of the world's goods. This minority is being challenged by a hostile majority.

In my opinion, this hostile majority does not want to trade on fair terms, it wants to trade on its own terms. And those terms are what most reasonable people could only call extortion.

Mr Dee offers simple solutions to his fellow company directors.

First, we can't deal with the Third World as a single customer. We must trade on a country-by-country basis. We should favour countries on whom reasonable economic policy is dawning. We should encourage and support these countries.

My second recommendation is that we put intense pressure on the UN—and on its health agencies—to give realistic instead of unrealistic advice to developing countries. . . . For this year and next, 70 per cent of WHO's budget will be paid by thirteen industrialized countries—thirteen out of 156 WHO member countries. Certainly this entitles the industrialized world to stand up to WHO. We must have the will to do so.[1]

So for Mr Dee it is the carrot and the stick, divide and rule, you need us more than we need you. It is a simple and aggressive response which matched closely the attitudes to the Third World of the new American president Ronald Reagan who made it plain that US support to developing countries should be restricted to those which were suitably docile in their relations with the 'land of the free'.

Mr Dee's is not the only voice from the industry. If he is the hard cop, there are, too, as in all good stories, the soft cops. So against the tough line cf Mr Dee, we can set the gentle tones of W. Clarke Wescoe, chairman of Sterling Drug Inc.:

The desire on the part of every country to have technology transfer is understood. The desire on the part of every country to export pharmaceuticals is also understood. The desire on the part of every nation to participate in pharmaceutical production from raw materials and packaging is understood, even if not practical or economically sound. There are limiting factors to all these desires . . . [but] there are needs enough for all to share in the fulfilling of the future. It is our responsibility to plan how to get there—and how we plan to deal with each other and with the world's health problems equitably—equitably for industry, for government and for all people. . . . Industry is interested in participating in a new and creative thrust on an equitable basis. I, for one, from the United States industry, would like to be a creative partner in that innovative thrust.[2]

Responding to the challenge

If the international pharmaceutical industry was difficult to locate when talking about its structure (see chapter 5) it is not hard to find when there is a challenge to which it must respond. Through the trade federation IFPMA, in which they have a dominant voice, through national governments and trade associations, and as individual companies, the multinationals have fought back strongly. Their response has been clear and has developed from a simple defensive posture against the attacks of their critics to a positive campaign aimed at winning the strategic ground from which to go on the offensive in the 1980s.

To analyse this response, it must be studied at a number of levels: (1) at the level of ideas, the companies actively try to shape, to

confuse, or to defuse the policy recommendations being elaborated by the United Nations and other agencies;

(2) at the practical level, action taken against countries which try to
implement policies perceived as hostile tends to be less subtle;

(3) at the level of corporate planning, new initiatives are underway
to exploit what the companies see as opportunities for growth in
emerging Third World markets.

Certain companies and trade organizations have not hesitated, on
occasion, to use all means available to achieve their objectives. They
systematically denigrate both their critics and their competitors,
particularly local companies in the developing world and the pharmaceutical producers of Eastern Europe. They exploit the national
self-interest which has prompted the governments of the richest
people in the world to oppose measures that could help bring
elementary health care to some of the poorest. Yet many of the
company representatives will privately admit, as individuals, that
the policies they oppose corporately make sense for the poor world.
There are those who believe that they can see ways to bring the
interests of their companies closer to those of the developing
countries. Always, though, corporate interests come first.

A corporate-eye view of the market's rise and fall

The corporate response obviously depends on its particular view of
the world. Here Klaus von Grebmer, an economist at Ciba-Geigy,
can help. He likes to use ingenious little sketches to illustrate his
arguments. One of his favourites is of a crane, a big box hanging
from its sling. That box, explains von Grebmer, represents the
pharmaceutical market. In it, the individual pharmaceutical companies are at each other's throats, fighting for their share of the
market. They have got it wrong, he says. 'In the past, pharmaceutical companies often concentrated too much on competing with each
other to gain market shares and higher turnovers.'[3] They have now
realized that it is as important, if not more so, to keep the overall size
of the market going up. Now the companies are turning on the crane
drivers—the politicians, health administrators, professionals and
journalists—who have their hands on the health policy levers which
make the value of the market rise or fall.

So when the pharmaceutical multinationals look at the policies
proposed for the developing countries, they are looking to see which
would restrict the growth of the markets and which would encourage
it. They then look at which policies would help them as a group to

maintain or enlarge their share of the market, and which would help their competitors. Taken together, there may be policies which, though reducing the multinationals' share of the market, still allow their total sales to grow by increasing the sale of drugs overall. Perhaps there will be, as Clarke Wescoe of Sterling suggests, 'needs enough for all to share in the fulfilling of the future'. This is a vital clue to understanding the corporate response to Third World initiatives on drug policy. It is also the only basis for answering the question with which we started—can the interests of the companies and the people of the Third World be reconciled?

What are the forces at work to make the Third World pharmaceutical market grow or shrink?

(1) *Population.* Populations will continue to grow faster in the Third World. As long as health care standards are maintained, pharmaceutical consumption will grow with the population.

(2) *Wealth.* There is good evidence to show that a country's expenditure on health care grows in direct proportion to its national income. Other things remaining equal, economic development in the Third World means expanded markets for pharmaceuticals.

These factors are outside the area of pharmaceutical policy. More pertinent are:

(3) *Health services.* An expansion of health services, whether in the private or public sector will generate new markets, provided drugs receive the same share of health spending. Where health services are not expanding, the market will remain stagnant even if there are populations with urgent drug needs.

(4) *Access.* In general, the easier it is for people to buy drugs—if they can do so without a doctor's prescription, for example—the more will be sold.

(5) *Utilization.* It follows that good drug use by health workers will dampen market growth, especially where they control access to the more potent and expensive medicines.

(6) *Price controls.* In rich countries, where the majority of people have the means to buy the drugs they want, the value of the market may be reduced if price levels are controlled. In poor countries where many people do not even have the means to buy the drugs they need, controls may not affect total market size since any money saved will be used to buy more drugs.

(7) *Brand names.* The marketing practices associated with branded specialities will promote market growth. A policy of using generic names only will reduce the incentives for intensive promotion and

will dampen growth, especially if combined with other curbs on marketing and the provision of information about drugs through independent channels.

A distinction must be drawn at all times between the size of the market in terms of money (which is what companies and finance ministers worry about) and in terms of the numbers of tablets and injections, units of treatment (which is what should concern health authorities).

Beyond the brute size of the market, the multinationals' next concern is their share of future markets. What decides this is considerably more complicated. Among the influences tending to reduce their share are: increasing local production by national companies; a slowdown in the rate of discovery of useful new drugs; the development of public *as opposed to* private health services; central buying on a 'best bid' basis; loose regulation in countries where there are local companies to take advantage of the market opportunities this allows. Influences tending to increase the share of the multinationals are: production technologies which grow more complicated or have greater economies of scale; the development of many useful new drugs; a bias towards the private rather than the public sector in health care; the recognition of patents; more bureaucratic and especially quality-control regulations which may penalize smaller competitors.

Best-buy packages

What matters to the companies is not the individual policies but the package of which they form a part. In most countries, two distinct policies will be found, one for the public sector, the other for the private. The object of the companies must be to remember their shareholders and fight for the best of the packages they can hope to get. It is on this basis that pharmaceutical industry analysts assess the potential of a market. Take, for example, this review of the future of the Brazilian market:

> Changes in the Brazilian pharmaceutical market are in the direction of more stringent regulation. Although this may open up opportunities for acquisition of smaller local companies by multinationals, it is doubtful if a wave of mergers is in the offing. The prime reason is that the industry is heavily controlled by the multinationals and the degree of incremental control that can be

obtained is minimal. However, the multinationals are still in the best position to cope with the extra regulation.

The general outlook for the pharmaceutical industry is positive. The major factors that will stimulate growth are population increase, urbanization, inclusion of a greater percentage of the population into the health care system, and the CEME [see chapter 5] program. The negative factors cannot overcome the general weight of the positive stimuli to growth. Multinationals will benefit most from the market growth but they may have to invest more heavily in the development of bulk medicinal production to maximize their profits.[4]

For the companies, a 'best-buy' package might be to have a developing country concentrate on expanding its public health service so as to reach under-served sections of the community, using a limited list of essential drugs but leaving the private sector alone. The country, particularly if it suffers shortages of foreign exchange, may want to increase the quantity of drugs it purchases without increasing the import bill. So they may wish to introduce controls on both public and private sectors. There is a clear conflict of interest. These are theoretical considerations. They are, however, reflected closely by the actual responses of the pharmaceutical multinationals to the various initiatives underway in the field of health and drug policy.

The early response

Switzerland is a good country in which to begin an examination of the corporate response. The Swiss pharmaceutical industry, unlike that of any other Western country, is of major national importance. Moreover, as an international financial centre, Switzerland plays a vital role in the operations of the drug companies of other countries, some of which have their international or regional headquarters there. It is also home to UNCTAD, IFPMA and WHO. In short, if there is a focal point from which the industry response will emanate, it is within the Basle–Zurich–Geneva triangle.

The three major companies, while nominally in competition, cooperate closely in many areas including public relations. Through their joint organization Interpharma, they plan and coordinate their public relations strategy as well as economizing on the costs of providing more mundane technical and economic information.

There are good grounds for taking the response of individual companies as a component of a joint position.

My first formal contact with the Swiss companies was made through Interplan, a public relations firm retained by Hoffmann–La Roche. The firm boasts that 'with its positive techniques, such as adversary relations, it can help clients to take well judged and successful initiatives'.[5] So, on the basis that the better you know your adversaries, the better you can counter them, Interplan had already set up meetings with Sanjaya Lall of UNCTAD and with other people who had criticized the operations of the multinational pharmaceutical companies in the developing world. While Roche was the client, there is every reason to believe that the results were shared with the other companies.

The fact that Roche was the client gives an interesting insight into the way in which the industry's public response to Third World policy issues fits into a larger framework. There were good reasons to bring critics to Roche—for one thing, a small part of the huge profits from Librium and Valium was going to a significant programme of research on tropical diseases. But there were other reasons for fixing the Third World debate on Roche, a company whose chief executive Adolf Jann had, until 1975, hardly deigned to acknowledge the press and who gave even his shareholders only minimal information. Suddenly he began to talk, to answer criticism. 'The reason for Jann's vocally scrappy posture,' explained the magazine *Business Week*, 'is that his company suddenly finds itself under attack on a number of fronts for its pricing policies.' The revelation that the USA was paying sixty times more for Valium than Britain, and the arrest of a former Roche employee, Stanley Adams, who told the European Commission about secret and probably illegal price-fixing schemes for Roche vitamins, were both good reasons for Roche to talk about something—anything—else.[6]

So the companies began to talk, but, as important, to listen, to learn and to plan. The change in tone, if not content, of the industry's response to criticism can be measured in terms of its distance from the strident report which Roche was circulating at the time as its response to Sanjaya Lall's first study for UNCTAD. Titled *A Blind Alley to Success*, it attacked Lall's work as irrational, utopian, full of theoretical and factual errors, wild accusations and polemics.[7] It was, to say the least, a negative reply.

Thus proposals to abolish brand names for drugs in developing countries were 'based on a concept of the existing situation which is either wrong or distorted . . . merely utopian proposals conceived at a conference table'. Of the suggestion that countries might consider limiting their purchases to a list of essential drugs:

> even if one conceded that the mechanics of the market do not always lead to the best possible results, a strategy promising success for the future could only lead to an improvement in the functions of the mechanism unless one intends to abolish completely the concept of market forces.
>
> Alleged national price discrimination is based on a comparison involving different dosages. . . . Any difference which exists is automatically designated as a price discrimination by the transnational corporations.

By 1976 Roche's tone had already become less strident and more positive. It began to address itself to the problems raised, rather than simply defend itself against its critics, and to sketch out the role it saw itself playing, albeit in simplistic terms:

> When you are going hungry, when you never have any free time because of a permanent struggle for bare survival, you cannot sit down and start to innovate. But in the industrialized countries where we have more than the basic necessities and the required educational level as well, innovation is a true possibility, a moral obligation, and in fact the only realistic answer to the main problems of our time.[8]

A Task Force on International Organizations

The problems to which the innovators of the pharmaceutical industry addressed themselves were their own rather than those of the broader community. In 1976, too, the informal coordination of public relations between a few companies gave way to an organized IFPMA 'Task Force on International Organizations', since when its fifteen members, taken from the highest levels in the corporations, have developed the formal industry response.

IFPMA made no attempt to defend untenable ground and conceded in principle the need to provide more accurate information on the safety and efficacy of its members' drugs. It was not prepared to give way on other issues, particularly not over suggestions that the use of drugs could be discouraged on grounds of their cost as well as for reasons of safety and efficacy. Regulatory control of promotion of medicines should be limited to ensuring that claims are 'consistent with available scientific and medical evidence for the individual products and should be clearly separated from the desire to exercise their control on economic rather than medical grounds.'[9]

The ground secured on questions of principle, the industry's attention passed to the practical problem of delivering essential drugs to developing countries at low cost. Professor Ludwig von Manger-Koenig, a West German health official, initiated the process with an offer to supply a limited range of essential drugs, specially labelled and packaged, at special prices, to the health services of the less developed African countries.[10] The offer may have been well meant and it certainly helped to generate long-running 'good news' stories about the drug companies. The depth of the dialogue that ensued is, however, in some doubt. A year after it was initiated, the German Pharmaceutical Industry Association BPI had to tell Dr Halfdan Mahler that he had misunderstood its offer—it was not for the whole African region, but only to help the most needy countries and then only with some of the most essential drugs.[11]

Other national associations and fifty individual companies also contacted the WHO offering to supply essential drugs at 'preferential' prices. Just what the WHO was supposed to do with these offers was not clear. Its mandate at the time was simply to advise governments on the best way to buy the drugs they needed at reasonable cost.[12]

In May 1978 the World Health Assembly decided that the Organization should 'develop further the dialogue with pharmaceutical industries in order to ensure their collaboration in meeting the health needs of large underserved sectors of the world's population.'[13] It still had no mandate to buy drugs on its own account, nor the mechanism to assess the merits of offers to supply them. In the case of specific rather than general offers, it was frequently not made clear on what basis they had been made. How much would have to be bought, how the drugs should be packed and labelled, where and when they would be delivered—such essential data was usually not specified. Without it, as WHO drugs division staff pointed out to me, it was not even possible to determine whether cheap drug offers were in fact cheap.

The intention seems to have been as much to embarrass the WHO as to supply essential drugs. One company, on discovering that the WHO's Geneva headquarters had not passed on the offers to regional offices, took it upon itself to do so. To communicate the offers would, say the WHO's officials, have been taken as a recommendation, and none could be given. Besides, since no formal call for offers had been made, many companies, particularly the

smaller national companies, which might well be interested in
supplying low-cost bulk drugs, had not had the chance to make
offers of their own. 'The WHO could hardly act as agent for the
multinationals without giving everyone a chance,' said one WHO
official. The companies on the other hand, continue to 'regret' the
WHO's 'delay' in acting on their offers.

Were the companies simply attempting to gain the initiative by
making positive offers which revealed the WHO as being apparently
incompetent to execute its own policies? Certainly, the possibility of
improving their image had not been lost on them:

> IFPMA wishes actively to encourage member companies from
> member associations to participate in this Action Programme. In
> cooperating with the WHO in this way they will not only be
> helping a worthwhile cause but *they will also do much to counter the
> criticism that as an industry we do too little to demonstrate our social
> responsibilities*. (My italics.)[14]

Gaining the initiative

The need for the companies to regain the initiative was highlighted
by the new president of the American PMA, Lewis Engman, shortly
after taking office. 'I believe that a trade association must have a
positive impact on public policy,' he said. 'It must not simply be
reactive.'[15]

It was in this spirit that IFPMA proposed a code of marketing
practice to be adopted voluntarily by the member associations of
each country.[16] The code has sufficient escape clauses to please the
most pedantic marketing manager. Thus

> statements in promotional communications should be based on
> substantial scientific evidence *or other responsible medical
> opinion*. . . .

> particular care should be taken that essential information as to
> pharmaceutical products' safety, contra-indications and side-
> effects or toxic hazards is appropriately and consistently com-
> municated *subject to the legal, regulatory and medical practices of
> each nation*

> samples may be supplied to the medical and allied professions to
> familiarize them with the products, to enable them to gain
> experience with the products in their practice, *or upon request*. (My
> italics.)

The importance of this code was not that it represented a major change in the position of the industry, nor that it was likely to produce major changes in the behaviour of individual companies. Its significance, noted an industry-watcher like *Scrip*, was that it anticipated by a month the 1981 World Health Assembly at which it had been expected that a resolution to control drug marketing practices might be presented. '*Scrip* understands that the drawing-up by the IFPMA of a Code of Pharmaceutical Marketing Practices may well have pre-empted any WHO activity in this area.'[17] The US PMA immediately became the first IFPMA member to adopt the code.

In similar vein, IFPMA member associations offered to give training in quality-control techniques to Third World technicians. 'The scheme has taken rather longer to get started than we had anticipated (not, I hasten to add, through any delay on the part of the pharmaceutical industry),' reported Michael Peretz to the Tenth IFPMA Congress in Madrid.[18] On the subject of the WHO/UNICEF Expanded Programme on Immunization, he continued to labour the tardiness of the international organizations:

> This programme is, of course, of special interest to those members of our industry who are involved in the manufacture of sera and vaccines and I should explain that these companies are most concerned at the lack of forward requirement estimates that should by now have become available from WHO and UNICEF.

These jibes can be seen as part of a calculated attempt to gain the initiative and also to discredit the recommendations of international organizations like the WHO, UNCTAD, UNICEF and UNIDO. This is important to the companies. 'Such resolutions and recommendations . . . have politically relevant effects,' says the formal version of Burkhard Wenger's 'bloop' theory.

> In fact, according to new theories in international law, a 'quasi-legal' significance. One refers in this respect to 'soft law'. It is to be assumed that the principles . . . will penetrate into the consideration of decision-makers and reappear, sooner or later, in the [enforceable] national laws.[19]

This is all part of the cut and thrust of international negotiations. Forget for the moment that the subject is the health, or at least the access to basic drugs, of the majority of the world's people. These are theoretical games played in political arenas far removed from reality. Corporate response to initiatives designed to put the theories into practice, be they by individuals, companies or governments, are more down to earth.

The personal and the political

Dr John S. Yudkin is interested in questions of drugs policy and in promoting the rational use of drugs. So, while in Tanzania between 1975 and 1977, he studied actual patterns of drug use in the country, with the encouragement of the Ministry of Health. His findings, some of which have already been referred to, were disturbing. He found dangerous drugs used without any need; ineffective drugs prescribed where more effective remedies were available; expensive drugs bought while cheaper and more appropriate products ran out of stock; promotion of drugs bearing little relation to the health needs of the country or the information needs of the doctors. Throughout, he focused on the major multinationals because, all too often, the expensive, dangerous, over-promoted or ineffective drugs were their products.

Yudkin's work has been widely and respectably published.[20] It runs counter to the interests of the multinationals. That was no reason, however, for Michael Peretz to allege, in conversation with me, that Yudkin 'admitted to me that he was a Marxist'; that 'he was thrown out of the country at twenty-four hours' notice and would not be allowed back'; or that 'his views are not worth tuppence to the Tanzanians.'

What appears to be a 'red smear' is just that. People present at Yudkin's one encounter with Peretz confirm that no such statement was made; the allegation that Yudkin was thrown out of the country at twenty-four hours' notice is untrue—as is clear from his passport, which I have seen. As to the value placed on his findings by the Tanzanians, a letter from the then Minister of Health confirms that his efforts were appreciated at the highest level and that they were having a useful impact on the resolution of local problems.

Sensibly, Michael Peretz declined to commit his comments to paper. 'I have no knowledge as to Dr John Yudkin's standing with the Tanzanian health authorities,' he wrote.[21] 'What I believe I said to you during our informal discussions was that in all my own talks with government health officials from Tanzania at United Nations Agency meetings, I have never heard them quote his views.'

The unwillingness of Mr Peretz to put his personal attacks on paper is nothing new. In 1977, over lunch with John Yudkin's former professor of pharmacology, he raised many questions about the factual accuracy of the Tanzanian work, in particular a report submitted to the Minister of Health. Yudkin wrote to Peretz, asking him to 'provide me with a list of those points which you feel are incorrect'.[22] Peretz, by then well on his way up the ladder to IFPMA as president of the British industry organization ABPI, ducked the challenge.[23]

I detail this specific case because it shows how sensitive the companies are to the opportunities offered by internal dissension among their critics. In all countries there is political tension between medical practitioners who would like the maximum of freedom and the maximum of resources and health ministry officials; it is particularly acute in a country facing financial problems as serious as those f Tanzania. There is tension, too, between expatriates who share tnese realities for just a short time and can act without fear of the long-term consequences for their careers, and local health workers. Yudkin's comment, in the report he submitted to the Tanzanian Minister of Health, that 'the main expenditure is at the larger hospitals and the Muhimbili is the front-runner among these', could not have endeared him to his superiors at the Muhimbili Teaching Hospital, putting as it did a powerful weapon in the hands of the Ministry men charged with making economies.

Clearly, it is in the corporate interest to foment these tensions if this helps to detract from the work of their critics. So starting from one partially justified complaint, 'that Dr Yudkin left the country without presenting [his study] before a practice seminar for criticism', the attack was mounted, by word of mouth.[24] (He did try to arrange a meeting in the fortnight before he left but it could not be incorporated in university schedules.) It was even suggested that Yudkin was the agent of British drug companies trying to discredit their European competitors.

Black propaganda against Zimbabwe

Character assassination of individual opponents is matched by the systematic denigration of individual companies which present a challenge to the multinationals. The experience of CAPS in Zimbabwe is educative. Thirty per cent of their pharmaceutical sales once went to South Africa. Immediately after independence in 1980 a disturbing phenomenon emerged. The word began to get around, as Henry Briscoe told me, that 'This is now a black country, so they'll buy any junk from anywhere, so be careful buying your pharmaceuticals from them. . . . this was a campaign by some of the competitor companies to get us out of the market.'

'Black propaganda' Briscoe aptly called it. But it was not his first experience of this tactic being used against his company by his multinational competitors. When CAPS was first established

> the representatives of the other companies lost no opportunities in those days of sowing the seed of doubt in the minds of doctors and pharmacists—'look, it is dangerous to buy from these guys'—we had a lot of trouble and a lot of black propaganda, if I may call it that, against us.

His experience is, of course, by no means unique. The constant references to the poor quality of Indian and Eastern European drugs are so much multinational *muzak*. The Indian drug exporters will testify to the way in which racism has been developed and exploited as a sales tool by the multinationals. In the field of cheap bulk drugs, India and the countries of Eastern Europe are formidable competitors. The multinationals have no desire to compete with them on price. So they have chosen quality as their field of battle. Where there are demonstrable shortcomings, or in the case of those few products where bio-availability is a particular problem, that is unobjectionable. Unfortunately, the multinational industry has shown itself prone to the temptation to invent evidence where none exists.

The best examples come not from the developing world but from the USA where these matters are well documented. There the FDA had to consider installing a special telephone to deal with reports that big companies were spreading false rumours about the quality problems of their generic competitors. Such false reports caused the hydrochlorothiazide (an out-of-patent Ciba diuretic) manufactured by the small generic company, Bolar, to be suspended from the valuable US Army market. The reports indicated that some patients improved only after the Ciba-made product was substituted for Bolar's generic equivalent, but FDA enquiries revealed that they had 'recovered' before they received the Ciba drug. At stake at the time were large government contracts for generic drugs. 'There is speculation', it was reported from Washington, 'that intensely competitive marketing measures by some firms have led to the generation of a number of unfounded reports of "therapy failures" at a time when government supply contracts are being renewed.'[25]

In fact, evidence from the USA suggests that the quality problems of drugs produced by small companies are not very different to those of the multinationals. Indeed, many multinationals have some of their products made by generic companies under contract. Donald Kennedy, then Commissioner of the FDA, concluded:

> The tests we conduct here . . . provide no evidence of widespread differences in quality between the products of large versus small firms. Only a small percentage of drugs do not comply with standards of quality, purity and potency, and when a drug deviates from the standard, it is just as likely to be a brand name as a generic drug.[26]

A widespread and insidious campaign

Against this background, the response of the multinational industry to the attempt of one country to rationalize its drugs policies can be better understood. The four main facets of the policy implemented by the Sri Lankan government in 1972 were:
—the centralization of all pharmaceutical imports;
—a reduction in the number of drugs imported and the liberalization of patent law to enable them to be bought from a wider range of sources;
—the replacement of brand names by generic names;
—the promotion of drug production geared to the health needs of the country rather than to the most profitable private markets.

These measures were a clear challenge to the five multinationals which manufactured drugs on the island. The aim was principally to save foreign currency, thus reducing, or at best maintaining, the value of the market. The multinationals' market share was also threatened. Their response was led by the American PMA whose president, Joseph Stetler, wrote personally to the Sri Lankan Prime Minister outlining his numerous objections to the scheme which, he said, 'calls in question the Government's position with respect to all foreign investment in Sri Lanka'. While Mr Stetler blustered in the USA, his member companies, through their local subsidiaries and agents, launched a formidable campaign intended to sow discontent with the policies.

> A widespread and insidious campaign of denigrating low-cost suppliers was launched. And a second source of opposition, the private practitioners, were drawn into the campaign. Reports were made of drugs being ineffective, substandard or toxic but little hard evidence was produced.[27]

The private doctors were also enlisted in the battle against the limited drugs lists. When drugs were to be chosen for the national formulary, the government brought private doctors on to the selection committee as a gesture of conciliation to a group potentially hostile to the new policies. The multinationals, through their salesmen, lobbied hard to promote their most profitable products as candidates for the lists. Here, the drug authorities took a self-confessed conciliatory line. They gave in over the more controversial products such as soluble aspirin, which has no benefit over its common equivalent except for the high profit margins which it can sustain.

The conflict reached a crisis over plans to rationalize production. These aimed to limit local production to the formulation of thirty-four basic drugs, raw material for which would have been imported through the State Pharmaceutical Corporation (SPC), to ensure that the price paid was reasonable. After protracted negotiations, four of the multinationals agreed to cooperate, although with great reluct-ance. The last, Pfizer, refused and stalled successfully for nearly four years. The company objected to being forced to use raw material provided by the SPC, on the grounds that its quality could not be guaranteed—although the main product in question, tetracycline, was to be supplied by Hoechst whose reputation for quality is at least as good as that of Pfizer. The real issue was that Pfizer had traditionally paid its parent company $99 per kilogram while Hoechst was offering to supply it for just $20.

When the Sri Lankan government considered nationalizing the company as a last resort to force its compliance, the company brought the big guns to bear. The American Ambassador called on the Prime Minister and indicated that the supply of food aid from his country would be put in serious jeopardy by such an action. This was a serious threat to a country then suffering from acute food shortages. So the government backed down, even though to do so meant spending more foreign exchange on drugs and thus increasing its dependence on 'food aid'.

The Sri Lankan experiment ended in July 1977 with the demise of Mrs Sirimavo Bandaranaike's government and the installation of the 'free trade'-oriented United National Party which had little sympathy for the pharmaceutical policies implemented by its pre-decessors.

To judge by the extent to which the multinationals have misrepre-sented the experience of those five years between 1972 and 1977 in Sri Lanka, they must have perceived it as an enormous challenge to their position. Even when the danger was removed, they apparently felt compelled to try to bury the experiment for ever. So when UNCTAD published the report prepared by the late Dr Senaka Bibile, former chairman of the SPC and professor of pharmacology at the University of Sri Lanka, the companies responded aggressively.[28] Attacking the report as 'unsound and distorted', they called for it to be withdrawn and given no further circulation.[29]

IFPMA's thirty-three-page response relies heavily on a paper prepared by the so-called Public Interest Committee. Since this subsequently formed the basis of the new government's pharmaceutical policy, its comments are of questionable objectivity. IFPMA's response itself leaves a great deal to be desired on questions of fact and accuracy. Thus Dr Bibile said in his report that local drug manufacture had traditionally been restricted to highly profitable but unimportant formulations. 'Without foundation,' retorted the IFPMA, justifying this by saying that all products made were included in the national formulary. What Dr Bibile had said is there for all to read:

> Vitamin preparations, soluble aspirin and cough remedies accounted for over 50 per cent of production. They were elegantly presented, heavily promoted, expensive and used by the affluent. For example, the two largest firms made eighteen combinations of vitamins, with or without iron, which were swallowed by the well nourished who did not need them. The undernourished could not afford to buy them.

IFPMA ducked this clearly defined criticism. Dr Bibile wrote:

> Profits after taxes and contributions to the government consolidated fund are marginal, as indeed they must be to provide drugs at minimal prices to the consumer.

Again, IFPMA wilfully misread the text.

> If this is intended to mean that the retail prices of products procured by the SPC were either lower than those applicable under the previous system of private sector importation or set at levels which gave the SPC a very low profit margin, it is not in accordance with the true facts.

Dr Bibile, of course, never intended anything of the kind. He made no claim that the SPC had reduced retail prices at a time of high inflation when the value of Sri Lanka's currency was falling:

Although inflation and adverse parity rates have resulted in increased prices for drugs, they are lower than might have obtained if traditional suppliers had been on the market.

What prompted IFPMA to fabricate such criticisms? Which elements of the policy were perceived as such a particular threat to the multinational industry? In themselves, the individual policy elements were neither unique nor particularly challenging, with the possible exception of the extension of limited drugs lists to the private as well as the public sector and the attempt by a small, relatively weak country to control the imports of raw materials for drug manufacture (as India does routinely). Perhaps the real challenge lay in the construction of an efficient, rational drug supply system in which the limited role for the multinationals was clearly defined and controlled. Had it succeeded, it might have served as a model policy package for other small, poor countries at a time when the industry urgently needed to delay such reforms.

Big brother and delaying tactics

Because of the wide-ranging nature of Sri Lanka's efforts and the industry's multi-faceted response, it is a good example of the forms that the companies' practical reaction may take. Usually the elements of their response are seen to be operating singly. A method that is frequently relied on is the quick recourse to home-country governments when the big-stick approach is needed.

In India, when the government proposed to introduce its generic name policy, the West German companies dropped dark hints that this would infringe the Indian-German free trade agreement. In Tanzania, the West Germans seemed to consider their embassy as a fully-fledged pharmaceutical company subsidiary. In Brazil, it was not the companies but the West German embassy itself which delivered a memorandum protesting about inadequate price increases for drugs and warning that this could affect German cooperation in other areas of industry.[30] Meanwhile, a British member of the European Parliament used that forum to protest against the apparently innocuous attempt by Nigeria to guarantee the quality of its drugs and reduce corruption in their purchase by using the international organization of SGS (*Société Générale de Surveillance*) to check financial and technical data for each consignment of imported drugs. To ask drug companies how their 'promotional costs' were calculated, constituted a restrictive trade practice which might breach the Lomé agreement, claimed Andrew Pearce, and he called for action to end the practice.[31]

Delaying tactics are also much favoured, a point not lost on the Indian *Eastern Pharmacist*:

> It is more than five years since the Union Health Ministry published draft regulations to curb the wasteful use of vitamins in pharmaceutical preparations. On one ground or another, implementation of these regulations has been delayed. The industry has also been adopting several tactics to stall the regulations. Its latest manoeuvre is to submit mass representations to the government stating that in the context of the inflationary conditions prevailing today, the prices fixed earlier for revised vitamin formulations cannot be valid.

The journal hoped that the government would not allow itself to be led back to the beginning again but would move to introduce the controls:

> If the regulations become effective, India would be one of the few countries in the world to regulate the content of vitamins in drugs, a measure which will not only safeguard the health interests of the population but also conserve foreign exchange substantially. It is needless to emphasize that regulations delayed are regulations foiled.[32]

Getting in close to write the agenda

As they entered the 1980s, delaying tactics on all fronts must have appeared eminently attractive to the multinationals. They had acknowledged the need for a new approach, but the bigger you are, the longer it takes to stop or change direction even when you know where you want to go. As Lewis Engman of the American PMA emphasized in 1979, the industry could not continue to be simply reactive. It had to start writing the agenda if it wanted to control the course of events. Engman went into detail. The industry had to be weaned away from 'firefighting' to seek 'a new positive impact on public policy'. 'We must help shape public understanding of the major issues involved.' He stressed the importance of talking to critics. 'Where Mr Stetler tended to be distant, Mr Engman will get in close,' commented *Scrip*, or—as Engman himself put it—'It's far harder for someone to stand up at a public meeting and abuse you if that morning you sat down together at breakfast; even if over breakfast you could not agree on a single issue.'[33] He chose not to mention that it is the industry's aim to be breakfast-time host as well as the arbiter of what gets talked about over the orange juice and coffee.

The American companies had been slow to respond to changing circumstances in the Third World. As late as September 1978 Joseph Stetler, then still head of the PMA, was saying that it would be poor business practice to support the WHO's essential drug lists, and that to sell drugs to poor countries at discount prices would also be against American business law.[34] The American response was in fact already in preparation. It began formally in January 1979 with a conference on pharmaceuticals for developing countries organized by the prestigious Institute of Medicine of the National Academy of Sciences; it was in fact as much the idea of the US PMA as of the American politicians who formally proposed it.[35] Senator Edward Kennedy, who opened it, enthused over the WHO's list of essential drugs. But the concrete proposals came from Dr William Hubbard, president of the Upjohn company. He outlined a strategy to increase the role of the US companies in solving the poorer countries' health needs. The first stage would be to set up aid programmes to get drugs to people who could not otherwise afford them. To do this, he said, it would also be necessary to reinforce their health services, the better to absorb the increased flow of medicines.[36]

The focus now shifts to 680 Fifth Avenue, New York, home of the Center for Public Resources, an American business and foundation-financed organization.

> created to develop new pragmatic methods to utilize business resources in meeting human needs, and to mobilize outstanding business and public leaders to implement those strategies. Its agenda is to construct business roles based on market incentives and on new approaches to public/private partnerships.[37]

To quote its own words:

> In keeping with its objective, CPR initiated a program with the Rockefeller Foundation and the pharmaceutical industry to increase industry roles in developing country health by improving drug development and availability for third and fourth world countries.[38]

It helped to draw up the agenda for the Institute of Medicine Conference:

CPR identified for the Conference a range of opportunities for stimulating industry roles in LDC [less developed countries] health: incentives, removal of regulatory and other disincentives, and opportunities for public–private partnerships.

Upjohn's William Hubbard was one of the eight-man steering committee which, after the conference, drew up the agenda for another get-together, the first meeting of the CPR Pharmaceutical Program. From this emerged the concrete plan for action. Initial proposals for execution by the Task Force were:
—the establishment of a Drug and Vaccine Development Corporation to help turn the products of academic research into available medicine with the help of the pharmaceutical industry;
—the establishment of a Scientific Tribunal 'to resolve issues relative to the safety and efficacy of existing drugs';
—promotion of a scheme by which US drug companies would sell their products to the government to be distributed to Third World countries in the same way as US farmers' surplus is distributed as 'food aid' under the PL 480 scheme.[39]
In addition, the Task Force also proposed the establishment of a pilot programme in one country 'carefully selected for its favourable environment' to treat specific diseases using a limited number of proven drugs, and the creation of an industry-sponsored 'fellows program' to train selected Third World health managers and researchers.

These decisions about the needs of the Third World once taken, it was then necessary to find people from the Third World to take part:

To be fully effective, the CPR Pharmaceutical Program will require involvement of representatives from the developing countries themselves. As an immediate next step, CPR will identify a group of 10–15 LDC advisors, who will assist CPR in its on-going program and will participate in various working groups.[40]

Dr Hubbard had emphasized at the Institute of Medicine meeting in 1979 that his strategy was unlikely to show any clear benefits for the first five years. Vaccine technologies were advancing so fast, however, that formation of the Drug and Vaccine Development Corporation had to be given priority if it were to be able to take advantage of the opportunities which were becoming available. Accordingly, CPR was able to report to the Task Force Meeting in March 1981 that 'the DVDC is fully incorporated and an outstanding Advisory Board has been formed.'[41] There is an air of inevitability about much of this. The Drug and Vaccine Development Corporation links many of the research activities of the Rockefeller Foundation and would, one suspects, have come into existence even without the CPR, given the many research efforts ready to leave Rockefeller-funded laboratories for field development.

Surrogate markets for drug aid

The same cannot be said of the considerably more complex business of turning the drug aid programme into a reality. CPR's analysis of the problem of drug supply in Third World health had focused on the shortage of money in general and on the shortage of money for health in particular. This, it said, affects both the purchase of drugs by the countries themselves and the willingness of the multinational companies to produce new drugs for the diseases prevalent in them.

> Until LDCs can afford adequate supplies of tropical disease drugs, the incentive for industry to provide these drugs lies in the creation of *surrogate markets*, with national or international aid programs absorbing the cost of supplying essential drugs.[42] (My italics.)

By November 1980 the proposal had begun to take shape. Operating on a similar basis to the US government's 'Food for Peace' scheme (PL 480), the aid programme would aim to 'improve the availability of pharmaceuticals in developing countries'.

> The US would provide loans . . . to selected developing countries to cover the cost of importing pharmaceuticals that are needed and requested by the recipient country. Such pharmaceuticals would be imported directly from the US or, with appropriate waivers, purchased from overseas subsidiaries of US companies located in developing countries. Procurement would be by competitive bidding.

Of course there would be strings attached for the countries on the receiving end:
—drugs would be supplied only if extra investments were made in health care generally;
—drugs and vaccines supplied were expected to reach appropriate target groups (mainly the urban and rural poor, said the working group);
—the drug aid must help to generate pharmaceutical consumption which would eventually be paid for by the country itself.

Drug aid would be popular with the governments of developing countries because it would not tie them to specific projects. It would be equally popular in the USA because it had 'the potential to significantly enhance the policy influence of the donor governments'.

Health officials in the developing countries were also expected to be enthusiastic about the scheme. While the bait for the finance ministries was the fact that foreign pharmaceuticals could be bought with local currency instead of hard dollars, the health ministries would be hooked by the idea that the loans would only be 'forgiven' if an equivalent amount of local money was pumped into health care:

Attaching this sort of condition to the loan forgiveness feature would give ministries of health additional leverage in requesting increased sector funding from ministries of finance and planning. An infusion of local currency into the health sector would cancel a dollar repayment obligation thereby both encouraging investment in the health sector and reducing the general debt burden of the economy.

Why, if the CPR is so concerned about helping to improve health in developing countries, do they not just lobby for a greater share of the US aid budget to go there?

There is one overwhelming practical reason for preferring the commodity approach: it is politically more acceptable in donor countries. This preference reflects . . . the desire to promote donor country [e.g. US] exports as part of the foreign assistance effort.

It would also enable sceptics to see where the money went. CPR estimated that the value of drugs distributed under this scheme could run into hundreds of millions of dollars.[43]

By April 1981 CPR felt that the task was now up to others, and its proposal was despatched to fight its way through the legislative underground of American government. While CPR would continue to offer support to interested parties, 'the Program has taken its role in this area to the limits of its mandate; the responsibility for further action rests elsewhere.'[44]

Drug utilization—a blank page

One maverick item appeared suddenly in the CPR Pharmaceutical Program 1981 Annual Report—a project to investigate drug utilization. The difficulty of achieving the final step in drugs delivery—appropriate use—is acknowledged. 'The myriad of technical behavioral barriers encountered at this stage of the delivery system are the most difficult to resolve,' says the report. So it proposed, not to investigate problems of drug use in a typical community, but to look at health schemes set up by private mining and plantation companies—to demonstrate the benefits of drug utilization under the best possible conditions. It seemed a particularly ill-conceived idea, reflecting the general lack of interest in the use as opposed to the supply of drugs.

Ciba-Geigy Pharma and the Third World: Facts and Issues, the bulky loose-leaf handbook which, with a companion volume about the rich countries, is given to all managers who might have to respond to public questions, has a page labelled 'drug utilization'. In April 1981 it was still blank. The Pharma Policy Unit had not managed to write it yet, they told me.

I went to see Ciba because they had, at the time, the reputation of being the most open and approachable company. Indeed, they were. Their directors had taken a policy decision that the best way to deal with critics was to meet them face to face rather than close the door on them. At Ciba, Lewis Engman's recommendations for the US companies were already standard practice. The company's 1979 annual report explains:

To ward off often quite unjustified attacks calls for a high level of political awareness. The fostering of this awareness both in Switzerland and throughout the Group by means of systematic training of managers was one of the prime concerns of the Pharmaceuticals Division during the year under review.

Before going into any more detail about Ciba's professed policy changes, it is as well to give a word of qualification. Ciba managers are advised to give information, but only up to a point. That at least is the gist of the advice in the first section of that fat handbook, 'How to Use *Ciba-Geigy Pharma and the Third World: Facts and Issues*'. It encourages users to offer copies of the book's loose-leaf pages to outsiders but says that in no circumstance should they be given access to the whole handbook. Further, specific questions should be avoided: 'Point 8. Try to generalize the issues whenever specific questions are asked.' With that caution, here is the story of Ciba's response to the new aspirations of the Third World, as they tell it.

A powerful approach to planning

In the 1960s and early 1970s, there was, among the pharmaceutical companies as elsewhere, a fashion for fancy mathematical models which tried to predict, with a high degree of accuracy, how companies would perform over a period as long as, in Ciba's case, eleven years. The mathematics failed to forecast essential, if unpredictable, factors such as oil price rises, world-wide inflation and the recession that marked the 1970s. The result was fiasco for the industry's planners. Ciba-Geigy for one had been projected to reach sales of well over 20 billion Swiss francs by 1980. It failed to reach half that target.

As a result, many companies gave less attention to planning and concentrated on short-term activities which seemed subjectable to a greater degree of control. Ciba opted for more planning, but of a different kind. They introduced a system that aimed to make the company more flexible and adaptable, better able to spread risks and withstand setbacks. In so doing, they changed drastically their style of management. The idea was deceptively simple—to work out a *leitbild* (which translates somewhere between strategy and guideline) for each part of the corporation as well as for the main group company itself. The *leitbilden* are general agreements about possible directions in which the company may develop over the next fifteen or twenty years, rather than precise plans. They are evolved through discussions within each level of the company and between the various levels of management, the process aiming as much to involve and establish consensus as to produce firm proposals.[45]

It was through this sort of planning that Ciba decided to get more, not less, involved in the Third World and to talk more, not less, to its critics. In 1976, after a *leitbild* had been successfully implemented in one division of the company, agrichemicals, the new process was introduced throughout. Soon each division had its own *leitbild*. These covered not only such questions as the type of products to be developed, the areas in which diversification might be profitable and so on; they also included broader issues like the Third World pharmaceutical policy debate.

Producing a future for the developing countries

Marketing man Fritz Schneiter is implementing part of the future vision. He explained how the company's current Third World outlook had developed:

In 1974, under the influence of the head of marketing, a project team was set up which proposed the establishment of a Task Force called PRODECO (Products for Developing Countries). This was intended to look more closely at the needs of those countries because it was recognized that a growing proportion of all research-based companies' production would be directed to these countries.

These were investigated in 'dialogues with the periphery', but progress was slow. Sure enough, the studies revealed that the countries of the Third World had problems of inadequate health structures, that they were committed to particular ideas about how drugs should be bought; and it was clear that the volume of drugs distributed within them had to be increased.

Was there a gap that Ciba could fill? Yes, said the authors of the divisional *leitbild*. So in May 1977 it was decided to set up a project team to establish an organization which would dedicate itself to supplying the drugs that later on in the year were to be selected by the WHO as 'essential'. There were good reasons for Ciba to do this. 'We had few drugs in the essential list,' says Schneiter. There were a few that were out of patent but the bulk of their range was not represented.

In April 1978 the new Ciba subsidiary, Servipharm, was officially launched. It offers, claims the publicity handout, 'top quality pharmaceuticals at economic prices' with more besides. Schneiter says:

> The aim of Servipharm is not just to supply drugs to countries but also know-how. About planning, distribution, storage, importing, control and even production. We can let the developing countries have the benefit of our know-how and experience. This we can give away without harming our business.

Where do the products come from? The original idea was that Servipharm should be merely a broker. 'Initially, we went out and bought the products of other manufacturers in bulk and repacked them.' In particular, it used the countries of Eastern Europe with which it had barter agreements. Then, because of quality problems, claims Schneiter, Servipharm switched to buying raw material to be formulated at Ciba factories. The number of tableting and bottling machines that were lying idle might also have had something to do with this decision, he admits. The company would not give details of the current size of Servipharm sales except to say that they were still insignificant in terms of the company as a whole. Its hopes were for the future. The company was already active in sixty countries and is expected 'to have a sizeable portion of the Third World market'.

Ciba's service package and its importance

Its 'service' activities were also slow to get off the ground. Help was offered to Kuwait in the design of a pharmaceutical factory. The United Arab Emirates was offered a feasibility study of a proposal to set up a quality-control laboratory there. In Uganda, help was offered in re-establishing the pharmaceutical services in that shattered nation. 'It is an antagonistic milieu,' Schneiter complained. 'People are so suspicious of anyone who is giving anything away.'

Fritz Schneiter is probably too close to the day-to-day life of the market place to have much taste for these soft activities. So I turned again to Klaus von Grebmer. He had joined Ciba in 1976 when his boss Dr von Wartburg was recruited to set up the pharmaceutical policy unit and Ciba's Director Ernst Vischer took on responsibility for IFPMA's Task Force on International Organizations. So he is well placed to put the service concept into the context of the general debate over Third World pharmaceutical policy.

Within the company, von Grebmer said, managers are too closely tied to reports and results. They cannot accept a policy that implies a temporary loss of business in return for gaining more later. What matters to them is getting the figures right on target. The conservatives fight shy of entering the government bulk supply business in a big way. They argue that promoting to the individual doctor is what Ciba knows best and should continue to do. 'What they have to realize is that although they talk about being a free market industry, much of the business is with the state.'

Since this is probably a trend that is beyond the influence of the drug companies, they should start adapting to it. What this has meant in the USA is that Ciba moved to join many of its US multinational rivals in selling generic drugs. In the Third World, von Grebmer reads major significance into the involvement in health of institutions such as the World Bank, with the likelihood that they will generate significant drug sales. It is in these areas that he sees the 'service' ideal of Servipharm being realized. If health care in the Third World is going to be packaged into aid projects with clear targets, companies like Ciba-Geigy could have an interesting role to play.

When I was in Peru, I talked to the health minister there and put it to him: What would be the possibility of setting up some sort of contract to reduce, say, the incidence of tuberculosis in the north-east of the country from 10 per cent to 1 per cent over a fixed period?'

In Latin America, says von Grebmer, the infrastructure already exists to make such ideas feasible. A company like Ciba could not actually treat patients—that would have to remain the prerogative of the local health workers. But they would be very well equipped to supply the necessary organization, support and drugs to enable them to do so.

The idea might arouse suspicions, he acknowledged. But Ciba had already worked like this for years in agrochemicals and no one had questioned it. The company has cooperated in a low-key way in this kind of health project for some time. In the Sudan, it tagged on to a programme of its agrochemical division to supply anti-malarials in a project intended to eradicate the insect vectors of disease. In Indonesia, it took part in small-scale tuberculosis control trials designed to be greatly expanded in the near future. Dr Oliver de S. Pinto spelled out clearly to Ciba managers the importance of such cooperation:

> Although most of the use of Rimactane is aimed to the individual treatment of tuberculosis, we are also deeply involved in several projects in which rifampicin is being used as part of schemes aimed at the overall prevention of tuberculosis in entire communities. Our active participation in such schemes can result in a preference for Ciba-Geigy Rimactane instead of someone else's rifampicin and at the same time helps us to identify other pharmaceuticals used in such schemes so that we can consider producing them as well, either as a service to sell our original product or to increase our product range.[46]

To serve the Third World? A question of structure

Ciba has seen that participation in community-health pilot schemes will help it acquire new business, just as clinical trials of new drugs are a routine form of promotion for new drugs in the rich world. So is its particularly positive approach to Third World drug needs nothing but a small adaptation of its present business methods?

The difference between its attitude to generic drugs, and that of Hoffmann-La Roche, gives some clues. Roche says that it is opposed to the idea of entering the market for generic drugs. This is something of a contradiction. Until the discovery of Valium and Librium, the company was best known as a producer of cheap bulk vitamins. It is still a leader in this field. But Roche does not consider vitamins as pharmaceuticals, but rather as fine chemicals. 'It is not generics, it is large volume chemical production,' says Peter Schurch. The fact is that its vitamins are sold as other companies sell generic drugs. What is agreed is that it would not be to Roche's advantage to expand disproportionately that side of its business. The investment costs are high and profits don't match those of speciality pharmaceuticals. 'We don't like it so much,' says Schurch of his company's vitamin business. 'It consumes an enormous amount of liquidity. We'd prefer to have two pharma divisions.'

There are, however, advantages in having some bread-and-butter business. Ciba's pharmaceuticals division is not particularly strong in the production of basic pharmaceuticals. There is a case for redressing the balance and developing the manufacture of basic pharmaceutical chemicals, especially if there are going to be generic markets to which the company can sell, trading on its reputation as a producer of speciality drugs. This will give it something to fall back on if the speciality market stagnates, a possibility which is very much in the minds of the company's directors:

sales increases should not be taken for granted, since despite the fact that the world pharmaceuticals market is growing, there are clear signs of stagnation in certain areas. . . . The increasing share of Third World countries, which together are now roughly equal in importance to the pharmaceutical market in the USA is in keeping with a deliberate policy on our part.[47]

Ciba's decision to enter with such gusto into the Third World, by contrast with Roche's reluctance, is as much a function of the two different corporate structures, and the opportunities and constraints which they present, as of any conversion to the cause of the poor. Underlying its planning process is 'the conclusion that the only constant factor in the business environment will be change itself—in other words, Ciba-Geigy managers must be continually re-thinking their attitudes, projects and actions.'[48]

The company may be better prepared for change and its managers more aware of the issues with which they are faced, but that does not necessarily make its actions very different from its competitors'. The evidence is that when it comes to controversial issues such as those catalogued in the first half of this book, Ciba's response is much the same as that of the less accessible companies.

Servipharm had entered first those markets where there was no drug registration and licensing procedure, or where it was perfunctory and therefore quick, Fritz Schneiter explained to me. These included countries where old-formulation Cibalgin had continued to be sold long after it was supposed officially to have been withdrawn. Yet Schneiter's boss, Gaudenz Staehelin, head of the Ciba Pharmaceuticals Divison, explained that the old amidopyrine-containing Cibalgin could not be withdrawn until the new version was approved by drug control authorities. 'They have to be informed and they have to give consent to any new formulation. This can take a very, very long time.'[49] Particularly, one may add, when the delay is to your advantage.

Similarly, one Ciba manager assured me that Servipharm products would not be manufactured in South Africa—this would not help them to enter other African markets. Yet they were at the time preparing to do just that, according to one of his colleagues.

There is a clear limit to the frankness which Ciba encourages in its employees. So investigators in the Philippines were assured by the local Ciba manager, Mr Lucas, that Filipino drug authorities had told the company that 'we could continue to dispose of existing stocks' of old Cibalgin. The interview terminated abruptly when they pressed for more details. 'I'm sorry, I think we should stop,' said Ciba's open-door man. For the record, Dr Arsenio Regala, the head of the Philippine Food and Drug Administration, emphatically denied that any such agreement had been made.[50]

Nevertheless, although Ciba has tried as hard as any other company to resolve the conflicts between Third World needs and corporate profitability, the problem remains.

The element of personal dishonesty

When the WHO essential drugs list was first published and I had to write a response to it, I went down to see one of the pharmacists, an old man, who knows about these things. 'I'll show you something,' he said, and reached into one of his drawers and pulled out a list of drugs. 'This is what we keep stockpiled for emergencies!' He belonged to the Swiss Chemical Industry Committee for Economic Planning for War and Emergencies, one of whose tasks it is 'to procure and assure the supply of vital goods in the sector of chemicals and pharmaceuticals needed for the population and the army'.[51] The list was almost identical to that of the WHO, with some obvious differences—more products for treating wounds and fewer for tropical diseases. Of course, he told me, the essential drugs list makes sense—in emergencies. And, for most of the developing countries, the situation is one of permanent crisis.

Well-briefed, my informant then returned to his office to write the industry's official response—a damning criticism of the WHO's essential drugs list.

This is what I mean when I say that for many of the people working within the industry there is a conflict or a problem which cannot be resolved. And it is not restricted to this one example. What, I asked Dr Berneker of Ciba's Medical Department, would you do if you had a drug like clonidine which had well-proven dangers for those who abruptly stopped taking it, if you were presented with a utilization survey from one of your markets which showed that the majority of patients did just that? The answer came easily, clonidine belonging to another company, a competitor at that, 'I'd recommend that it be taken off that market.' Yet Dr Berneker still defends the sale of amidopyrine over the counter with no adequate warning.

There was also a comment from a manager whose job appears to be to dissuade international agencies and national governments from taking too great an interest in drug purchasing. He agreed that centralized buying made sense. It didn't even have to be too formally organized.

What those countries need to do is to come over here and find somebody like that Hans, you know, someone who really knows the markets; pay him three times the salary and get him to take charge of drug buying. He'd save them his salary within months. The trouble is that in too many countries, they don't get good people to do the job; it goes to a friend of the Minister or a cousin who knows nothing about it.

Michael Peretz also has a personal point of view. 'Surely,' I put it to him, at the end of our discussion, 'the most sensible policy for a poorer developing country would be to set up a central buying agency and buy only cheap generic name drugs.' 'If you can guarantee the quality, yes,' he agreed. Quality would, I concurred, cost a little more, but that need not upset the basic conclusion. So why then did IFPMA obstruct moves by the international organizations such as the WHO to promote such policies? 'You can't expect us to support policies which run counter to our own interests.'

Coming out ahead

The industry's response has certainly been positive. The majority of companies have now explored, with more or less enthusiasm, the primary health-care needs of the Third World. They have taken stock of their own capacities to contribute to the delivery of this care. Companies geared to the needs of the rich and the old may now choose to stay out—Astra of Sweden's decision to leave the Brazilian market is a pointer here. Some companies may find other areas of business more attractive, especially those US-based companies whose entry into the Third World has been relatively recent and for whom the prospect of expansion through generic drug sales may not promise much in the way of profitability.[52]

Meanwhile, those companies which find themselves with the right production capacity and market presence have already geared themselves to doing business in primary health care. They will sell essential drugs at cut prices. But always, they will have their eyes on the bottom line of the balance sheet: 'They are not interested in becoming welfare organizations. . . . It's just their perception that they will come out ahead in the long run by doing it that way.'

That is not my opinion. Those are the impeccably authoritative tones of the pharmaceutical industry speaking with the voice of Joe Stetler about the plans of the German and Swiss companies to cooperate with Third World countries in the supply of essential drugs, just months before the US PMA decided to do the same.[53]

The other side of their response is the companies' admitted efforts to obstruct, their apparently deliberate lack of cooperation with attempts to deliver primary health care and end the wasteful abuse of medicine where these will cost them money. So they will accept essential drugs for under-served poor communities but not the application of rational drugs policies in the richer strata of the community where they already have profitable markets; local production may be acceptable if the companies can trade their know-how in establishing it for patent rights or the freedom to use their brand names; even generic name policies might be acceptable if they were introduced with a package of regulations that made it difficult for small local companies to compete.

What the multinationals cannot and will not accept are policies that aim to improve drug use if this means restricting, where necessary, the quantity of drugs sold. Now if things are as bad as at that health post in Ghana where it was chloroquine and penicillin with everything, then you could cut the volume of drugs sold by 75 per cent without noticing the difference in terms of health. Or, in Brazil, if you halved the number of antibiotics prescribed, the most noticeable result would probably be a halving in the rate of antibiotic-induced diarrhoea.

'It cannot be our responsibility'

The drug companies talk long and lovingly about the benefits that their products bring to the rich world; about the money they save by keeping people out of hospital; about the productivity gained by getting people back to work quicker. They talk about the needs that their drugs *could* meet in the Third World if only governments would buy them.

They prefer not to discuss, and certainly not to accept responsibility for, the costs of misuse of the drugs which they *do* sell in the Third World. They avert their corporate gaze from the people hurt or killed by drugs they did not need in the first place. They are not concerned if the Third World poor spend their money on medicines for children whose main need is food; nor do they allow themselves to wonder whether, in their efforts to ensure a profit for the shareholders, they divert people's anxiety about the health of their families from action which might really improve it.

What does Peter Schurch of Roche feel about people who buy vitamins when their need is, clearly, for food? 'Is it our problem?' he asks rhetorically, and then answers in the negative. 'It can't be. We promote to the physician. The promotion reaches the public through the physician in nearly all cases I know.' This is an absurd argument, to hide behind Third World doctors, blaming them for the fact that millions of people waste money they cannot afford on vitamin pills for hungry children.

People die of TB in Bangladesh because it is resistant to streptomycin. The drug should have been restricted to this use alone, to avoid the development of resistance. Instead it was made available over the counter in, for example, Pfizer's best-selling Combiotic. The product was finally taken off the market, under pressure. Pfizer still disclaimed responsibility for misuse, against all the evidence: 'Since Combiotic is not an oral drug but one that must be administered by injection, it is extremely unlikely that it is used by other than qualified members of the medical profession.'[54] Yet it is common knowledge in that country, as in many others, that the abuse of injectable drugs is just as widespread as that of other forms.

In South-East Asia, the companies bribe doctors by giving them free samples to sell—but disclaim responsibility for any excess prescribing that follows. In Brazil, they deliberately mislead doctors about the value of their products—then turn their backs when these are used beyond the limits of their effectiveness. Ciba's Butazolidin, that effective if hazardous relief from rheumatism, is used well beyond its indications in many countries, as a general painkiller. 'It is not our fault. We are not promoting the drug as such,' says Dr Berneker.

What the industry wants is sales without responsibility. This corporate response to the dangers and waste inherent in the misuse of their products is familiar. For a few years in the mid-1970s I worked with small groups of people in Europe, the USA, Asia and Africa investigating the way baby milks were actually used in the Third World. Some of the companies of whose activities we were most critical are better known for their drugs than their baby foods. So it was no surprise to find the International Council of Infant Food Industries (ICIFI) still sharing offices with IFPMA in Zurich.

'I'm glad I don't have his job,' said Michael Peretz of the man who left the elevator as we entered. It was Dr Stanislas Flache, Secretary-General of ICIFI. We were at the time a month short of the rout of the baby milk companies at the thirty-fourth World Health Assembly. 'Nestlé and the other companies made a lot of mistakes to get to the point they did,' he went on, as we descended. They certainly had. They had allowed the debate over baby foods to centre on the way the products were actually used. So they were confronted by proof that many Third World children were dying through the unavoidably inappropriate use of those products—and then refused to accept any responsibility. So crass was their response that they succeeded in uniting 118 of the 122 WHO member countries which voted to recommend that all governments introduce stringent controls to force the companies to face their responsibilities.[55] 'We won't ever get to that stage if I can help it,' said Peretz as he saw me safely out on to the front step.

Twelve: Towards the Year 2000

The patient has been thoroughly examined. Like good clinicians, we have looked not just at the immediately apparent illness but at the patient's social and economic environment as well. The diagnosis is easy—the patient is motivated by a powerful sense of self-interest and, although a little confused by the onset of his middle age, there can be no question of treatment. What concerns us is the prognosis.

The multinational pharmaceutical companies have a positive contribution to make to Third World health care, of this there can be no doubt. They can contribute to the development of new drugs, either under agreement with non-profit institutions, as Roche has done in its development of mefloquine with the WHO and the Walter Reed Institute, or on their own initiative, like Wellcome with its malaria vaccine, in the simple expectation of reasonable profits. They can contribute by supplying essential drugs either paid for by the developing countries themselves, or as aid donations from their home governments. They can help by building, or providing the know-how for, factories to produce drugs within the developing countries themselves. Such are the pressures of the market, that the prices of the drugs they sell for primary health care will probably be reduced in relative terms, a vital contribution since this will increase significantly the number of tablets, bottles of syrup and ampoules available.

They will contribute to the delivery of better health care for those in the Third World who can afford little or receive none. Indeed, some already are. But their contributions will be conditional. The conditions will include freedom from interference, particularly in their more lucrative existing markets, concessions over commercial issues such as the recognition of patents and the right to use brand names, protection against special treatment for local competitor companies and more. These conditions will exact their cost. 'Future developments can be surprisingly well predicted in specific fields,' says pharmaceutical industry consultant and forecaster Leif Schaumann. 'It is more difficult to figure out how they mesh.'[1]

As we return through the rice paddies and cotton fields to that initial question, 'Is the positive contribution of the multinational pharmaceutical companies outweighed by, even incidental to, the damage they do and the bad health care they promote?', it is precisely this mesh, this interaction of events, that we must address.

The technological stage . . .

The technological environment in which the companies will operate over the next decade us becoming clearer. Despite all the talk about the importance of the multinationals in the development of new drugs, the evolution of bio-engineering has shown that the world is not as dependent on them as they would pretend. Many advances have come, and will come, from laboratories outside the pharmaceutical industry, be they of governments, universities or private industry. With their existing infrastructure and experience in turning new chemicals into marketable drugs, the multinationals are obviously well placed to exploit the scientific advances of the past few years. Latterly, though, their large cash reserves—used to acquire the most promising independent research units—have been even more important.

Under whoever's aegis they develop, the new technologies will bring products of importance to the Third World. Many of these will be vaccines of particular value to primary health care directed towards prevention. The multinationals will not gain great commercial advantage from these, although they will provide sound business for companies already having a vaccine base. The commercial importance of the new technologies will, in the first instance, be the opportunities they create to make the production of existing drugs more efficient.[2]

The WHO essential drug list shows that the bulk of pharmaceutical needs can be met by well-established products. With many of these old enough to have lost their patent protection, and with the traditional technologies for their manufacture now more accessible, the larger and more advanced developing countries will be able to undertake a greater share of their production. The eventual share they capture depends, particularly in export markets, on how successful the multinationals are in using the new technologies to produce the old and tried drugs at prices which undercut these new competitors.

This basic chemical production is 'a field far more important than most industry observers realize', says Leif Schaumann.[3] Certainly, those developing countries not able to produce pharmaceutical chemicals from basic raw materials are likely to find that, while the prices of finished medicines become less variable in an increasingly 'transparent' world market, their drug-formulating plants will confront frequent problems in the acquisition of bulk drugs. Prices of these will fluctuate widely as the multinationals, claiming that cheap suppliers cannot guarantee a continuity of supply, make this prediction come true in the supply of those bulk drugs which they control.

. . . and the political actors

The political stage for the 1980s has also been set by the efforts of the international organizations and their Third World backers on the one hand and the responses and emerging alternatives put forward by the corporations on the other. The WHO says that the challenge of primary health care is primarily political rather than technical, and it does not make the mistake of locating the political opposition exclusively outside the developing countries:

> Success will depend very heavily on changes in the socio-economic setting and in the political climate; a significant breakthrough in improving the health status of the majority of the world's population cannot be expected unless the main causes of poverty and underdevelopment, such as obsolete socio-economic structures, can be removed. . . .[4]

Some of these internal conflicts are clear for all to see. The strikes of doctors in Kenya, Nigeria and Tanzania during 1980 and 1981 are excellent examples. Underlying these actions was a demand for a larger share of their countries' health budgets, either through higher salaries, through the right to have (or expand) private practices in addition to government jobs, or both. This is not the place to debate the rights and wrongs of their case. It is pertinent simply to point out that these are very visible conflicts which affect a large population and that they are thus high on the agenda of the governments concerned.

The medical profession itself is seen as a clear obstacle to the introduction of primary health care in countries like India: 'Government authorities are now convinced that a new cadre of medical personnel should be created,' comments the *Eastern Pharmacist*.[5]

The medical profession and the Medical Council of India are

uncompromisingly opposed to the creation of a second category of medical practitioners. The common man is unable to understand the stance adopted by the present class of practitioners. The truth is that the medical profession is apprehensive that if people are taught to depend upon self-medication for common ailments and are also made wiser about preventive health care methods, its practice and income will shrink!

The industry can, and does, build up immensely powerful support for itself from doctors in developing countries by judiciously contributing to their living standards where more subtle means are ineffective. The process is seen in its early stages in Nigeria, where, as William Connelly of Sandoz put it, 'samples in the form of trade-size packages are well received by the physician.'[6] As the market matures, it reaches the point where, as Klaus von Grebmer of Ciba says of the Philippines, the doctors 'earn more on pharmaceuticals than on all their other activities'. It should come as little surprise, then, to find that when a reforming government tries, as in Sri Lanka, to rationalize drug use, private doctors oppose a move that interferes with an important part of their livelihood.

Less well-known, but equally obvious, is the conflict of interest faced by the people who actually sell the drugs to the public, the pharmacists. Henry Briscoe explained what happened when he went out to sell the products of his new company in what was then Rhodesia:

'Look,' he would tell a pharmacist, 'instead of selling that for 30 shillings, we're going to let you have it for 5 shillings.' And he'd say, 'Well, fine, but where the hell do I get my profit?' I'm sorry to say that some professional people adopted that attitude. . . . if you were cheap, that meant less for them. I'd like to think that a professional person would say, 'I'll take the value for my client', but when you get a profession like pharmacy, you have a very difficult dividing line between what's business and what's professionalism.

The multinationals don't sell drugs by cutting their price. But they too know on which side of the dividing line they want to keep the pharmacist. In India, companies like Merrell would send their representatives to check whether he was recommending their product—if he wasn't, he lost his special discount. In the Philippines, the pharmacist is the intermediary who is expected to allow drug company representatives to check the prescriptions their clients bring—to make sure that local doctors are prescribing what they ought to.

In many countries, the pharmacists are not even professionals. But they are still supplied with 'ethical', prescription-only drugs even where it is against the law for non-professionals to trade in them.[7] Bode Ladejobi writes of Nigeria's patent medicine sellers:

> it is not unusual to buy ethical drugs from these individually located stores. One significant factor which is not readily recognized by some executives of pharmaceutical companies in Nigeria is that the patent medicine dealers have a strong political base and they will continue to be an important outlet for drugs in Nigeria.[8]

It would be wrong to imagine that the pharmaceutical companies are not aware of the political power of these trade groups. Indeed, my hosts at Ciba expressed surprise at the general ignorance of the importance of the local lobby in opposing such measures as price reductions. They could name five or six countries off the cuff where the wholesalers or agents were either ministers or health officials or held high office in the drug control organization. Clearly, the multinational companies know who their friends are, and, in countries where things work like that, they know how to behave.

Spreading risks in the public sector

Private doctors, pharmacies and the wholesale business which supplies them are a formidable lobby for the pharmaceutical industry. But in the multinational's form of business came into existence, in part, to spread risks. So the companies should not be expected, especially in volatile developing countries, to rely solely on such a well-defined, one-sided interest group. The worldwide trend, highlighted by Klaus von Grebmer, towards more involvement by the state in health care is at least as strong in the developing countries as in the developed. So how are the companies planning to spread their risks and maintain their influence in this changing world? How can they protect their interests in countries where their main customer is going to be the state, and government buying has moved beyond the stage where a free lunch and an appropriate gift is enough to clinch a sale?

The initiatives of CPR and Ciba-Geigy provide some pointers here, although their specific projects may never be realized. Whether or not intended as such, the CPR's plans for fellowships and demonstration programmes look like a system of legitimate incentives for Third World opportunists. A cloud of suspicion must hang over any industry-sponsored fellows programme. Even if only serious research workers benefit, its mere existence will be powerful persuasion to the hopefuls to stay in line.

There is scope, too, for influencing scrupulously honest and dedicated Ministers of Health. Who could resist compromising on a few, perhaps relatively important points of policy if, as compensation, you could be included in a programme which would, overnight, relieve you of the foreign currency problems that obstruct the development of your primary healthcare programmes? Your old friend, the Minister of Finance, would finally have to stop laughing when you came to see him. At last, you could show him an economically feasible way to get those rural health-care programmes started.

Servipharm's 'services' have a similar appeal, one which I believe is to the lazy and incompetent, giving help to them to hide their failings; to the ambitious and accomplished, help in gaining the recognition of their peers and superiors.

Do I read it all wrong? Unfortunately, I know too many people, some of whom work for Ciba-Geigy, who read it, just as I do. The company has marketing representatives based in Beira to promote agrochemicals. In the safety of expatriate circles, they talk scathingly about the basis on which they do business here. When the agricultural authorities find themselves in a sticky situation, due to lack of staff, disorganization or plain incompetence, Ciba is there to help. If an insecticide order is late and the cotton crop is in danger, Ciba arranges to have it airfreighted in. Never mind the cost, we've saved our necks, or so the corporate interpretation goes. And remember, it is in dialogues with this kind of 'periphery' that Ciba's *leitbilden* are drawn up.

The attractions of community medicine

With suitably tailored incentive packages, the multinationals aim to win friends and influence people in the state sector in order both to maintain their present interests and to exercise their influence over future health policies. More directly, through the promotion of package deals, they hope to gain a profitable share of the market for pharmaceuticals used in primary health care.

There are good reasons for them to want a share of this market, even though prices will have to be low and profit margins small. In the rich world, there is an especially profitable future in drugs for chronic diseases which guarantee stable sales over a long period. In the poor world, the equivalent will be drugs for mass treatment campaigns covering whole communities. Dr Jannssen, head of the Johnson and Johnson subsidiary, Jannssen Pharmaceuticals, has called attention to the low cost of medicines for animals in relation to similar products for human use. 'In those countries where there are so many sheep, tens of thousands of sheep are being treated simultaneously, and the distribution costs are virtually negligible.'[9] Similarly, he implies, if you treat humans *en masse*, the drug cost will be very much lower than for individual treatment. This does not mean that the market will be unattractive to the multinationals, many of which run profitable veterinary medicine divisions.

Nevertheless, the multinationals do not want to have to compete for markets in primary health care against cheap suppliers, be they the generic producers of Europe and the USA or the factories in Eastern Europe and the developing countries. So they must rely on the extras they can offer. Quality is one sales point they will use, though they recognize it will not be enough. It is the sales and service package deals which they now hope will give them their competitive edge.

The agricultural parallel

Both Ciba and CPR choose to draw a parallel between their proposed programmes and existing activities in the field of agriculture. A further examination of this comparison is educative. In Beira, we already benefit from Ciba's agrochemical services. So when I went in search of guidance as to the best way to deal with the various insect pests that afflict the water company's orange grove, the easy answer I was given was Ciba's booklet, *The Protection of Citrus in Mozambique*. Its introduction highlighted the importance of citrus in the government's agricultural plans and modestly acknowledged that 'there are without doubt more scientific and more complete sources of information on the subject,' immediately going on to suggest that these perhaps have little application to real life, and to reassure the reader that Ciba has already done the thinking. 'Here we try to provide simply a practical guide, conceived for Mozambique, the result of the permanent confrontation between scientific data and actual experience on the ground.' Predictably, neither the generic names nor the generic equivalents of the Ciba products are mentioned. Although a spraying timetable is given, it is useless unless Ciba products are applied, and these are certainly not among the cheapest. In truth, though, since the Ciba salesmen are in town to help with the trying importation procedures, it is unlikely that any but the most determined buyer would bother with alternatives. Ciba's name is in front of everyone. The give-away notepads on the best people's desks say 'Avirosan for Better Rice'. Very popular too are the Ciba T-shirts and jaunty caps.

Far from the marketing of agrochemicals demonstrating, as Klaus von Grebmer would like to think, how the corporate service ideal should work in practice, it simply exhibits many of the failings that have been criticized in the drugs business. But the issue is broader than this. Through the involvement in the supply of agricultural service packages, the agrochemical multinationals have succeeded in giving undue priority to the chemical contribution to better agriculture in ways which appear to boost corporate turnover more effectively than peasant crop yields. It was Hoechst that I observed in East Africa single-mindedly selling their insecticide Thiodan (endosulfan) in a World Bank-funded project to improve peasant cotton yields on the shores of Lake Victoria. They, too, gave away caps and T-shirts emblazoned 'Thiodan for Better Cotton'. They provided all the resources needed to ensure that the insecticide part of the project went as planned. The problem was that insecticide spraying was just one of the items in the plan for improved cotton yields. There is no point in peasants spending money on insecticide for cotton planted at the wrong time, or without fertilizer, or on cotton that is not weeded correctly. That was no concern of Hoechst's, however. It was there to distribute chemicals, which it did most efficiently.[10]

The complex business of food

The debate about agribusiness and its contribution to the world food problem is at least as complex as that of the contribution made to health by the pharmaceutical industry. It is significant to find that there, too, the 'packages' offered by the multinationals are subject to serious criticism. Canadian Pat Roy Mooney writes in his important study *Seeds of the Earth*:

> Global companies have virtual control over the second phase of the Green Revolution, allowing them to 'package' inputs of seeds and chemicals with the help of government subsidies, foreign aid and higher farm prices.[11]

Among the agribusiness companies he investigates are familiar names—Pfizer, Sandoz, Upjohn and Ciba-Geigy.

Agrichemical corporations seek the development of plant varieties best able to stimulate chemical sales. The resulting bias can lead to greater crop uniformity and disease vulnerability as well as increased financial and environmental costs. . . . Because of their involvement in several phases of the total food system, agribusiness plant breeders look to profits from several sectors. This enables them to breed seed suitable to their chemical, processing or retail interests, but not necessarily suitable to the profitability of the farmer or the nutrition of the consumer.

The food analogy continues to be particularly appropriate when investigating the broader political implications of the pharmaceutical industry's programme for the future. When I returned from Europe, there was no rice in Beira. The US government indefinitely held up a scheduled shipment promised under the PL480 scheme (for which, it is worth noting, Mozambique would have paid, albeit at concessional rates). The interruption in the normal 'Food for Peace' trade was US retaliation for the Mozambican government's temerity in expelling six people alleged to have conducted CIA activities hostile to the country from the shelter of the local US embassy. The evidence against them looked convincing, the more so in the absence of any denial from the USA that the expelled had CIA connections. What is of interest here is the fact that the food shipment should automatically be stopped.

A little help for our friends

The experience of Sri Lanka has shown that such aid will always be used for political purposes should the need arise. More fundamental, though, is the way in which the aid is used to reinforce allies at the expense of other countries. The implications for this in the field of health are particularly pernicious. The CPR proposal for a drug-aid scheme parallel to PL480 is strongly oriented towards selected countries which are friendly to the USA, in line with current US foreign policy which is to give aid in accordance with US priorities and to downgrade the importance of aid through the agencies of the United Nations and World Bank over which it has less direct control. This will mean that some countries which have historically ignored the health needs of their people will be favoured. Many countries where real efforts have been made to bring health care to all will meanwhile be left to struggle on by themselves.

Mozambique is surely no candidate for US drug aid. Neighbouring Malawi will be. Yet Mozambique has made great efforts to bring primary health care to its people. In his twenty-odd years in power, Malawi's president Banda contented himself with bringing a sizeable part of his country's pharmaceutical trade under the control of his private companies, leaving the health care of his people to their own woefully weak resources, and to the missionaries still scattered along the shores of what was Livingstone's lake.

Of Nicaragua and El Salvador, it will be the USA's friend which gets preference, regardless of its carelessness for the lives of its people. The Philippines, for staying faithful, will be rewarded. Other countries in South-East Asia will be blacklisted, despite demonstrated commitments to primary health care. It is particularly appropriate to find Robert Dee's Smith Kline corporation already collaborating with the Zaire regime in the supply of essential drugs.[12]

Health care delivered by governments is very visible. In communities whose main contact with their government is through its tax collectors or paramilitary police, it will make a welcome change, one that may mute hostility. The pharmaceutical industry knows this:

> We in the pharmaceutical industry recognize, more than most other people, that pharmaceuticals are important not only because they are a necessary part of the health component but also because *they provide tangible evidence to the people concerned that something is being done to help them.* (My italics.)[13]

Supporting these friends, persuading them to devote more resources to their peoples' health care, will pay political dividends to the donor countries. With the rest of the aid package, it will continue to stabilize tottering regimes. More specifically, it will also serve to confuse the political essence of primary health care which is that the health of poor communities can ultimately only be improved in parallel with broad social and economic development which takes account of their needs and in which they participate. To those who still choose to measure health care in terms of the number of hospital beds available or the number of tablets distributed, the countries which care less will appear to be doing more.

The companies' two-tier future

On the one hand, the multinationals are the protectors of self-seeking medical conservatism in the developing countries; on the other, they are collaborators in primary health care, even promoting it to selected partners for whom it might not otherwise have had a high priority. How will they balance these two, apparently opposed interests?

There is, in fact, no conflict. The United Nations Centre on Transnational Corporations (representing the poor world) and the researchers of the Organization of Economic Cooperation and Development (which represents the rich) agree that the pharmaceutical industry has a two-tier future. A handful of big multinationals will dominate the research-based business of producing new drugs, while smaller companies have to content themselves with the supply and production of cheap generic products.[14]

For the multinationals, a two-tier world of a different kind would be the ideal. In it, their friends would have drugs, if not health, for all by the year 2000. Their opponents would have to manage as best they could alone. The poor would be served with cheap drugs while the rich continued to buy expensive remedies in profitable free-for-all markets. The under-served could be allowed rationally selected essential drugs so long as existing consumers continue to take their richly packaged placebos.

In this two-tier world, the extravagance of the uncontrolled market for the rich would be a permanent advertisement for the multinationals, a goal to which the poor might aspire. The poor peasant farmer will not believe that the basic drugs he gets from the health centre are as good as or better than the expensive vitamin tonic which the prosperous village shopkeeper claims is the source of his well-being. The washerwoman from the squatter shanty town will not believe that her child's diarrhoea is best treated with sugar and salt when the family for whom she works in the suburbs gives three different tablets to their children when they are ill.

It will work on an international scale as well. As long as rationally chosen essential drugs are tarred with the brush of poverty, countries with rising incomes will be vulnerable to the suggestion that they are getting less than the best. IFPMA already promotes this idea:

There is . . . no sound basis in medical science for restricting available therapy to a limited list of drugs. It is clear that for authorities to do so would be consciously to elect an inferior standard of health care for their people.[15]

But health is indivisible

The multinationals would be more comfortable in their two-tier world. Rather than just defending the policies of privilege, they would be dealing in the more pragmatic and less controversial business of defining who will have access to which system of health care. In this they would be just one more group of actors among many. But this two-tier strategy is in direct conflict with the concept of health for all, as Halfdan Mahler has emphasized:

> It is obvious . . . that health is indivisible. This indivisibility is of paramount importance within each country where it encompasses the different components and different levels of the health system. . . . Deficiencies in one will lead to defects in the others and weaken the total effort.[16]

It will, in practice, be a hard political point to make, especially while the multinationals strive to avoid open conflict. They will not, nor will they need to, set themselves up in opposition to government attempts to regulate the sale of drugs. Just as at the turn of the century Mahlon Kline, of Smith Kline, campaigned for the introduction of the Pure Food and Drug Act to bring order to the anarchy of patent medicine marketing in the USA,[17] so, in the 1980s, it will be in the multinationals' interest to do just this in the developing world. It may already be that the majority of ineffective and dangerous drugs are sold by the national companies of the developing countries or by the multinationals' other competitors. Perhaps this is why Michael Peretz of IFPMA was so insistent that I should not write this book without mentioning that dangerous drugs like chloramphenicol and amidopyrine are sold without due caution by Eastern European companies as well as by the multinationals and that, in these countries, they use anabolic steroids to put weight on Olympic athletes rather than on hungry children as do his member companies. (I promised I would.)

What of the costs and benefits of the multinationals' contribution in the face of this pragmatism? The rich world already has a clear idea of what the balance sheet looks like from its side. The OECD concludes:

> It seems probable that the makers of national policy will take a more positive view of the industry, and especially of its innovative sector. . . . If national incomes are to be maintained, industries in which the developed nations enjoy a comparative advantage must be emphasized. The high-technology sectors, of which pharmaceuticals are a prominent example, are an obvious choice.[18]

As late as 1978, Halfdan Mahler had promoted health as a common cause, a focus for political cooperation between rich and poor worlds:

> Political leaders of the world, use the neutral ground of health to promote global development dialogue. WHO has already shown in shaping its policies that such a dialogue among countries of all shades of political ideology is not only possible, it is highly fruitful. Use health as a lever for social and economic development. More than that, use it as a lever for peace.[19]

Ultranational interests

Harsh economic realities which threaten the rich world's elevated living standards have changed that, and the debate about pharmaceuticals, as about 'health for all' in general, has been tempered by the new climate.

During the 1970s, it was the *multi*nationality of companies that drew attention. They operated beyond national boundaries. They could transfer their profits, jobs, and even the base of their operations, from one country to another at will. The perception is now changing. What will emerge in the 1980s is that these are not just *multi*nationals which operate in many countries, nor *trans*nationals whose dealings transcend frontiers but *ultra*nationals, each an enterprise whose activities, while they extend beyond national borders, are nevertheless intimately linked with and strongly oriented towards the economic welfare of its home country. The support which the pharmaceutical ultranationals already get from their home governments demonstrates this. And, as ultranationals, the pharmaceutical companies will contribute to Third World health just as long as this is in the economic interests of the rich world in which they are based.

When UNIDO looked to the future and concluded gloomily, 'A review of the demographic, social, economic and political factors shows that the prospects of attaining the goal of "health for all by the year 2000" are very dim,' they were looking at precisely these broader national interests; 'the only positive way to achieve this . . . could be through a genuine cooperation between developed and developing countries at all levels.'[20] by 1980, Halfdan Mahler was echoing UNIDO's gloom:

> We have to face a new reality. The results of the so called North–South dialogue, whether within the United Nations system or in

other fora are, to say the least, meagre. The developing countries fear, perhaps with some justification, that soft social programmes are being offered to them to conceal the intention of the developed countries to maintain economic supremacy. On the other hand, the developed countries are contending that their own economic predicament is such as to make disinterested dialogue with the developing countries impracticable. All this has created a climate that could easily give rise to political, economic, social and psychological obstacles to the realization of health for all in the foreseeable future.[21]

Promoting health for all in a two-tier world

On the other side of the balance sheet, those committed to the ideal of 'health for all' will also work in a two-tier world. They will continue to press for the introduction of policies to promote rational drug use. They will take advantage of what Schaumann foresees —'less doctrinaire management thinking in the future when it comes to joint ventures, licensing, joint marketing' on the part of the companies with 'much evidence of such strategies in the developing countries as the leading countries among them continue the pursuit of their national aspirations in the pharmaceutical field.'[22]

Just as drugs can serve to still political dissent, they can also be effective as 'preventive placebos'. Adequate drug supplies will do much to ensure that front-line health workers are accepted by their communities. This will in turn make the other, more important, facets of their primary health care work more effective. The health promoters will not allow their cooperative ventures with the industry, nor their limited successes in primary health care in underserved communities that these will allow, to blind them to the damage that will continue to be done by the ultranationals through the wasteful, harmful and ultimately irrational medicine they promote. During the past two decades attention has focused on the safety, efficacy and cost of drugs. In the 1980s, this will change. It may confidently be predicted that attention will switch to the gross mismatch between actual drug usage and real drug needs.

Third World health workers will be supported in their attempts to attack the problem at source by the international spotlight which will be kept on the ultranationals. A foretaste of this comes from the inaugural conference of Health Action International, a coalition of consumer, professional and development action groups from twenty-seven countries in both rich and poor world.

The stranglehold of the international pharmaceutical industry on the provision of health care is one of the main issues on the agenda of the Group of 77 [the formal organization of the developing countries]. We shall seek full working cooperation with them to bring about long-overdue changes in the way medicines are produced and marketed—and also withheld . . . . If the industry is to continue in its customary ways, our prescription for it will inevitably cause it irritation and pain.[23]

Last word, though, goes to the health authorities of Mozambique:

The battle against the pharmaceutical transnationals will not be easy. But the debate must be rekindled wherever possible, since the positive achievements to be realized and already in sight will represent an immeasurable benefit for the health of all the people in the world, especially those least protected: those of the developing countries.[24]

Epilogue

Back at the Beira Water Company, life goes on at its usual pace. We, too, are looking towards the year 2000, trying to work out how to provide everyone with enough water for their basic needs as well as supplying the factories, railways and harbour. We would like to buy the big pipes for the 50 kilometres of new pipeline that is needed from Zimbabwe. They have a purpose-built factory there, shut down for lack of orders. Our $1.5 million a year would be useful business for them. French pipes, the alternative, are more expensive, as they have a long way to come. But the French government, unlike that of Zimbabwe, can afford to give loans to encourage their industry's exports, and these are a powerful incentive.

Meanwhile, death goes on too. Ernesto Vilanculos, for whom the medicine ran out in chapter 6, died shortly afterwards. It was, in truth, not just the shortage of medicines. He had abandoned treatment before and his death was inevitable, medicine or no. I've lost count of the sons and daughters, nieces and nephews, of my colleagues who have died during the year in which this book has been in the writing. Insofar as work is concerned, this has made me harder and meaner than I thought possible. 'Do you realize,' I said to Inacio the other day, 'just what would happen if everyone in the company used a company van to carry relatives to and from the hospital whenever they had a sick child there? We'd never get any work done.'

'I know,' he said. 'But what am I supposed to do? He was uncontrollable when he heard that the boy had died. We couldn't just leave him there like that.'

Inacio had to take another day and a half off work to arrange the funeral. It was not the first time this year. Like so many of his colleagues who are lucky and have jobs, this brings with it family responsibilities which create problems at work.

The import of chemicals needed to treat the water is at last going smoothly. But we cannot do as much as we would like to extend the supply of water in the *bairros precários*. There is now a shortage of foreign currency for the import of plastic, raw material for a little factory here in Beira which makes small-diameter pipe. So many people knock on our door, with money in their pockets, to whom we cannot offer any hope this year of the outside tap which they want. Inacio bears the brunt of this pressure. I won't be surprised if his headaches start again. He'll be queuing up for a *consulta* soon, for another prescription. That last eleven-item prescription of his cost, according to my calculations, nearly as much as a family has to pay for a water connection.

Yesterday, another worker at the company drove into town with me. How was his family? Only so-so? He'd been up all the previous night with the youngest child who was suffering from bad stomach pains and diarrhoea—they don't have water piped to their home yet either. 'We took him to the health centre but there they just gave him chloroquine and Resochin [chloroquine]. For diarrhoea! It was all there was. So we took him to hospital to emergency. They have lots of good medicine there.' And the child? 'Still no better. . . .'

Notes and References

Part I: The 1970s

One: The Issues

1 Proceedings, IFPMA 9th Assembly, Zurich, 1978.
2 *Prophylactic and Therapeutic Substances*, A28/12, WHO, Geneva, 1975.
3 Lall, *Major Issues in the Transfer of Technology to Developing Nations: A Case Study of the Pharmaceutical Industry*, TD/B/C.6/4, UNCTAD, Geneva, 1975.
4 McKeown, *The Role of Medicine*, Blackwell, Oxford, 1979.
5 Doyal and Pennell, *The Political Economy of Health*, Pluto Press, London, 1979.
6 Independent Commission on International Development Issues, *North–South: A Programme for Survival*, Pan, London, 1980.

Two: Safety

1 Meyler and Peck (eds.), *Drug-Induced Diseases*, vol. 3, Excerpta Medica Foundation, Amsterdam, 1972, p. 316.
2 Discombe, *British Medical Journal*, 1952, pp. 1270–3.
3 WHO, *Drug Information*, July–September 1977, p. 16.
4 Epstein and Yudkin, *Lancet*, 2 August 1980, pp. 254–5.
5 ibid.
6 Hammond, *New Scientist*, 13 March 1980, p. 811.
7 Sim, *New Scientist*, 19 June 1980, p. 341.
8 This and much of what follows is derived from *Competitive Problems in the Drug Industry — Chloramphenicol (chloromycetin): Summary and Analysis*, prepared for the Select Committee on Small Businesses of the US Senate by the Congressional Research Service, Library of Congress, Washington, DC, 9 April 1979.
9 Aladjem, *New England Journal of Medicine*, vol. 281, no. 24, 1969, p. 369.

10 Sarastri, *New England Journal of Medicine*, vol. 282, no. 14, 1970, p. 813.

11 Ghitis, ibid.

12 Dunne *et al.*, *Lancet*, 6 October 1973, pp. 781–3.

13 Silverman, *The Drugging of the Americas*, University of California Press, Berkeley, 1976.

14 Yudkin, *Lancet*, 15 April 1978, pp. 810–12.

15 Breckon, 'Pharmaceuticals in the Third World — the Remedies', BBC World Service, transmitted 2 September 1979.

16 *Drugs for Today and Tomorrow*, IFPMA, Zurich, 1979.

17 Victora *et al.*, 'Drug Usage in Southern Brazilian Hospitals', School of Medicine, University of Pelotas, 1980 (mimeo).

18 Silverman, *International Journal of Health Services*, vol. 7, no. 2, 1977, pp. 157–66.

19 Haines, *Medical Marketing and Media*, November 1976, pp. 22–31.

20 US Senate Health Subcommittee, *Drug Regulation Reform Act 1979, Hearings*, pp. 534–9.

21 Tiefenbacher, *Proceedings*, IFPMA 9th Assembly, Zurich, 1978.

22 Holmes, circular letter dated 20 February 1973.

23 Pinto, *Drug Monitoring*, Ciba-Geigy Pharma Registration Symposium, 15 March 1977.

24 In Vankowski and Dunne (eds.), *Trends and Prospects in Drug Research and Development*, CIOMS, Geneva, 1977.

25 *Proceedings*, Geneva Press Conference on SMON, Organizing Committee, Tokyo, 1980.

26 Medawar, *Insult or Injury*, Social Audit, London, 1979, and Medawar, *Drug Disinformation*, Social Audit, London, 1980.

27 Cited in Minkin, *Depo-Provera, a Critical Analysis*, Institute for Food and Development Policy, San Francisco, 1980.

28 *Daily News*, 16 July 1973, Dar es Salaam.

29 *Daily News*, 22 July 1973, Dar es Salaam.

30 Derived from Table 1 in Atkinson *et al.*, *Studies in Family Planning*, vol. 5, no. 3, 1974, pp. 242–9.

31 Upunda, Yudkin and Brown, *Therapeutic Guidelines*, African Medical Research Foundation, Nairobi, 1980.

Three: Efficacy

1 *Scrip*, 11 July 1979.

2 *Scrip*, 3 October 1979.

3   *Scrip*, 16 June 1980.
4   *Scrip*, 8 December 1980.
5   *Scrip*, 24 September 1980.
6   Meyers *et al.*, *Review of Medical Pharmacology*, Lange, 1970.
7   Silverman, *The Drugging of the Americas*, University of California Press, Berkeley, 1976.
8   *Scrip*, 11 March 1981 and 6 May 1981.
9   In Victora, 'Drug Promotion in Brazil: How to Deceive with Statistics', Department of Social Medicine, University of Pelotas, Brazil, 1979 (mimeo).
10 *New Internationalist*, April 1977.
11 Muller, *New Scientist*, 31 March 1977.
12 *Mike Muller: A Case of Moral Incontinence*, Circular to Representatives, Divisional Managers, Regional Managers, Searle (UK), April 1977.
13 Letter to author, 22 May 1981.
14 Schiller *et al.*, *Gastroenterology*, vol. 80, no. 5, 1981, p. 1275.
15 *International Product Disclosure — Lomotil*, Searle, Chicago, 1980.
16 Bala *et al.*, *Indian Pediatrics*, vol. 16, no. 10, 1980, p. 903.
17 *Economic Priorities Report*, vol. 4, nos. 4–5, Council for Economic Priorities, New York, 1973.
18 *Washington Post*, 8 February 1976, K1.
19 Letters, Searle–Beirut and Searle–Bombay, 1977.
20 *In Sickness or in Wealth*, transcript of radio programme transmitted 26 June 1979, BBC, London.
21 *Bulletin of the WHO*, vol. 58, no. 1, 1980, p. 23.
22 For a recent review see Noah, *New Scientist*, 14 August 1980. The author concludes: 'With the wealth of antibiotics and chemotherapeutic agents available at present it seems difficult to believe that none can be recommended for treating traveller's diarrhoea but this is indeed so.'
23 Dunne *et al.*, *Clioquinol, Availability and Instruction for Use*, IOCU, The Hague, 1975.
24 *Proceedings*, Geneva Press Conference on SMON, Tokyo, 1980.
25 Dunne *et al.*, *Clioquinol, Availability and Instruction for Use*.
26 *Proceedings*, Geneva Press Conference on SMON, Tokyo, 1980.
27 Sim, *Clioquinol in South East Asia — Preliminary Report*, IOCU, Penang, 1980.
28 Ciba-Geigy, *1979 Annual Report*, Basle, 1980.
29 *Sunday Nation*, Nairobi, 6 April 1980.
30 Letter KL 5.1/KA/b, Ciba-Geigy, Basle, 5 August 1976.

31 *Proceedings*, Geneva Press Conference on SMON, Tokyo, 1980.
32 National Health Programme 1977/8 – 1983/4, Khartoum
    University Press, Khartoum, 1975.
33 *Diarrhoea Dialogue*, AHRTAG, London, no. 1, May 1980. This
    WHO-funded newsletter gives a coherent review of the
    development of appropriate therapies for diarrhoea and their
    application.
34 *Diarrhoea Dialogue*, no. 1.
35 Mahler, *Social Perspectives in Health*, address to 29th World
    Health Assembly, Geneva, 1976.

Four: Research

1 *Chemical Week*, 4 February 1981.
2 *Scrip*, 24 January 1979.
3 *Scrip*, 13 December 1978.
4 Shimamoto, *Proceedings*, IFPMA 9th Congress, Zurich, 1979.
5 *Scrip*, 7 March 1979.
6 Lall, *Major Issues in the Transfer of Technology: A Case Study of
    the Pharmaceutical Industry*, UNCTAD, TD/B/C, 6 April 1975.
7 *Prophylactic and Therapeutic Substances*, WHO A, 28 April
    1975.
8 *Transnational Corporations and the Pharmaceutical Industry*, UN
    Centre on Transnational Corporations, ST/CTC 9, 1979.
9 Sarrett in *Proceedings*, Pharmaceuticals for Developing
    Countries Conference, National Academy of Sciences,
    Washington, 1979.
10 *Proceedings*, IFPMA 9th Congress, Zurich, 1979. The increase
    to $40 million cited for 1978 is the consequence of WHO's
    Special Programme for Tropical Disease Research.
11 Reis-Arndt, *Pharmaz. Ind.*, vol. 40, no. 11, 1978, p. 1116.
12 The upper figure is that cited by Max Tiefenbacher and is the
    estimate of the market research company IMS for sales to low-
    and middle-income countries which, with the exception of
    Spain, Portugal and Yugoslavia are those countries usually
    considered to be 'developing', in *The Pharmaceutical Industry
    and The Third World*, PMA, Washington, 1980.
13 Sarrett, *op. cit.*
14 Behrman, *Tropical Diseases — Responses of the Pharmaceutical
    Companies*, American Enterprise Institute, Washington, 1980.
15 Sarrett, *op. cit.*
16 *New Drug Evaluation Project Briefing Book — 1980*, FDA,
    Washington, 1981.

17 *Proceedings*, CIOMS Round Table, CIOMS/WHO, Geneva, 1977.

18 Janssen, *Journal of Medical Pharmacology and Chemistry*, no. 1, 1959, p. 299.

19 Chloroquine was first synthesized in Germany in 1935, patented and named Resochin. Despite its anti-malarial activity, concern about its side-effects is said to have led to its abandonment. In 1942, the US War Production Board initiated a crash programme to develop new anti-malarials following the Japanese capture of Javanese plantations which had been the main Allied source of quinine. The most successful synthetic derivative, codenamed SN 7618, turned out to be identical to Resochin.

20 Dunning *et al.*, *Impact of Multinational Enterprises on Scientific and Technological Capacity: The Pharmaceutical Industry*, OECD, DSTI/SPR/77.34 –MNE—draft, 1977.

21 Wegner in *Proceedings*, IFPMA 9th Congress, Zurich, 1978.

22 IFPMA, 'Memorandum on the WHO Special Programme for Research and Training in Tropical Disease and the Role of the Pharmaceutical Industry' in *The Pharmaceutical Industry: International Issues and Answers*, PMA, Washington, 1979.

23 Etronol Injectable IST4 305/564 31976/566.

24 McMahon *et al.*, *British Medical Journal*, vol. 2 no. 6202, 1 December 1979, p. 1396.

25 *Transactions of the Royal Society of Tropical and Medical Hygiene*, vol. 74, no. 5, 1980, p. 558.

26 *Schisto Update*, vol. 2, no. 4, October 1980.

27 Mackenzie, *Transactions of the Royal Society of Tropical and Medical Hygiene*, vol. 71, no. 3, 1977, p. 183.

28 *The Pharmaceutical Industry: International Issues and Answers*, PMA, Washington, 1979.

29 Wegner, *op. cit.*

30 Behrman, *op. cit.*

Five: Market Power

1 Muller, *New Scientist*, 3 February 1977.

2 *Ibon*, no. 13, 28 February 1979.

3 *Scrip*, 12 December 79.

4 *Scrip*, 19 September 1979.

5 *Signs of the Times*, Manila, 14 November 1975.

6 Lall, *Major Issues in the Transfer of Technology to Developing Countries: A Case Study of the Pharmaceutical Industry*,

UNCTAD, TD/B/C.6/4, 1975.

7 Schaumann, *Guidelines for the Analysis of Pharmaceutical Supply System Planning in Developing Countries*, DHEW 79–50086, Office of International Health, Washington, 1979.

8 *Transnational Corporations and the Pharmaceutical Industry*, United Nations Center on Transnational Corporations, New York, ST/CTC/9, 1979.

9 Dunning *et al.*, *Impact of Multinational Enterprises on National Scientific and Technological Capacities: Pharmaceutical Industry*, OECD, DSTI/SPR/77.34, 1977.

10 Kallett and Schlink, *100,000,000 Guinea Pigs*, Vanguard, New York, 1933.

11 *Global Study of the Pharmaceutical Industry*, UNIDO, ID/WG. 331/6, 1980. These figures are for bulk chemicals and should be multiplied three or four times to give the selling price of the finished drug.

12 See *Transnational Corporations in World Development: A Re-examination*, UN Economic and Social Council, E/C.10/38, 1978.

13 *Multinational Monitor*, March 1980, p.8, for example.

14 *Scrip*, 2 July 1977.

15 Economic Development Administration, *The Drug and Pharmaceutical Industry in Puerto Rico*, Puerto Rico, 1980.

16 *Scrip*, 29 November 1978.

17 Burstall, *The Transfer of Pharmaceutical Technology to the Developing World*, OECD, 1980 (draft).

18 *Guardian Weekly*, 1 March 1981, p. 8.

19 *Transnational Corporations and the Pharmaceutical Industry*, op. cit.

20 Dunning *et al.*, op. cit.

21 Schaumann, op. cit.

22 *Scrip*, 3 December 1980.

23 Giovanni, *A Questão dos Remedios no Brasil*, Polis, São Paulo, 1980.

24 Dunning *et al.*, op. cit.

25 Gareis, 'Pharmaceuticals in the Year 2000, as Suggested by Present-Day Trends', paper presented at Hoechst Pharma Press Conference, November 1980.

26 Information Research Limited, London, 1980.

27 Burstall, op. cit.

28 *Update: The International Pharmaceutical Market*, Hoenig and Strock, New York, 1980.

29 Dunning *et al.*, *op. cit.* The evidence is that the oligopolies are not particularly short-lived. In the USA, in six of the nine therapeutic sub-markets reviewed, the 1960 market leader was still in first or second place in 1973, although not necessarily with the same products (ref. 8. p. 125). The average life of a drug is reported by Dunning to have increased from five to fifteen years.

30 *The Pharmaceutical Industry and the Third World*, Pharmaceutical Manufacturers Association, Washington, 1979.

31 *The Selection of Essential Drugs*, WHO Technical Report Series, No. 615, 1977.

32 Ciba-Geigy, *1979 Annual Report*, *Scrip*, 26 November 1980.

33 *The Pharmaceutical Industry: International Issues and Answers*, Pharmaceutical Manufacturers Association, Washington, 1979.

34 Yudkin, *International Journal of Health Services*, vol. 10, no. 3, 1980, p. 458.

35 *Case Studies in the Transfer of Technology: Pharmaceutical Policies in Sri Lanka*, UNCTAD, TD/B/C.6/21, 1977.

36 *Scrip*, 28 February 1979.

37 *Economic Cooperation Among Developing Countries in Pharmaceuticals. The APEC/TTI Experience*, UNCTAD, CAR/PH/WP17, 1980.

38 *Case Studies in the Transfer of Technology: Pharmaceutical Policies in Sri Lanka*, *op. cit.*

39 Hye, *Bangladesh Pharmaceutical Journal*, January 1978.

40 BBC World Service radio reports, 1981.

41 *Scrip*, 6 April 1981.

42 *Africa Health*, February 1980.

43 Information Research Limited, London, 1980.

44 *Scrip*, 31 May 1980.

45 Ladejobi, *Medical Marketing and Media*, January 1977.

46 Connelly, *Medical Marketing and Media*, October 1975.

47 *Scrip*, 11 November 1978.

48 *Technology Policy in the Pharmaceutical Sector in the Philippines*, UNCTAD, TT/34.1980, 1980.

50 *Scrip*, 3 November 1980.

51 *Scrip*, 19 September 1979.

52 *Scrip*, 12 December 1979.

53 Advertisement in *Correio da Manha*, 31 May 1942, Rio de Janeiro, cited in Giovanni, *op. cit.*

54 Giovanni, *op. cit.*

55 *Taticas Promocionais*, Sandoz, Brazil, 1970, from Giovanni, *op. cit.*

56 *Scrip*, 13 October 1979.

57 Giovanni, *op. cit.*

58 From Cordeiro, 'A Politica dos Medicamentos', in Guimaraes (ed.), *Saude e Medicina no Brasil*, Graal, Rio de Janeiro, 1978.

59 *Diario do Congresso Nacional*, 12 May 1977, supplement cited in Giovanni, *op. cit.*

60 *Transnational Corporations in the Pharmaceutical Industry of Developing Countries, Brazil Case Study*, UN Center on Transnational Corporations, 1981.

61 *Update: The International Pharmaceutical Market, op. cit.*

62 *Transnational Corporations in the Pharmaceutical Industry of Developing Countries, op. cit.*

63 *Case Studies in the Transfer of Technology: The Pharmaceutical Industry in India*, UNCTAD, TD/B/C.6/20, 1977.

Six: Drug Use

1 Perine *et al.*, *East African Medical Journal*, vol. 57, no. 4, April 1980, p. 238.

2 Breckon, 'In Sickness or in Wealth', transcript of radio programme transmitted 26 August 1979, BBC, London.

3 Victora *et al.*, 'Drug Usage in Southern Brazilian Hospitals', University of Pelotas 1980 (mimeo).

4 Adjepon-Yamoah in *African Health*, September 1980.

5 Simasthien *et al.*, *Lancet*, 6 December 1980.

6 Heyman *et al.*, *Lancet*, 7 March 1981.

7 Dukes in Bergmann (ed.), *Studies in Drug Utilisation: Methods and Applications*, WHO Reg. Publics, Euro Series no. 8, 1979.

8 Wade in Bergmann, *op. cit.*

9 *Schisto Update*, vol. 2, no. 4, October 1980.

10 *Report of Committee on the Selection of Essential Drugs*, Technical Report Series, No. 615, WHO, 1977.

11 Wade, *op. cit.*

12 Dukes, *op. cit.*

13 *Scrip*, 25 May 1981.

14 Schaumann, *Guidelines for the Analysis of Pharmaceutical Supply System Planning in Developing Countries*, DHEW 79-50086, Office of International Health, Washington, 1979.

15 Blum, Herxheimer, Stenzl and Woodcock (eds.), *Pharmaceuticals and Health Policy: International Perspectives on Provision and Control of Medicines*, Croom Helm, London, 1980.

16   *Global Study of the Pharmaceutical Industry*, ID/WG.331/6, UNIDO, 1980.
17   This is freely derived from illustrations in various papers by Dr John S. Yudkin.
18   Meyers *et al.*, *Review of Medical Pharmacology*, Lange, 1970.
19   Wellstein, 'Prices of International Low Price Sources for Drugs and Raw Materials of Essential Drugs of WHO', Institute of Tropical Hygiene, Heidelberg, 1978 (mimeo).
20   'Transnational Corporations in the Pharmaceutical Industry of Developing Countries: Egypt Case Study', UN Center on Transnational Corporations, 1981 (draft mimeo).
21   Nadim, *Rural Health Care in Egypt*, IDRC, TS15e, Ottawa, 1980.
22   *Health Needs and Health Services in Rural Ghana*, IDS Health Group, University of Sussex, 1978.
23   Tiefenbacher in *Proceedings*, Pharmaceuticals in Developing Countries Conference, Institute of Medicine, Washington, 1979.
24   ibid.
25   Beria *et al.* in 'Consumo de Medicamentos em Tres Grupos Sociais', paper presented at the 32nd Annual Meeting of the Brazilian Society for the Advancement of Science, Rio de Janeiro, 1980.
26   Giovanni, *A Questão dos Remedios no Brasil*, Polis, São Paulo, 1980.
27   Johnston, *Lancet*, 17 May 1980.
28   For a description of traditional medicine in Nigeria in the mid-1960s see Maclean, *Magical Medicine*, Penguin, Harmondsworth, 1971.
29   Amah, *East African Medical Journal*, June 1980.
30   See, for instance, Blum, in Blum *et al.*, *op. cit.*
31   *Surveillance for the Prevention and Control of Health Hazards due to Antibiotic-Resistant Enterobacteria*, Technical Report Series, No. 624, WHO, 1977.
32   US Senate Subcommittee on Monopoly, *Competitive Problems in the Drug Industry*, Hearings, Part 32, 1977, p. 15428.
33   Wasielewski, 'Do We Really Need More New Drugs?', Hoechst Pharmaceutical Division Press Conference, Hoechst, November 1980 (mimeo).
34   *African MIMS*, January 1980.
35   See, for example, von Grebmer, 'Drug Therapy and its Price', Ciba-Geigy, 1980 (mimeo).

36 *Surveillance for the Prevention and Control of Health Hazards due to Antibiotic-Resistant Enterobacteria, op. cit.*
37 *Bangladesh Pharmaceutical Journal*, 1977, 1978.
38 *Ciba-Geigy Pharma: Facts and Issues*, Ciba-Geigy, undated.
39 In Dupuy *et al.*, *A Invasão Farmaceutica*, Graal, Rio de Janeiro, 1979.

Part II: The 1980s

Seven: Towards Resolution

1 *International Herald Tribune*, April 1981.
2 *Swiss Chemical Industry in Figures*, Swiss Society of Chemical Industries, 1980.
3 *Tages-Anzeiger*, 28 March 1981.
4 US Senate Subcommittee on Monopoly, *Competitive Problems in the Drug Industry*, Hearings, Part 32, 1977, p. 15472.
5 Pletscher, *Proceedings*, IFPMA 10th Assembly, Zurich, 1981.
6 Beecham's first mentioned amoxicillin in a patent application in Britain in 1962. The company later claimed that the 'true' date of discovery was 1968, an argument accepted by the British court, but not in Ireland. *Scrip*, 25 August 1979 and 22 August 1979.
7 *Scrip*, 16 March 1981 and 8 April 1981.
8 US Senate Subcommittee on Monopoly, *op. cit*, p. 15475.
9 Reekie and Weber, *Profits, Politics and Drugs—the Strong Answer*, Macmillan, London, 1979.
10 Peretz, *Proceedings*, IFPMA 10th Assembly, Zurich, 1981.
11 *Wall Street Journal*, 10 March 1976 and 29 March 1976.
12 Blum, Herxheimer, Stenzl and Woodcock (eds.), *Pharmaceutical and Health Policy: International Perspectives on Provision and Control of Medicines*, Croom Helm, London, 1980.

Eight: Primary Health Care

1 *Area Handbook for Mozambique*, US Govt. Printing Office, DA PAM no. 550–64, 1969.
2 *Directivas Economicas e Sociais*, Frelimo, Maputo, 1977.
3 *Primary Health Care*, WHO/UNICEF, Geneva/New York, 1978.

4   *Primary Health Care*, Earthscan, London, 1978.
5   *Health Needs and Health Services in Rural Ghana*, IDS Health Group, University of Sussex, 1978.
6   Nordberg, *Ethiopian Medical Journal*, vol. 12, 1974, p. 25.
7   *Primary Health Care*, Earthscan, *op. cit.*
8   Mburu, Society, Science and Medicine, vol. 13A, 1979, p. 577.
9   *Health Sector Policy Paper*, World Bank, 1975.
10 ibid., 1980
11 ibid.
12 ibid.
13 *Proceedings*, 31st World Health Assembly, WHO, 1978.
14 *Draft Strategy for Health for All by the Year 2000*, WHO Executive Board, WHO, May 1981.
15 *Proposed Programme Budget for 1982/3*, WHO, 1980.
16 *National Health Programme 1977/8–1983/4*, Khartoum University Press, 1975.
17 *Proposed Programme Budget for 1982/3*, WHO, 1980.
18 ibid.
19 Gish, *Planning Pharmaceuticals for Primary Health Care*, American Public Health Association, Washington, 1979.
20 *The Selection of Essential Drugs*, Technical Report Series, No. 615, WHO, 1977.
21 *Case Studies in the Transfer of Technology: Pharmaceutical Policies in Sri Lanka*, UNCTAD, TD/B/C.6/21, 1977.
22 Hye, *Bangladesh Pharmaceutical Journal*, vol. 7, no. 1, 1978.
23 *Proceedings*, Geneva Press Conference on SMON, Tokyo, 1980.
24 Hye, *op. cit.*
25 See Yudkin, *International Journal of Health Services*, vol. 10, no. 3, 1980.
26 Personal communication.
27 *Case Studies in the Transfer of Technology: Pharmaceutical Policies in Sri Lanka, op. cit.*
28 *Transnational Corporations in the Pharmaceutical Industry of Developing Countries, Brazil Case Study*, UN Center on Transnational Corporations, 1981 (draft).
29 *Scrip*, 29 November 1979.
30 *Peruvian Basic Drugs Program*, PAHO, CD23/29, 1975.
31 Decreto Lei 18/77 and 19/77 and Diploma Ministerial 42/80, Maputo, Mozambique.
32 *Normas de Tratamento de Diarrheia Aguda Nas Criancas*, Ministerio de Saude, Maputo, 1979.
33 Diploma Ministerial 105/77, Maputo, Mozambique.

Nine: Rational Policies

1 Epstein *et al., Lancet*, 2 August 1980.
2 Mahler, *The WHO You Deserve*, WHA33/DIV/4, WHO, 1980.
3 Nand, *Technology Planning for Developing Countries*, UNCTAD, 1979.
4 *Case Studies in the Transfer of Technology: Pharmaceutical Policies in Sri Lanka*, UNCTAD, TD/B/C.6/21, 1977.
5 Nand, *op. cit.*
6 *Peruvian Basic Drugs Program*, PAHO, CD23/29, 1975.
7 *Scrip*, 4 March 1981.
8 *Transnational Corporations in the Pharmaceutical Industry of Developing Countries*, UN Center on Transnational Corporations, 1981 (draft).
9 *First Consultation on the Pharmaceutical Industry — Report*, UNIDO, ID/WG.331/10/Rev 1, 1980.
10 *Drug Information*, WHO, PDT/DI/77.1, 1977. The confusion over technical names has not in this case been resolved by the WHO's decision to call the two drugs aminophenazone and *nor*amidopyrine respectively, which fails to emphasize their close structural similarity.
11 Nand, *op. cit.*
12 *Health Sector Report*, World Bank, 1980.
13 *Case Studies in the Transfer of Technology: Pharmaceutical Policies in Sri Lanka, op. cit.*
14 Lall, *Major Issues in the Transfer of Technology to Developing Countries: A Case Study of the Pharmaceutical Industry*, UNCTAD, TD/B/C.6/4, 1975.
15 Agarwal, *Drugs and the Third World*, Earthscan, London, 1978.
16 *Statement to UNCTAD on UNCTAD Document TD/B/C.6/21*, IFPMA, 1978.
17 *Scrip*, 29 June 1981.
18 Ministry of Petroleum and Chemicals, *Report of the Committee on Drugs and the Pharmaceutical Industry*, New Delhi, 1975, and *Scrip*, 21 November 1974, for instance.
19 Chudnovsky, *World Development*, vol. 7, no. 1, 1979, p. 45.
20 *Drugs and Pharmaceuticals*, vol. 3, no. 5, May 1980; *Scrip*, 4 March 1981, and *Eastern Pharmacist*, August 1980.
21 *Economic and Political Weekly*, vol. 13, no. 12, 27 May 1979.
22 ibid.
23 *African Health*, September 1980.
24 *Scrip*, 14 January 1981.

25 Nordberg, *Ethiopian Medical Journal*, vol. 12, 1974, pp. 25–32.
26 Obel, *East African Medical Journal*, July 1980.
27 *Drug Policy in the Context of Primary Health Care in Thailand*, WHO, SEA/RC32/TD/IP8, 1979.
28 Obstoj, *Scrip*, 21 November 1974.
29 *Economic and Political Weekly*, *op. cit.*
30 *Scrip*, 25 February 1981.
31 *Drug Information*, WHO PDT/DI/77.1, 1977, and subsequent issues.
32 *Eastern Pharmacist*, July 1980.
33 From Gustaffson *et al.*, *Lancet*, 3 January 1981.
34 Upunda *et al.*, *Therapeutic Guidelines*, African Medical Research Foundation, Nairobi, 1980.
35 *Normas de Tratamento de Diarreia Aguda nas Criancas*, Ministerio de Saude, Maputo, 1979.
36 Connelly, *Medical Marketing and Media*, October 1975.
37 *Pharmaceutical Policies in Guyana*, UNCTAD, CAR/PH/WP.5, 1980.
38 *Mortality and Morbidity Weekly Report*, 14 December 1979.
39 *Proposed Programme Budget 1982/1983*, WHO, PB/82–83, 1980.
40 *Final Report*, Conference of South Pacific Countries on Technical Cooperation in Pharmaceutical Industries, WHO Regional Office, Manila, 1980.
41 *Scrip*, 22 April 1981.
42 Kingham, *Preliminary Observations on UNCTC Draft Report*, US PMA, Washington, 1981.
43 Schaumann, *Guidelines for the Analysis of Pharmaceutical Supply System Planning in Developing Countries*, DHEW79–50086, Office of International Health, Washington, 1979.
44 Mahler, *World Health is Indivisible*, 31st World Health Assembly, WHO, 1978.

Ten: Producing What's Needed

1 Burstall, *The Transfer of Pharmaceutical Technology to the Developing World*, OECD, 1980 (draft).
2 *Pharmaceutical Price List*, CAPS, Zimbabwe, August 1978.
3 Burstall, *op. cit.*
4 Data from *Assessment of the Pharmaceutical Industry in Developing Countries*, UNIDO, ID/WG.292/2, 1978; and *Reports on Drugs from the National Drug List which because of their Essentiality Could be Produced in the Developing Countries*, UNIDO, ID/WG.267/5, 1978.

5 Lall, *Growth of the Pharmaceutical Industry in Developing Countries: Problems and Prospects*, UNIDO, ID/204, 1978.
6 *Lima Declaration*, UNIDO, ID/Conf 3/31, 1975.
7 *Global Study of the Pharmaceutical Industry*, UNIDO, ID/WG.331/6, 1980.
8 Lall, *op. cit.*
9 See, for example, Tiefenbacher in *Proceedings*, Pharmaceuticals for Developing Countries Conference, National Academy of Sciences, Washington, 1979.
10 Lall, *op. cit.*
11 *Report of First Consultation on the Pharmaceutical Industry*, ID/259, UNIDO, 1981.
12 *Assessment of the Pharmaceutical Industry, op. cit.*
13 AAB (Consultores de Relacões Publicas), *Saude Pela Pesquisa*, Saraiva, São Paulo, 1966.
14 *Scrip*, 7 February 1979.
15 *Scrip*, 16 July 1980.
16 *Scrip*, 15 December 1980.
17 *Scrip*, 8 November 1978.
18 *CAPS 1980 Annual Report*, CAPS, Zimbabwe, 1981.
19 BBC, Service for Africa, 28 July 1981.
20 *Eastern Pharmacist*, December 1979.
21 *Drugs and Pharmaceuticals — Industry Highlights*, vol. 4, no. 1, Lucknow, January 1981.
22 *Scrip*, 29 March 1980.
23 *Scrip*, 15 December 1980.
24 Lall, *Major Issues in the Transfer of Technology; Case Study of the Pharmaceutical Industry*, UNCTAD, TD/B/C.6/4, 1975.
25 *Scrip*, 31 December 1980.
26 *Resolution on Cooperation Among Developing Countries in the Production, Procurement and Distribution of Pharmaceuticals*, 5th Conference of Heads of State of Non-Aligned Countries, NAS/CONF.5/S/RES.25, 1976.
27 *Scrip*, 22 April 1981
28 *Report of a Consultation on the Development of Guidelines for Local Formulation and Distribution of Essential Drugs in Developing Countries*, WHO, DPM/80.1, 1980.
29 *Scrip*, 4 April 1979.
30 *Scrip*, 7 February 1979.
31 *Scrip*, 22 April 1979.
32 *Scrip*, 28 January 1981.
33 *Scrip*, 25 May 1981.

34   For a comprehensive list of twenty common restrictive business
      practices which the Third World say unreasonably obstruct
      their industrial development, see *Draft International Code of
      Conduct on the Transfer of Technology*, UNCTAD,
      TD/CODE.TOT/25, 1980.
35   *Eastern Pharmacist*, April 1980.
36   *Pricing and Availability of Intermediates and Bulk Drugs*,
      UNIDO, ID/WG.331/4, 1980.
37   *Case Studies in the Transfer of Technology: The Pharmaceutical
      Industry of India*, UNCTAD, TD/B/C.6/20, 1977.
38   *The Availability, Terms and Conditions for the Transfer of
      Technology for the Manufacture of Essential Drugs*, UNIDO,
      ID/WG.331/5, 1980.
39   *Drugs and Pharmaceuticals, op. cit.*
40   *4th Annual Report*, Special Programme for Research and
      Training in Tropical Diseases, UNDP/World Bank/WHO, 1980.
41   Canfield, *Bulletin of the WHO*, vol. 50, no. 203, 1974.
42   Peters in *Proceedings*, Pharmaceuticals for Developing
      Countries Conference, *op. cit.*
43   *4th Annual Report, op. cit.*
44   Thus a new plant to manufacture ethylene from petrochemicals
      costs around $600 million (*International Construction*, December
      1980) while Indian estimates put the cost of a multipurpose
      plant to produce eighteen different bulk pharmaceuticals at
      under $11 million (*Reports on Drugs from the National Drug List,
      op. cit.*)
45   *Chemical Week*, 19 November 1980.
46   *Transnational Corporations and the Pharmaceutical Industry*, UN
      Centre on Transnational Corporations, ST/CTC/9, 1979.
47   *1978 Annual Report*, Glaxo, London, 1979.
48   Burstall, *op. cit.*
49   O'Brien, *Futures*, August 1980.
50   *Scrip*, 18 March 1981.
51   *Chemical Week*, 25 February 1981.
52   *Tages-Anzeiger*, 13 February 1981.
53   Nand, *Technology Planning in the Pharmaceutical Sector in
      Developing Countries*, UNCTAD, 1979.
54   Agarwal, *Drugs and the Third World*, Earthscan, London, 1978.
55   *Report of the Ad-Hoc Committee on Drug Policies on the Action
      Programme on Essential Drugs*, WHO, EB 63/19, 1979.
56   *Resolution on Cooperation Among Developing Countries, op. cit.*
57   Burstall, *op. cit.*

Eleven: The Corporate Response

1   Dee, *Proceedings*, IFPMA 10th Assembly, 1981.
2   Wescoe, *Proceedings*, Pharmaceuticals for Developing Countries — Conference, National Academy of Sciences, Washington, 1979.
3   von Grebmer, 'Drug Therapy and its Price', Ciba-Geigy, 1981 (mimeo).
4   *Update: The International Pharmaceutical Market*, Hoenig and Strock, New York, 1980.
5   *Campaign*, 22 April 1977.
6   *Business Week*, 16 June 1975.
7   'The Blind Alley to Success', Hoffmann-La Roche, 1975 (mimeo).
8   Nowotny, *Proceedings*, IFPMA 8th Assembly, Zurich, 1977.
9   *Transfer of Information Relating to Drugs and Their Registration*, statement to the WHO as adopted by IFPMA Council, IFPMA, 1977.
10 Muller, *New Scientist*, 21 July 1977.
11 *Scrip*, 12 May 1979.
12 *Resolution WHA.28/66*, WHO, 1975.
13 *Resolution WHA.31/32*, WHO, 1978.
14 Peretz, *Proceedings*, IFPMA 10th Assembly, Zurich, 1981.
15 *Scrip*, 24 October 1979.
16 *Scrip*, 13 April 1981.
17 *Scrip*, 22 April 1981.
18 Peretz, *op. cit.*
19 *International Codes of Conduct and Ciba-Geigy Pharma*, Ciba-Geigy, undated.
20 See, for instance, *Lancet*, 15 April 1978; *International Journal of Health Services*, vol. 10, no. 3, 1980; Yudkin in *More Technologies for Rural Health*, Royal Society, London, 1980.
21 Letter, 21 April 1981.
22 Letter, 14 October 1977.
23 Letter, 21 November 1977.
24 *Daily News*, Dar es Salaam, 20 June 1977.
25 *Scrip*, 4 July 1979; 18 July 1979; 8 August 1979.
26 US Dept. of Health, Press Release P78–34, 13 September 1978.
27 Lall and Bibile, *World Development*, August 1977.
28 *Case Studies in the Transfer of Technology: Pharmaceutical Policies in Sri Lanka*, UNCTAD, TD/B/C.6/21, 1977.

29   *Statement to UNCTAD on Document Number TD/B/C.6/21*, IFPMA, 1978.
30   *Scrip*, 4 February 1981.
31   *Scrip*, 30 March 1981 and 8 April 1981.
32   *Eastern Pharmacist*, August 1980.
33   *Scrip*, 24 October 1979.
34   *Scrip*, 7 October 1978.
35   *Scrip*, 7 February 1979.
36   Hubbard, *Proceedings*, Pharmaceuticals for Developing Countries Conference, National Academy of Sciences, Washington, 1979.
37   *CPR at a Glance*, CPR, New York, 1980.
38   *Pharmaceutical Industry Roles in Developing Country Health*, CPR, New York, 1980.
39   ibid.
40   ibid.
41   *Pharmaceuticals Program 1981: Annual Report*, CPR, New York, 1981.
42   ibid.
43   *Improving the Availability of Pharmaceuticals in Developing Countries: A Strategy for Action*, CPR, New York, 1980, from which all the previous description is taken.
44   *Pharmaceuticals Program 1981: Annual Report, op. cit.*
45   Levitt, *Planning Systems in the Pharmaceutical Industry*, PJB Publications, London, 1980.
46   Pinto, *Drug Monitoring*, Ciba-Geigy Pharma Registration Symposium, Ciba-Geigy, 1977.
47   *1979 Annual Report*, Ciba-Geigy, 1980.
48   Lorenz in 'Planning in an Age of Uncertainty', *Financial Times*, London, 1980.
49   Interview transcripts, Belbo Film Company, 1981.
50   ibid. Although Dr Regala said that he would know of any such agreement, Ciba-Geigy apparently knew more than he did about his organization's affairs. In a humiliating about-face, he was obliged to retract his statement: 'Following subsequent investigation, we confirm our agreement with Ciba-Geigy (Philippines) Inc. allowing them to exhaust their remaining stock . . . . Any statement to the contrary previously expressed by the undersigned should be disregarded.' In *De Medicijnen Markt*, Novib, The Hague, September 1981.
51   *National Association for the Swiss Chemical Industry*, Swiss Society of Chemical Industries, Zurich, 1980.

52 *Transnational Corporations and the Pharmaceutical Industry*, UN Centre on Transnational Corporations, ST/CTC/9, 1979.
53 *Scrip*, 7 October 1979.
54 Breckon, 'In Sickness or in Wealth', transcript of radio programme transmitted 26 August 1979, BBC, London.

Twelve: Towards the Year 2000

1 Schaumann, *Pharmaceutical Perspectives in the 1980s*, SRI International, 1980, pp. 80-485.
2 This is the view taken by the US Office of Technology Assessment: *Impact of Applied Genetics: Micro-organisms, Plants and Animals*, US Government Printing Office, 1981, supported by the example of Ciba-Geigy and rifampicin, *Tages-Anzeiger*, Basle, 13 February 1981.
3 Schaumann, *op. cit.*
4 *6th Report on the World Health Situation*, WHO, 1981.
5 *Eastern Pharmacist*, August 1980.
6 Connelly, *Medical Marketing and Media*, October 1975.
7 *Scrip*, 14 January 1981.
8 Ladejobi, *Medical Marketing and Media*, January 1977.
9 Jannssen, *Proceedings*, CIOMS Round Table, Geneva, 1977.
10 Muller, *New Scientist*, 25 April 1974.
11 Mooney, *Seeds of the Earth*, ICDA, London, 1979.
12 *Scrip*, 20 May 1981.
13 Peretz, *Proceedings*, IFPMA 10th Assembly, Zurich, 1981.
14 Dunning *et al.*, *Impact of Multinational Enterprises on National Scientific and Technical Capacities*, OECD, DSTI/SPR/77.34, 1977, and *Transnational Corporations in the Pharmaceutical Industry*, UN Centre on Transnational Corporations, E/C.10/38, 1978.
15 *The Pharmaceutical Industry: International Issues and Answers*, PMA, Washington, 1979.
16 Mahler, *World Health is Indivisible, op. cit.*
17 *Eastern Pharmacist*, September 1980.
18 Burstall *et al.*, *Multinational Enterprises, Governments and Technology: Pharmaceutical Industry*, OECD, 1981.
19 Mahler, *World Health is Indivisible, op. cit.*
20 *Global Study of the Pharmaceutical Industry*, UNIDO, 1980.
21 Mahler, 'The WHO You Deserve', address to World Health Assembly, May 1980.
22 Schaumann, *op. cit.*

23 Inaugural statement, Health Action International, Geneva, 1981.
24 *Politica Farmaceutica em Mocambique*, Summary report presented at WHO sub-regional conference on pharmaceutical policy, Ministerio de Saude, Beira, April 1981.

Index

SOCIAL SCIENCE LIBRARY

Manor Road Building
Manor Road
Oxford OX1 3UQ
Tel: (2)71093 (enquiries and renewals)
http://www.ssl.ox.ac.uk

WITHDRAWN

This is a NORMAL LOAN item.

We will email you a reminder before this item is due.

Please see http://www.ssl.ox.ac.uk/lending.html
for details on:

- loan policies; these are also displayed on the
  notice boards and in our library guide.

- how to check when your books are due back.

- how to renew your books, including information
  on the maximum number of renewals.
  Items may be renewed if not reserved by
  another reader. Items must be renewed before
  the library closes on the due date.

- level of fines; fines are charged on overdue books.

Please note that this item may be recalled during Term.